MODERN JAPAN

ORIGINS OF THE MIND

Japanese Traditions and Approaches to Contemporary Life

Alexander Prasol

Niigata University of International and
Information Studies, Japan

古往今来

MODERN JAPAN
ORIGINS OF THE MIND

Japanese Traditions and Approaches to Contemporary Life

W World Scientific

NEW JERSEY · LONDON · SINGAPORE · BEIJING · SHANGHAI · HONG KONG · TAIPEI · CHENNAI

Published by

World Scientific Publishing Co. Pte. Ltd.

5 Toh Tuck Link, Singapore 596224

USA office: 27 Warren Street, Suite 401-402, Hackensack, NJ 07601

UK office: 57 Shelton Street, Covent Garden, London WC2H 9HE

British Library Cataloguing-in-Publication Data
A catalogue record for this book is available from the British Library.

MODERN JAPAN: ORIGINS OF THE MIND
Japanese Traditions and Approaches to Contemporary Life

ISBN-13 978-981-4295-63-5 (pbk)
ISBN-10 981-4295-63-9 (pbk)

Typeset by Stallion Press
Email: enquiries@stallionpress.com

Printed in Singapore.

Dedicated to the memory of my friend and colleague,

Masao Ichioka

Preface

What is this Book About?

This book reveals the lifestyle of the people of modern Japan. It describes how the Japanese perceive nature, the universe and themselves as well as how they interact with other people, their surroundings and the ideas of others. This book also discusses how the Japanese behave toward close friends and outsiders. In short, it answers the question of why the Japanese think and act in the ways that they do.

I have based my discussion on personal observations, impressions and thoughts accumulated over years of living in Japan which I find a very remarkable country. I have made use of the works of many talented authors, both Russian and non-Russian, who have studied and puzzled over Japanese culture.

Why Japan?

The growing interest in Japan is fueled by two main sources.

First, Japan is the only non-Western country to have achieved global economic success. Europeans and Americans are intrigued about how Japan has emerged among the world's leading nations. Westerners have a common stereotype that a non-Western country just cannot be as successful as Japan has been. Interest in Japan is further intensified by the media, researchers, writers and analysts throughout the world. Be it the "Made in Japan" automobiles and TV sets that are readily available in any country or the *Yamato-nadeshiko* women tiptoeing in kimono with ikebana in their hands at every corner, the entire international community is interested in this extraordinary country.

Second, it is Japanese culture itself that fascinates the world. For centuries, Japan has been absorbing, like a giant sponge, all of the best of the outside world. Long periods of isolation gave Japan time for thoughtful absorption and further assimilation of the borrowed ideas and technology that were later polished into a uniquely Japanese style. The principle of social energy conservation says that the weakening of external links intensifies internal links. Through the efforts of several generations who knew almost nothing of the outside world, a unique cultural tradition was created in Japan. Out of isolation has evolved its unique attraction and allure. One hundred years ago, A. Nikolaev, a Russian traveler, wrote that Japan possesses "a gorgeous natural environment combined with the complete absence of serfdom and foreign domination [that] has endowed this nation with many valuable qualities in a combination that is rarely seen anywhere else" (Nikolaev, 1905).

Obviously, the best way to understand a culture is to live in it for several years, working with its people and observing their everyday lifestyle. Short-term visits, even if they are rather frequent, cannot provide this same opportunity. Japanese society is still tightly closed to outsiders, and foreigners usually find it difficult to assimilate. Therefore, the knowledge gained by those who have lived in Japan and who have managed to comprehend its culture from the inside is of considerable value. Notwithstanding every individual experience is necessarily limited and subjective, there are certain aspects that any foreigner cannot fail to notice while living in Japan. These shared observations and reflections can provide a detailed picture of this distinctive country and help to illuminate its uniqueness for all those interested in Japan. This is the main goal of this book.

What is the Main Idea?

The traditions, character and mentality of any nation are the result of its age-long development. These characteristics are an intricate combination of historical events and ethnological patterns. Any exclusive national feature normally has its origins rooted in the past. However, it is not easy to explain these features adequately since human society is a result of complicated cause-and-effect relationships. People usually find it difficult to take an abstract view of the present or to comprehend fully the implications of the remote past. It is not easy to understand what really happened during those times; how did it happen and why? Japanese history is much better documented than that of many other countries, since manuscripts have always played an important role in Japanese culture. Our knowledge of Japanese history may be subtle but it is still sufficient to attempt looking into the changing times of Japan and exploring the mechanisms of and reasons for her transformations.

This book not only reveals the mentality and national character of the modern Japanese people but also tries to explore and to present the roots of their mannerisms. As you begin navigating Japanese culture, you might ask yourself several seemingly naïve questions. Everyone knows that the Japanese are generally more polite than people from other countries, but why is this so? Why does their behavior change so much when they are among strangers? Why do they relax so much when being served by others? Generally speaking, why is the service in Japan the best in the world? Why is their public transportation so accurate and dependable? Why do the Japanese like gift-giving but dislike disclosing their true thoughts and feelings? Why do they value loyalty and commitment so much? For how long have they done so? Why, when interrogated by the police, do they easily confess to crimes that they have not committed without being beaten or tortured? What are the reasons for such behaviors?

These are just a few of the many questions that can be answered by a survey of the history of Japanese society. I have included credible facts from historical and contemporary Japanese society to present a coherent picture in trying to comprehend the Japanese people.

What is NOT Included in this Book?

Knowing firsthand the difficulty of navigating the rough sea of literature today, I feel that it is helpful to inform you of what is not found in this volume. There is no romanticism of Oriental martial arts which therefore receive very little mention. Thrilling legends about samurai warriors and intriguing secrets of the ancient past are left for other writers to explore. The inscrutable nature of ancient Oriental culture in its modern conception, as well as esoteric philosophy and sacred rituals, poeticism of everyday aestheticism, the unfathomable secrets of the enigmatic Japanese soul — all of these of a more exotic nature are not found here. If you imagine Japan as a crystal temple set in foamy white clouds, you should probably stop here.

About the Author

I was born and raised on the coast of the Japan Sea in the Russian city of Vladivostok. I graduated from the Faculty of Oriental Studies at the Far Eastern National University, and have dedicated almost 40 years to studying Japan, having defended both my MA and PhD theses on various aspects of Japanese culture. For the last 18 years, I have been living in Japan where I teach Russian history, language and culture. I have drawn upon my personal experience and observations in this book in an effort to explain how ancient traditions and cultural mentality work in contemporary Japan to make her a fascinating and attractive subject.

Acknowledgments

The completion of this book would not have been possible without the help of an unseen team of supporters. First and foremost, I thank the Niigata University of International and Information Studies for making it financially possible for me to publish this volume. Part of the book was written during my sabbatical leave at two universities; my heartfelt gratitude to the Faculty of Japanese Studies of the Far Eastern National University (Vladivostok, Russia) and its Dean, Professor Alexander Shnyrko, as well as the Center for Japanese Research at the University of British Columbia (Vancouver, Canada) and its Director, Professor David Edgington. Through participation in seminars, discussions and events, I was also able to meet a number of highly qualified colleagues, all of whom willingly shared their expertise. Such expertise contributed in no small measure to the completion of this volume. My deepest thanks to them all.

I also thank Alyona Sokolova, Olga Leshkova and Natalia Betankurt for their help in translating the manuscript into English, as well as Gregory Twomey and Gregory Hadley for proofreading. Finally, I express my deep gratitude to both Vladimir Tereshchenko and Viktoria Ivanova for designing the graphics.

Technical Remarks

The Japanese names are given in the European manner: a personal name followed by the surname. This book was originally written in Russian and for this reason the quotations of English-speaking authors were also translated into Russian. In this English version, some quotations have undergone a double translation. In cases where I could not reinstate the original English quotations, the translations may differ grammatically from the original, but the integrity of their meanings have been preserved.

Brief Historical Background

However odd it may appear at first glance, the Japanese way of life can be easily explained by the country's traditions and customs derived from the past. Therefore it seems appropriate to present a brief summary of some peculiarities of Japanese history, government system and terms used in this book.

According to official historiography, the Imperial House of Japan is the oldest continuing hereditary monarchy in the world. It has 1,500 years of history. The mythological chronicles of the eighth century *Kojiki* (712) and *Nihon Shoki* (720) state that the first legendary Emperor Jimmu with the blessing of the gods took the throne in 660 BC. However, the Japanese historians believe that the imperial dynasty was formed much later — in the third or fourth centuries AD. In the middle of the seventh century, the Japanese emperors accepted the title *tenno* (literally "heavenly sovereign"), and since then the phrase "we rule the world as the gods' descendants" was used in every emperor's edict. The divine origin of the emperor's image manifested itself in almost absolute sanctity: for centuries it was forbidden to depict the image in paintings or describe it in words. Unlike European monarchs or ordinary Japanese families, the Imperial dynasty had never had its own family name. Even a skillful investigator will not be able to detect any human qualities in a succession of Japanese emperors' names and that is logical — direct descendants of the gods were not supposed to possess any.

In the beginning of the eighth century, the Imperial House of Japan and system of government were reorganized according to the Chinese model in a strictly centralized order. During that period the

Emperor acted both as the country's ruler and high priest and originator of the worship of goddess Amaterasu who was believed to have given birth to the first emperor of Japan. However, that period when the emperors enjoyed the fullness of social and religious power was comparatively short.

Flourishing of the bureaucratic system of governance and absence of real threats from the outside world resulted in the rise of the aristocracy, especially the Fujiwara clan. This tradition of having powerful allies from influential clans close to the throne was born in Japan a long time ago. Until 456 the clan of Katsuragi remained the major ally of the Imperial House, and it was then succeeded by the Heguri clan which was in power until 498. The Otomo clan kept its influence until 539, and then it yielded to the clan of Mononobe that was succeeded by the Soga family in the second half of the century. In 645 the shintoistic clan of Fujiwara pushed its way forward to the throne.

Soon after the system of regents had been introduced in Japan, *tenno* lost their power and turned into sacred and symbolic figureheads. The clans, who had in their hands political and military power, clashed fiercely with each other for the reigning authority so the favorites would change from time to time. The divine status of the emperor, however, remained unquestioned. The concept that the emperor could or could not rule but should always be at his place had been embedded for centuries in the minds of the citizens of the Yamato country — an ancient name for Japan.

The strengthening of provincial feudal lords' influence as well as the spreading of Buddhist temples forced the emperors to look for new ways of keeping their power. Emperor Shirakawa (1053–1129), who fought against the growth of power of dominant land-lords, became the first emperor to ostensibly abdicate the throne in favor of a monastery, a curious maneuver called *insei*. In fact he continued to rule the country but did not take any official rank. Emperor-monks remained the most powerful landlords and controlled almost half of the land in the country; they had armed troops and guards of public order at their personal disposal.

The system of private landownership developed in Japan in the eighth century, bringing with it the first landowners. Because of frequent disturbances and clashes, many armed themselves very quickly to protect their land. Landlords formed their own armed units, with some naturally becoming leaders. This practice spread quickly especially in remote rural areas. Some noble aristocratic clans upon receiving plots of land far away from the capital joined the class of warriors, as did, for instance, the well-known clan of Taira. That was how the warrior caste was formed, which played a crucial role in the history of Japan later as first mentioned in the chronicles of the ninth century. Units of professionally trained warriors, always armed and alert, were also of great use for aristocrats inveigled in endless conspiracies and intrigues against each other. Even the emperors would use the services of distinguished warrior clans. The warriors serving the court aristocracy named the future caste of leaders from the verb *samurau* which means "to serve" and gave us the well-known word, "samurai".

For several centuries, the ancient Japanese country of Yamato sought to subdue the neighboring Ezo tribes that inhabited the north-eastern territories of Honshu Island. From time to time the emperors would send troops led by a commander who was called "shogun". Shoguns were appointed from noble and distinguished warrior clans close to the Imperial House. Like many other words, the name of this title was borrowed from the Chinese language (*jiāngjūn*, meaning general). With time, this military rank acquired a more pompous description: "great warlord, conqueror of barbarians" (*seii taishogun*). By the beginning of the 10th century, the Ezo tribes had weakened and ceased to threaten the country of Japan; the campaigns against them stopped and commanders were no longer appointed. The rank *seii taishogun* was forgotten for some time and when it was later revived, it had acquired a fairly different meaning.

In the 12th century, Imperial authority (and also the power of Fujiwara regents) started to fade; in fact, the country was ruled by different warrior clans that had grown stronger in the course of inter-clan clashes. At the end of the 12th century the first commander posts were held by warrior clans of Taira (descendants of Emperor Kammu who ruled the country from 781 to 806) and Minamoto (descendants of Emperor Seiwa who reigned from 858 to 876). In 1184 the Minamoto family had the crucial superiority and Yoshinaka Minamoto (1154–1184) entered Kyoto, an ancient capital of Japan, with a massive army. The Tiara clan and their allies had to flee to the south of the country. Actual power over the country was almost entirely in the hands of Yoshinaka Minamoto. He was the de facto ruler of the country, but he remained de jure an impostor as he did not have the Imperial mandate for the post of Chief Commander. Therefore in 1184 he had the Emperor grant him the title *seii taishogun*. Together with the highest warrior rank, Yoshinaka Minamoto was granted the sole right to gather and train the army, this giving him a considerable advantage in clashes with rival clans.

Nevertheless, his cousin, Yoritomo Minamoto (1147–1199) managed to amass his own army and later defeated his relative. He then completely defeated the Taira clan and led a campaign against the north-eastern tribes, thus ending their independence. This accomplishment led him to demand the highest warrior rank from the Emperor, which was granted in 1192. Since then, the rank *seii taishogun* (later used simply as shogun) was no longer given for temporary commanders but for a constant military head of the country who would pass it to his heirs. For almost seven centuries from 1192 to 1867, the title shogun was a subject of inheritance in the clan, though it was formally granted by the Emperor. During these seven centuries Japan had three shogunates with several clans bearing this highest rank.

Kamakura shogunate (*Kamakura bakufu*, 1192–1333)

Minamoto clan (1192–1210), three shoguns.
Fujiwara clan (1226–1252), two shoguns.
Imperial princes (*shinno*) (1252–1333), four shoguns.

Kyoto shogunate (*Muromachi bakufu*, 1338–1573)

Ashikaga clan (1338–1573), 16 shoguns.

Edo shogunate (*Edo bakufu,* 1603–1867)
Tokugawa clan (1603–1867), 15 shoguns.

From 1573 to 1603 Japan did not have shoguns and the country was ruled by warlords Nobunaga Oda (1534–1582) and Hideyoshi Toyotomi (1536–1598). They had full power like all the preceding shoguns but did not formally possess this title.

While the shoguns were busy ruling the country, the Imperial House was entertained by pompous ceremonies, performances of ancient dances *gagaku*, contests of poets and calligraphers and sporting competitions. The emperors kept only ritual and religious power from the past. The first half of shogunate rule was not peaceful: rival warrior clans and even the emperors regularly made attempts to seize power. In the 14th century Emperor Godaigo (1288–1339) decided to wrest power by starting a war. The attempt failed and the warrior clan of Ashikaga played a major role in this struggle. In 1335 Ashikaga Takauji (1305–1358) confronted the Emperor and soon became a shogun. With a small group of his supporters, Godaigo left for the mountains of Yoshino to set up the Southern Court in competition with the Northern Court in Kyoto. The two courts were facing off each other from 1337 to 1392, until the weakened Southern Court ceased to exist.

It is worth mentioning that during the reign of the Ashikaga clan, the Hojo family received much power. For more than 100 years, its representatives ruled the country as regents for Ashikaga shoguns. They assumed the same role as the Ashikaga clan which had previously ruled the country as servants of the Emperor.

The warrior class attained its greatest power in the era of Tokugawa (1603–1867), when 15 shoguns of the clan ruled the country consecutively after defeating their rivals in battle. As part of the tradition, the new government set up a new capital in the city of Edo (present Tokyo). The end of internecine wars and establishment of a sole government contributed to the rapid development of all aspects of social life. For two and a half centuries, Japan had very little contact with the outside world and developed in isolation. Many of the habits and traditions which were formed during Tokugawa rule are the basis of the distinctive Japanese culture well-known to the rest of the world.

The Imperial Dynasty managed to regain full government powers only in 1868 after an armed clash with the shogunate. Thus began the Meiji (enlightened rule) era under the reign of a young emperor. At that time when Japan was struggling to defend its independence, the revival of imperial power ignited the renaissance of deep-rooted traditions in the national government system. In February of 1889, the Constitution of the Empire of Japan was adopted, announcing Japan a constitutional monarchy. The Emperor and his court moved to Edo and renamed it Tokyo since the capital city of the shogunate and the capital city of the Emperor were to have different names. Emperor Meiji (1852–1912) became the first powerful and legitimate Emperor of Japan after a long break, meriting special attention in the modern history of Japan. During his reign, the country achieved a striking revolution in its development by industrializing all aspects of life according to the Western model. Japan's victories in its wars against China (1894–95) and Russia (1904–05) boosted the international image of this Asian country which had been regarded as backward until then.

In 1926 Emperor Showa (1901–1989) took the throne and brought about the greatest upheaval. During his rule Japan initiated aggressive invasions against her Asian neighbors and occupied their territories; Hiroshima and Nagasaki were destroyed by an atom bomb; Japan lost World War II. On the eve of 1946, Emperor Showa publicly renounced the divine origin of the ruling dynasty. The legend which had been carefully tended for more than 12 centuries had ceased.

The change of government was documented in the new Constitution of Japan which came into effect in May, 1947. Under its provisions, the Emperor of Japan is "the symbol of the state and of the unity of the people." Since then all sovereign power has resided with Japanese nationals who are referred to as "the Japanese people" in the Constitution. The Emperor exercises purely ceremonial and formal functions — approval of appointments and dismissals suggested by the government, endorsing documents, receiving ambassadors' letters of credence and giving awards. All activities of the Emperor connected with the state are to be performed in accordance with the advice and approval of the Cabinet.

After the death of Emperor Showa on 7 January 1989, his eldest son Akihito acceded to the throne. He is the 125th Emperor according to Japan's traditional order of succession. In 1991, his eldest son Naruhito was declared the Crown Prince of Japan, heir apparent to the throne.

As a whole, the monarchical system of Japan has rather successfully adjusted to present democratic rule, though Japanese democracy still has a long way to go. The Imperial House is not viewed as a key element of Japan's political system; despite this, it still plays a significant role in society. The Japanese people display a generally positive attitude to the Imperial dynasty, regarding it as a special part of their national history and culture.

Contents

It's highly unlikely that you can find anywhere in the world
a country more interesting and original than Japan.

— N. Bartoshevsky

Chapter 1

The Outside World and Japanese Creativity

Japan's "Three-Cycle Response" for Innovative Change

The geographic location of Japanese civilization has a significant impact on both its character and its relations with the outside world. According to UCLA Professor Jared Diamond, the southeastern islands of the Pacific and Indian Oceans, including the Japanese Archipelago, were populated by *Homo sapiens* somewhat later than was the interior of the Eurasian continent. The routes of global migration created a situation in which Japanese culture developed in the shadow of that found in India and China. Over the centuries, India and China have influenced their neighbors, including Japan, with their rich cultures. Neighboring nations have reacted in different ways to this influence. Some have willingly absorbed new knowledge while others have resisted foreign innovations and stuck to their own traditions, preserving them for posterity. Japan, as we shall see, has done both.

If Diamond's theory is correct, the first inhabitants of the Japanese Archipelago came from what later became known as China and Korea. Migrants from the southern islands of the Pacific Ocean might have joined them later. Island culture and continental culture developed in their own separate ways, but cross-cultural contacts between Japan and the continent were frequent. Nourished by numerous contacts with neighboring countries, continental culture grew more rapidly than island culture.

Successive waves of immigrants to the Japanese Islands brought with them new knowledge, practical skills and religious beliefs.

Ancient Japanese chronicles reported numerous groups of newcomers from the continent during the third century AD. By the middle of the fifth century there were about 20,000 hereditary silk spinners, all of whose ancestors had come from abroad. As for the trips of the proto-Japanese people to China, chroniclers dated them as far back as the second century AD (Hasegawa, 1965). Earlier contact could not be determined because of the absence of written language. Therefore, the conclusions of the authors of *The Ancient History of Japan* that "the population of ancient Japan consisted mostly of immigrants from the continent and Japanese culture itself was formed from their active participation in the process" (Meshcheryakov and Grachov, 2002) seems entirely convincing.

Profiting from an abundance of seafood and the practical knowledge obtained from skilled craftsmen in neighboring countries, the ancient Japanese had little need for their own innovations. From the dawn of their culture, they learned a formula that has proven itself over the ages: go to China for something new. For example, there was no writing system in Japan before the introduction of Chinese characters. After adaptation of the Chinese script, a tradition of awe for all things Chinese was inscribed on the written page. This habit of looking toward China eventually developed into a tradition that was passed from one generation to the next. There are few things more enduring in Japan than a sacred compliance to traditions.

The reaction of the Japanese to foreign ideas and technology can be seen as a "three-cycle response" of imitation, adaptation and improvement, each of which is described below. As we shall see, this pattern has played itself out over and over again throughout Japan's history.

The process of imitation, however, was not chaotic. The Japanese accepted only those things that they considered useful and suitable. For example, rice-sowing techniques were adopted rapidly, but cattle breeding did not prove to be practical on islands with little pastureland. After the first flush of Confucian learning, Confucian thought was established as the organizational foundation of state structure and ideology. However, the Japanese divested Confucianism of its key teachings about the status of the ruler. Chinese emperors originated from common backgrounds, but they received their authority from the Mandate of Heaven. Chinese emperors could be deposed if they ceased to follow virtuous and humane rule. In contrast, the Japanese believed that their emperors, or *tenno* (literally, heavenly sovereign), had reigned "since time immemorial" and were considered to be the direct descendants of the gods. Therefore, the imperial dynasty had to reign forever.

Although Japan utilized the significant achievements of Asia's continental civilizations, the *Yamato* dynasty (ancient name for the country of Japan) nevertheless considered itself equally great and uniquely independent. Although the ancient Japanese did not lend any valuable ideas to their neighbors (but instead learned from their neighbors) they still held themselves in equal esteem to the Chinese. Everything that the Japanese borrowed from the outside world was carefully filtered, selected and contextualized to the needs of the local culture. This is the second important aspect of Japan's interaction with the outside world — adaptation.

After centuries of intensive cultural contact with China, the process of interaction slowed and then stopped completely by the end of the ninth century. Connections with the Korean kingdoms had been cut off even earlier. At the beginning of the 10th century, Koguryo, a reconstructed Korean kingdom, asked Japan to become its suzerain, but the request was rejected. Japan entered a period of isolation in which it processed and adapted the cultural information it had received from abroad.

During the following centuries, the Japanese applied continental knowledge to statecraft, science and culture. "This kind of Japanization can be seen in many cultural areas that are accessible to our observation (paintings, sculptures, architecture, costumes, etc.)" (Meshcheryakov and Grachov, 2002). As Vladimir Alpatov wrote, in modern times "the process of adaptation of European linguistics in Japan was singularly purposeful: only those things that helped to deepen and to develop national traditions were taken into consideration" (Alpatov, 2003).

The development of national traditions while using Chinese characters has led to a curious situation. Original Korean and Chinese personal and geographic names are unknown to most Japanese people unless they read international periodicals where these names are

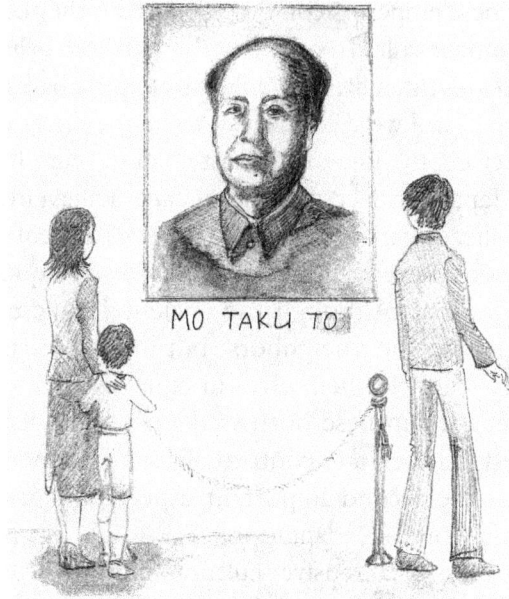

Figure 1.1:   Japanese reading of names.

written in Roman script. In Japan, Chinese and Korean names are read according to their Japanese pronunciation. For this reason, Mao Zedong is known in Japan as Mo Taku To, the name of Chinese premier Wen Jiabao is read as On Ka Ho and the former President of South Korea Chun Doo Hwan is routinely called Zen To Kan.

Given the fact that even famous people's names are dealt with in this way, it goes without saying that in present-day Japan, the average Chinese or Korean cannot expect to hear the proper pronunciation of their names. The Reverend Choi Chang Hwa, a South Korean Protestant minister, spent 13 years in Japanese courts insisting that television announcers of the NHK, Japan's public broadcast network, pronounce his name as he wished. In Japan, Mr. Choi was widely known as Sai Sho Ka. In 1988, the presiding Supreme Court justice Atsushi Nagashima admitted that a person's name "symbolizes his individuality and constitutes a part of his human rights," but nevertheless ruled against Mr. Choi, saying that the announcers did not violate his rights because the Japanese reading of the ideographs was an accepted social custom (Haberman, 1988). It is worth mentioning that this is not necessarily a uniquely Japanese phenomenon. In China, Japanese names are read according to Chinese conventions.

The lawsuit of the South Korean minister did, however, help achieve something of a compromise towards changing this long-standing tradition. After this court case, NHK announcers began to read according to Korean convention for people living in North and South Korea. However, it is often the case that many Koreans living in Japan readily assume the Japanese version of their names in order to further assimilate within Japanese society. As for private Japanese radio and TV stations, the old practice of reading Korean names according to Japanese conventions is maintained. This means that geographic and famous personal names in China and Korea, as they are known both in their countries and to the outside world, will remain unknown to the majority of the Japanese for a while.

Modification and perfection of knowledge and technology received from the outside world is the third and final stage of Japan's borrowing mechanism. It differs from the two previous stages by its emphasis on the creative component. Improvement of borrowed ideas is at the very core of the Japanese creative process. Not found in the imitation stage and showing only a limited presence in the adaptation stage, this component is the climax of improvement.

Currently, foreign-born ideas that have been improved upon beyond recognition by Japanese developers are often labeled as "Made in Japan" and then re-exported. Examples abound: watches and green tea, bonsai and ikebana, cars and electric appliances, and more. Many technological solutions resulting from the improvement of patents and licenses purchased from Western inventors are marketed as uniquely Japanese.

Ig Nobel Prize Winners

The telephone was invented in the United States in 1876. Within one year, the Japanese became the first to import the new device. Despite Japan's readiness to obtain the technology, it took them

13 years to decide who would be responsible for implementing the new invention: the government or private companies. Eventually, the government's Mail and Telegraph Department established the first telephone line between Tokyo and Yokohama in 1890.

The Japanese tend to have a thirst for everything new. To study hard and to investigate the unknown have long been viewed as the honorable duty of every loyal citizen. Every novelty triggers a certain craze in Japanese society resembling commuter behavior before the departure of the last train. Companies rush to develop a new product and to implement it into everyday life, a phenomenon so common that it has been given its own names: *kato kyoso* and *yokonarabi*.

Following World War II, the Japanese have not only been imitating and borrowing new skills and experiences, but have been constantly and thoroughly improving upon them. The pursuit of intensive improvement is deeply rooted in the Japanese mind. Everything of which the Japanese are proud has been borrowed from China and then improved upon and enhanced. In the second half of the 20th century, this was especially noteworthy in the areas of science and technology.

For example, Japanese car makers are the world leaders in upgrading and implementing new models. Here, it is also worth mentioning the "quality clubs" organized by Japanese manufacturers to encourage their workers to come up with new suggestions for improvement. Consumers usually expect a commodity to have only one specific function, but the Japanese are famous for developing functionality as well as devising new and unusual functions for the most ordinary of things. Although the Japanese did not invent the radio, the clock or the flashlight, they were the first to combine them into one commodity. Office desks manufactured in Japan are equipped with additional extendable shelves, built-in lamps, thermometers, electric pencil sharpeners and other devices, the utility of which consumers only learn of after seeing the finished product. A camera auto-adjustment device that ensures the optimal quality of a picture was also invented by Japanese innovators. Robots are developed in Japan more rapidly than in any other country; these are truly Japanese inventions. Recently, Japanese supermarkets have begun printing the following day's weather forecast on customers' receipts.

The Japanese pursuit of improving everything sometimes results in innovations that can hardly be invented by anybody else. In 2002, the major Japanese toymaker Takara offered for sale a portable dog-to-human language translation device that converts a dog's bark into text. A sensor and a transmitter are built into the dog's collar which sends a signal to a receiver used by the dog's owner. The device sells for about US$110. According to the company, more than 250,000 units were sold in Japan during the product's first year, although some are skeptical about this number. Former Prime Minister Jun'ichiro Koizumi has reportedly given it as a gift to the former Russian-President Vladimir Putin, a well-known dog lover.

On 4 June 2006, the central Japanese newspapers wrote that Atsumi Agricultural High School in the small town of Tahara (Nagoya prefecture) had invented and cultivated cubic melons in a project that took four years. The cube-shaped melons taste the same as regular melons but are easier to transport. One melon costs 10,000 yen (about US$82) and the planned harvest is 50 pieces per

Figure 1.2: Dog-to-human communication.

season. (*Yomiuri:* 4 June 2006). The leader of the "cubic project" expressed hope that the new melon would stimulate the local economy. One could laugh at the news; is this worth four years of effort? But the leader was completely serious. He truly hoped that the logistical convenience and unusual shape of the melons could revive the economy of the small town. This is a very Japanese project in terms of scale.

It is widely known that Japanese companies try to create a family atmosphere in the office by providing various bonuses to their employees in celebration of significant events in their lives. The company provides both moral and financial support to its employees when they get married, experience a happy event, suffer the death of a relative and on other significant occasions. Much as this is appreciated, companies would like to make it even better through the very Japanese way — via overall improvement and intensification.

Figure 1.3:　Cube-shaped melon.

Pet food manufacturer Hills Colgate Japan started paying its employees one-time allowances and giving gifts on the occasion of a pet's birth or death. The head of the company, Yoshio Koshimura, suggested that the pets of the employees should be considered as full members of their families. The employee gets 10,000 yen (about US$82) when he or she buys a pet or when the pet produces off-spring. The same amount of money is paid to the employee on the death of the pet, together with a condolence letter and a day off for the funeral. To obtain the allowance, an employee has to present a picture of the pet and have its name registered. Within a few months of the rule taking effect in November 2005, 32 employees registered 30 dogs and 24 cats, with two of them having received the allowance.

In 1991, the Harvard Committee established the Ig Nobel Prizes to be awarded for improbable researches. The Ig Nobel Prizes are a parody of the Nobel prizes, but the laureates are real people who have invested much time, resources and effort on their discoveries and achievements. As of 2008, Japan has had 12 Ig Nobel laureates. In 1992, the prize was awarded for the discovery of the chemical components that make sweaty feet smell unpleasant; in 1997, for identifying how different chewing gums affect brain electromagnetic radiation; and in 1999, for inventing the substance that, when applied to men's underwear, helps to reveal marital infidelity. Although amusing, the Japanese inventions are nevertheless very practical. One has to have a very special worldview to conduct research of this kind.

Winners of the genuine Nobel Prize are not as numerous as Ig Nobel Prize winners in Japan. In 2008, Japan was ranked 9th in the world for its number of Nobel laureates (nine winners in the category of natural sciences). The United States and Great Britain hold the top positions on the list (222 and 74 awards, respectively). Among the G8 countries, Japan was ahead of only Italy and Canada; its current status based on Nobel Prizes does not match Japan's economic status in the world. "The government's 2009 science and technology white paper shows that the foundation for basic science research is crumbling... From 1996 to fiscal 2010, the government earmarked more than ¥60 trillion for its three 5-year science and technology basic plans. But it is questionable whether the money spent so far has been used effectively to develop talented scientists. Of the scientific papers written in Japan, the average frequency of one of them being quoted was 0.94 times in 2007. The corresponding figure was 1.51 for the United States, 1.37 for Britain, 1.24 for Germany, 1.23 for Canada and 1.12 for France. The white paper says that frontline researchers lament the paucity of specialists in basic science" (*The Japan Times:* 30 June 2009).

The Most Creative of Imitators

Japan has experienced four waves of foreign influence throughout its history, each wave contributing to the development of her civilization. Between the seventh and ninth centuries, China served as the major information provider. From the mid-17th to the 19th century, scientific and technical knowledge was imported by Europeans, mainly the Dutch. In the second half of the 19th century, the United States and the developed European countries (England, France, the Netherlands and Germany) became the dominant influences. These countries continued to be influential following World War II, although the role of the United States has increased.

The secret to Japan's progress during the last 150 years lies in the improvement of borrowed ideas and products. Having neither natural resources nor a tradition of invention, the Japanese have managed to achieve quite a bit, showing that they have a good command of competitive activities. As discussed above, they rapidly borrow, implement, adapt and ultimately improve upon borrowed ideas and technology.

In the early 1900s, educated European observers wrote that "Japan has adopted all of our new inventions and discoveries, has tested all systems found in Europe and has applied them in a different form, altering them as much as it was necessary to make their country more powerful. Japan used Europe as the ladder to climb onto the top of the Far East" (Hesse–Wartegg, 1904). Half a century later, the president of Sony, Masaru Ibuka, echoed this comment by saying that the Japanese manage to outrun their foreign competitors through their ability to understand the missed opportunities of foreign inventions rather than through their own inventiveness. Thanks to this ability, Japan has been able to get to the top, and not just in the Far East.

How do the Japanese manage to do this? They value skills and technologies that pay off quickly. Fundamental scientific discoveries that have an indefinite practical significance are postponed until such time when their significance becomes obvious. Centuries-old experience has made the Japanese global leaders in borrowing technology. The Americans had barely invented the transistor radio when Sony began mass production of pocket radio receivers, an area in which they became a global leader. This is one example of where the centuries-old commitment to miniaturization and attention to detail was of great help.

In 1946, the United States occupation forces ordered the first lot of Japanese furniture and home appliances for their military personnel stationed in Japan. More than 950,000 items were delivered to the 200,000 apartments rented for this purpose. This was the first major order for the emerging Japanese home furnishings industry. In 1949, the first Japanese fans, scooters and cameras appeared in Western stores and, within a few years, had successfully defeated their Western competitors due to superior function, quality and design.

Until the mid-19th century, the Japanese could neither construct nor navigate ocean vessels. Vasily Golovnin once wrote that the Russian sailing vessel *Diana* had greatly impressed the Japanese when it entered the port at Hakodate and changed tack in a headwind. The delighted Japanese did not hesitate to express their admiration to the Russian sailors (Golovnin, 2004). A century later, Japan was a global leader in ship construction. In 2007, Mitsui Engineering & Shipbuilding Co. launched the world's largest dry cargo vessel, the *Brazil Maru*, which was designed to transport iron ore from Brazil to Japan. The ship has a 327,180 ton displacement, is 340 meters long and 60 meters wide with a 21.13-meter draft. In comparison, the *Titanic* had a 66,000 ton displacement, was 269 meters long and 28 meters wide.

Railways were invented in Europe, but the fastest and most punctual trains appeared in Japan. In 1964, the Japanese were the first to exceed the 200 km/h speed barrier and remains a global leader in the rail industry. The current Japanese railway network is the most developed and dynamic in the world. The imminent demographic crisis and vague prospects for the domestic transportation market have driven Japanese manufacturers to export rail products and technologies.

The aluminum used to construct the cars for the Hitachi express trains make them 20 percent lighter than European rail cars. Japanese trains are more efficient and more environmentally friendly. They are also less noisy and vibrate less at high speed. Japanese express trains are considered the most reliable in the world, a fact that must have encouraged the British Ministry of Transport and the South East Railway to order several dozen Javelins (as they are named in London) from Hitachi, the first of which appeared in Great Britain in 2009. Great Britain will be the third foreign market for Hitachi, after the United States and Taiwan where these trains are already running. Japanese manufacturers, including the machine-building giant Kawasaki, have long ago established themselves in the American transportation market; the majority of New York City subway trains are made by Kawasaki.

It is the same with many other inventions originally imported into Japan. Regardless of the original plans of the inventors of GPS, the Japanese actively adjust this foreign innovation to satisfy their own needs. All new inventions are tested in the light of security applications.

On 13 November 2006, Kyoto University tested an evacuation guide system based on GPS technology and wireless network communications. The system was developed by post-graduate students under the supervision of Toru Ishida and was designed to coordinate rescuers' actions during natural disasters and acts of terrorism. The system covers a 2-kilometer-wide area and displays an evacuation guide on the rescuers' mobile phone screens, showing evacuation centers, other groups' routes, the location of the telephone owner and information received from the rescue headquarters. Thirty post-graduate students from the University participated in the search and rescue drill.

In 2008, two Japanese ministries ran a joint full-range experiment that developed the main parameters for building next-generation houses with central control systems. Except for the northernmost island of Hokkaido, there are no central heating systems in Japan; Japanese houses are very cold in the winter and hot in the summer. Consumers want to be able to turn the heating/cooling system on before coming home to warm (or cool) the air. The Japanese market now offers separate electronic control systems that can adjust TV sets and air conditioners from mobile phones via the Internet. The systems currently on the market are mostly non-compatible, so the goal of this project is to unify the external control systems and to add some new functions. For example, in case of an earthquake, the TVs will automatically switch to emergency broadcast stations and the heating appliances will be turned off. The houses of senior citizens living alone will be optionally equipped with devices to transmit information about their health (body temperature, blood pressure) as well as information about the contents of their refrigerator to social centers. These systems will make it possible to ensure the rapid dispatch of social workers to the places of greatest need. The project, based on the latest IT innovations, will make it possible to begin mass production of systems that will exercise external control over home electrical appliances. About 50 major home appliance manufacturers (including Sony and Toshiba) and communication corporations (headed by NTT and KDDI) are involved in the project.

Standup comedian Arkady Raikin once suggested special driving gear to be powered by a squirrel running in a cage in order to tap the squirrel's energy for electricity for the national economy. The Japanese are hardly familiar with Raikin's performances but they definitely think in a similar way. The Shibuya District is one of the fashion centers of Japan and about 700,000 people pass through its central square daily. This never-ending stream of pedestrians gave the local administration the idea to harness the movement. Four slabs were incorporated into the sidewalk and connected to a generator. The vibrations from the step of a 60-kilogram person are sufficient to generate 0.5 watts of electricity. The generated power is used for festive illumination. Why waste the energy of pedestrians' footsteps when it can be used to make life brighter and less polluted?

The Japanese approach to innovations does not always lead to success. In the 1970s, the astronautical world faced the challenge of how to increase the capacity of spacecraft. The goal was to determine a way to place the maximum payload into orbit by using a limited fuel supply. Engineers from different countries participated in the international contest. A Japanese engineer suggested the idea of the springboard: first, the spacecraft is launched by a springboard and only switches on the engines at the separation point. The project involved the latest (at that time) technological materials to minimize friction during acceleration so as to provide a higher starting speed for the spacecraft. This would save fuel and increase the spacecraft's capacity. The plan was considered solid and comprehensive but not innovative.

In recent decades, a lack of creative potential has greatly slowed the progress of Japanese science, which has led several Japanese companies to begin experimenting with their usual thoroughness and accuracy. The Omron Company conducts monthly creative thinking seminars for its managers. At these seminars, employees are assigned the roles of 19th century reformers, modern private detectives or Formula 1 pilots. The Fuji Company offers unusual and non-routine subjects to be studied by their top managers, for example, the history of Venice or the peculiarities of ape group behavior. The construction giant Simizu combines annual seminars with recreation at a resort area. To stimulate their creative thinking, employees are given unfeasible tasks, like developing a plan for flying a non-functioning spacecraft from the surface of the Moon (Thornton, 1993).

The tremendous efforts of Japanese companies to encourage their employees to think creatively are worthy of deep respect. There is, however, something in all these experiments and innovations reminiscent of projects that receive Ig Nobel prizes, such as the study of the influence of chewing gum on brain electromagnetic radiation.

The originality of these efforts is virtually unquestionable. But what are the results? First of all, it is difficult to expect creative thinking from a person who has been taught (as we shall see in later chapters) to approach problems consistently in one way from kindergarten to university, and then encouraged to approach them in another way after he turns 25 years old. Progress in this sphere is impossible without altering the entire educational process to include the elements of creative problem-solving at all stages of personal development. But these changes will undoubtedly shake the very foundations of the Japanese national personality and mentality, and furthermore will require changing certain attitudes that no one has yet dared to change. I do not know if these changes are possible, but if they are, then to what extent are they possible? In light of the respect the Japanese have for past experiences, these changes do not seem feasible at all. Educational reform started in Japan around 20 years ago with some positive results, but no effective fundamental changes have yet been made. Japanese senior management recognizes this problem. "Says Takashi Kamiya, a human resources manager at Fuji Film: 'You can't just tell your employees, 'Be creative!' You have to create an environment that caters more to the individual so that employees can learn how to draw their own maps for the company's future. We've never had to do that before.' But before poking fun at Japan's often naive efforts at fostering creativity, Americans and Europeans should remember that immediately after World War II this modern colossus was often ridiculed for its clumsy attempts at industrialization. If Japan's global companies sow even a few seeds of flexibility and inventiveness in their ranks, they won't just be competitive. They could well set the industrial agenda for the rest of the world" (Thornton, 1993).

If we look to the late 19th century, we will find a similar opinion expressed by a prominent Russian figure: "The Japanese have been making mistakes, but they learn easily, and never make the same mistake twice. They learn their past lessons and correct all mistakes quickly and efficiently" (Mechnikov, 1992).

Chapter 2

Perception of the World and Nature

Abbreviating the Nearest Space

Japanese culture developed with strong contributions from Chinese civilization, but did so under the conditions of self-sufficiency characteristic of an island state. In all things, the Japanese have looked to the so-called nearest space, or only those ideas and objects within their immediate reach. Eventually, such an environment furnished the country with its national identity. Being dependent on craftsmen and thinkers of the mainland for innovations, the Japanese learned to detect useful knowledge and adapt it to their own needs.

Japan's relations with the outside world began to change around the end of the first millennium AD, in a time known as the Heian Period. The country entered a phase of isolation where the people lost interest in outside influences which subsequently paled into insignificance. Traveling to remote countries held no appeal. The Japanese preferred to stay inside their own small and properly arranged, familiar and predictable world. Alexander Meshcheryakov (2004) noted this feature of the Japanese perception of the world: "The Heian man remained static in the middle of his artificial park-and-garden world, observing the scene of changing nature through his window. Obviously, the Heian man's field of vision shrank...to what we can now call 'curtailed' space. Thus, the Japanese became short-sighted and remained so for the rest of their history."

This specific perception of the world has become an essential component of Japanese culture. The feeling of internal comfort and serenity generated by a restrained community or space is still peculiar to the Japanese mentality. This is especially evident to foreigners who have been raised in an open and unrestrained space, both literally and figuratively. Robert March, who spent many years in Japan, compares everyday Japanese life with staying in a box-like confined space:

- Living in a box or compartmentalized society means that great familiarity prevails.
- People know what others think about many matters, and the extent of interpersonal communication is reduced.
- Privacy is minimal.
- People believe that a society in harmony is possible (and essential) in small spaces.
- Manners, customs, rituals, methods of communication, etc., are standardized and made routine to enable everyone to look good and to protect their honor in order to sustain a "harmonious society".
- People learn to cooperate with others by suppressing aggression.
- Dependence upon an identity that is developed within the confines of four walls is overwhelming.
- People believe that their world is the only world and that there is nowhere else in which to escape.
- The exact coordinates of the box are used to make efficiency, precision, status ranking, space saving, compacting, economy, waste avoidance, etc., ways of life.
- The control and organization of life in the box induce a strong sense of order and security.

(March, 1996)

As their space contracted around them, Heian aristocrats started to take aesthetic pleasure in contemplating their limited sphere, including nature, handmade amenities and art. As a result, the objects with which the Heians surrounded themselves were reduced to obtain a charming elegance in their simplicity. According to experts in literature, "The Japanese revealed the everlasting source of beauty in simplicity. They discovered discreet beauty" (*Zapiski u izgolov'ya*, 1988). A single flower or a branch in a vase seems to be more aesthetically acceptable to the Japanese than a lively bunch of flowers. The hop of a single frog in a pond and circles on the water inspire them with feelings and associations more genuine than a whole choir of frogs singing at sunset. As a rule, Japanese poets and writers express their admiration for nature by focusing on a single feature, and often not even on the feature itself but on the human perception of it. The Japanese perception of the world, as reflected in the arts, places the single above the multiple and gives priority to details instead of the whole.

Renga (collaborative poetry) became a very popular poetic genre among the samurai in the 14th century. One of the poems by Fujitaka Hosokawa (1534–1610) is devoted to his close friend, warrior and poet Chokei Miyoshi (1523–1564). The poem reads:

> "[He] was sitting like a statue, with his fan lying slightly aslant at his knees. If it were hot, he would take his fan with his right hand very carefully, open it gracefully with his left hand four or five sticks wide and fan himself trying to make no noise. Then he would close the fan with his left hand and put it back. He would be extremely careful in his movements so that the fan would not wander from its original position for even a tatami straw's width" (Sato, 1999).

It is not easy to answer the question of "what is this poem about?" There is no action, just a tentative image of it. The author's imagination penetrates minute details, leading his readers along. In Japanese terms, the details are expressive, aesthetic and self-sufficient enough for the poet to be inspired.

Modern Japanese writers are still peering into the details. In his novel *Reflected Moon*, Nobelist Yasunari Kawabata (1899–1972) focused his spiritual eye on a simple set of drinking glasses: "Glasses, turned upside-down, are standing in strict order as if they were parading... They are standing so close to each other that their surfaces merge. Naturally, the glasses are light by the morning sun only in part as they are turned bottom up, so only the bottom edges are shining and sparkling like diamonds..." (Kawabata, 252). The full description of the glasses light by the morning sun is twice the length of the quotation.

Figure 2.1

Source: Website of Rakuten Ichiba, accessed from [http://www.rakuten.co.jp].

Focusing attention on the nearest space has become a tradition and a distinctive feature of the Japanese world view, one that has developed at both the individual and governmental levels. Restriction of external communication in the second half of the Heian Period was followed by the almost complete isolation that began in the 17th century and lasted for more than two and a half centuries. In total, the Japanese had no full-fledged official relations with the outside world for about a thousand years. Some trade and cultural contacts on a regional or a personal level were maintained, but they were not part of official policy. One's community of residence became the essential criteria for self-identification with the nation. Those who left the country for any reasons automatically became strangers.

In 1782, 17 Japanese were shipwrecked in Russia; after being adrift for 8 months they were washed ashore and stayed abroad for 10 years. On 24 June 1793, the two remaining survivors, the Japanese merchant Kodayu Daikokuya (1751–1828) and a friend, returned to Japan. The Tokugawa government (*bakufu*) could not decide what to do with them as there was no precedent for someone returning from abroad after such a long absence. On 17 August, the "returned migrants" were brought to the capital for examination. The *Bakufu* (literally, tent government) vacillated for 10 months before entering a resolution on 6 June 1794 to place the strangers into a special settlement. They were to live on a medicinal plantation, given an allowance under governmental supervision and restricted in their movements. Every year they were given short-term leave to visit their homes. Daikokuya spent the last 34 years of his life in his native country in the civil service, under conditions akin to house imprisonment.

Until quite recently, the more than 100,000 Japanese residing abroad, including diplomats, were not entitled to vote in Japanese elections. The message is that you are a stranger as long as you are outside Japan. As soon as you return, restitution will be kindly granted. The final restrictions on electoral legislation were eliminated by the parliamentary elections of July 2007. Masao Takahashi, who lives in Australia, observed: "I have lived in Sydney for 19 years now, but this is the first time I can vote from abroad" (*Yomiuri:* 14 July, 2007).

Japanese is the only language that uses three main systems of writing: one character-based (*kanji* — ideographs from Chinese characters) and two phonetic (*hiragana* and *katakana*). Words that are borrowed from other languages, including personal and place names, are written by using characters of the *katakana* alphabet. By using this alphabet, even children who are not familiar with the word's meaning can nevertheless recognize that the word represents a foreign item, place or idea. Words that originated in Japan, however, are written in the *kanji* and/or *hiragana* alphabet. In the Japanese writing system the foreign terms cannot be written by using the same characters as for Japanese words.

It is widely known that Japanese houses tend to be very cold in the winter. Most houses, even those of the wealthy, have no central heating except for those in Hokkaido in the north. Heating is provided directly in the room instead of through a central unit that heats the entire house. To keep warm, people put on warm clothing or place a heater under the table for the family dinner. Often people sleep under an electric blanket. Although these can be considered as

Figure 2.2: Three writing scripts.

cost-saving measures, they reflect a desire of the Japanese to manage their most immediate vital space. In this context, one should not be surprised to see hot packs tucked under a person's arms to keep warm in cold weather.

Focusing on the nearest limited space is likely the cause of the renowned Japanese love for miniaturization. Gardens and parks, minia-ture natural landscapes, the art of raising miniature trees (bonsai), the small neat houses, pocket TV sets, calculators, watches and many other things result from the incessant desire to contract and to refine the nearest space. By the time Japan was discovered by foreigners, this fea-ture had matured and was evident to every observer. "A single Russian cart and a yoke can hardly turn around on the largest Japanese field...

Figure 2.3: Bonsai.

Nevertheless, through incredible painstaking efforts, the Japanese manage to earn a living with these toy fields" (Shreider, 1999).

The goal of miniaturization seems logical. The size of things within the nearest space must psychologically match the volume of available vital space. After several centuries of continual miniaturization, the unreality of the Japanese world would arrest the attention of the beholder. A Russian who was invited to a Japanese dinner at the end of the 19th century observed: "When I watched the undersized community, … the numerous tiny cups, bottles, saucers, teapots and, finally, the tiny dishes that would perhaps suit midgets or infants, it occurred to me suddenly that I had found myself among a group of grown-up children playing with their small household and having their meals for fun and entertainment, rather than for appeasing their hunger" (Shreider, 1999).

The Japanese are stereotypically light eaters. According to surviving records, the Japanese of 200 years ago consumed, on average, only one-third to one-half the average daily consumption of Russians. Although this comparison with Russians who live in the coldest country of the world (the colder the climate the more calories that must be consumed) is, of course, relative, the difference in appetite is still impressive. "The Japanese eat very little compared to Westerners. Each of us, imprisoned and motionless, ate twice as much as a Japanese, while on the road each of our sailors could take food that would probably be enough to fill three Japanese" (Golovnin, 2004).

Even in modern times, the Japanese typically consume less than do people of other nations. Japanese restaurants are known for serving miniature portions arranged for presentation rather than for satisfying hunger. Following World War II, however, Japanese people quickly became accustomed to continental-style meals and all the attendant calories, animal fats and carbohydrates. Japanese people became taller, thicker at their waists and, unfortunately, suffered more

Figure 2.4:   Living in a miniature world.

of the weight-related health problems seen in the West. Overweight people are no longer a curiosity on Japanese streets. Despite this trend, Japan can still boast some of the healthiest people in the world. According to the Organization for Economic Cooperation and Development (OECD, 2005), Japan comes last of the 30 countries for which statistics on obesity-related problems are available. Overweight people in Japan make up one-fourth (25 percent) of the population, while South Korea is next (31 percent). The United States leads with 66 percent of its population being overweight. As for obesity, of the 59 nations tallied Japan stands in 55th place with 4 percent of its population being obese. (For reference, 29 percent of the people in the United States are obese; Russia, 19 percent) (WHO, 2005).

Polished Simplicity

Long isolation did not prevent the Japanese from mastering the knowledge that they had gained from abroad. They improved the processing and storage of rice, while silk manufacturing and fabric dyeing were uniquely perfected. The Japanese craving for all things simple, clear and reliable drove them to skillfully divide complicated processes and phenomena into their simplest components, as well as to perfect the details. They adhered to these principles both at work and in art.

The tea ceremony, as borrowed from China and quite simple in nature, became a profound ritual in Japan. Moreover, tea houses and all of the items used during the ceremony were miniaturized. The Japanese extended the ceremony and divided it into phases. They set a strict time limit and attached special meanings to the details such as: how to enter (to creep in, to be exact) the tea house, how to move while preparing tea, how to hold a cup, how long to look and what to look at. These were repeatedly deliberated upon, tested and improved upon. Just a tea cup, let alone other items, could be subject to many considerable manipulations, if treated in the right way. One expert said: "For the uninitiated…cup worship seems to be exaggerated and bordering upon archaic fetishism. A cup is treated like a living person. It is given a name, its biography is traced and recorded on the walls of the cases in which it is kept, and it is wrapped in silk of special grade... Before use, a cup is bathed in hot water (a bit longer in winter) to let it 'revive', then it is wiped with a linen napkin. On a hot day the napkin is brought in a cup, but it should not be wringed and folded. Instead it should be floating free in cool water, triangle-shaped. Having put a cup on the tatami, one's hand must not proceed to the next movement; it must bid good-bye slowly to the cup in a 'maintained perception' mode, as if two friends were parting unwillingly" (Mazurik, 2003).

With such attention to ceremonial details and a desire to fill each detail with philosophical meaning, the slightest deviation can be viewed as impertinence and the violator can be shunned.

This is true not only for the tea ceremony, but for other aspects of Japanese life and culture. In 1967, when *Nihonjinron* (Japanism) was at the peak of its popularity, the 13th symposium of the All-Japanese Scientific Society for Psychological Analysis (*Nihon seishin bunseki gakkai*) was held in Tokyo. The only topic of discussion was

Figure 2.5:   Tea ceremony.

the meaning of the idea of *amae* (dependence upon and presumption of another's benevolence), an abstraction lacking any deep philosophical meaning and not exclusively attributed to Japan. Nevertheless, a pitched argument raged at the symposium where opponents irrationally confronted and blamed one another of complete ignorance of the meaning of *amae* (Doi, 2001).

The constant craving for differentiating between trusted friends and outsiders inevitably generates several schools of thought, with each denying recognition of others. Similar conflicts can be observed in any sphere of activity, whether it be Buddhism or Confucianism, sumo or martial arts, a tea ceremony or ikebana.

Striving for simplicity of form underscores many aspects of Japanese life. For instance, traditional Japanese music has a simple harmony and is mainly used to fill in the background in theatrical performances. The music supplements the text read by the actors and their body language which is the main medium of expression. The contextual nature of the musical accompaniment and the fact that the music itself is devoid of any significance make it difficult for foreigners to understand its meaning. The notion of "program music," well known to Western culture, was introduced to the Japanese relatively late. Traditional Japanese composers were not aware of complicated orchestral polyphony.

Japanese vocal performance is rather specific as well. It is based on the mid-range of the voice and is distinguished by the absence of lower and higher sounds; there is no soprano or bass. Such a manner of singing is democratic and therefore accessible to the common people. It is mass entertainment rather than a refined art. Japanese singers do not aspire to demonstrate the power or range of their voices. A good singer in Japan is a person with an ear for music and expressive mid-range voice. It is for this reason that Japan is known as a singing nation, and Japan boasts a tremendous number of karaoke clubs. A person wishing to sing to an "empty orchestra" can do so at a hotel, bar, special lounge, on a tourist bus or elsewhere according to his mood. Japanese television regularly holds various singing contests for common people, many of whom might have no singing ability at all. The level of performance might be so "democratic"

Figure 2.6:   Traditional landscape painting.

that some countries would probably hesitate to broadcast the contests.

Temple architecture and sculpture that arrived in Japan from China and the Korean Peninsula originally had very complicated forms. Christians, who are accustomed to magnificent church build-ings, are always surprised at the empty halls and passages of plain oak and the minimal décor of Japanese temples. The grand samurai of the Tokugawa Age (1603–1867) lived in castles and estates that were startling for their simplicity and austerity. A French diplomat wrote that "the uniform décor of Edo palaces bore the impression of noble simplicity" and "public buildings and residences of *daimyo* [landowning feudal lords] were decorated for a New Year in almost the same fashion as commoners' houses" (Humbert, 1870).

The Japanese borrowed the tradition of placing stone pyramids on graves from the Indians, but, with time, that tradition was also sim-plified to merely vertical wooden plates. Currently, gravestones have regained their pyramidal shape but the strict and pure simplicity

Figure 2.7:   Japanese gravestones.

Source: Website of Hokuriku Sekizai Co. Ltd, accessed from [http://www. hokurikusekizai.com].

remains clear. Japanese monuments have no photos, sculptures or any other ornaments.

The most popular Japanese poem patterns are *tanka* (31 syllables) and *haiku* (17 syllables). At one time Japanese poets used a more complicated form called *choka* (literally, long poem), but this died out in favor of *tanka* which was later shortened to *haiku*. Such short poems are widely recognized as characteristically Japanese. Japanese poetry does not rely on rhyming, which makes the poet's task much easier. Because of this, Japanese poetry is less attributed to the upper classes than is the poetry of other countries. The poetry of Basho (1644–1694) generated thousands of admirers and imitators. The total number of *tanka* and *haiku* composed by amateurs vastly outnumber the number of poems composed by professionals. A successful *haiku* by an unknown author could be engraved on the gates of a local temple and become popular in the community, while a neighboring town remained unaware of it. Nyozekan Hasegawa believes that, however it is manifested, Japanese art is closer to the common people and is simpler than that of other countries (Hasegawa, 1965).

Compared with Japanese culture, the Western culture appears sophisticated and abundant in extravagant ideas, images and supernatural phenomena. It is inhabited by heroes like the American John Henry or the Russian *bogatyr*, with magic carpets, giants, ogres, snow queens and other figures of fantasy. There is nothing of the kind in Japanese folklore. The characters of Japanese fairytales are common people living their common lives. Sometimes they are distinguished by a small funny feature, such as a very long nose, for example. The characteristic simplicity of Japanese fables is striking to any Western reader.

This is true not only of folklore. One Japanese aristocrat wrote about his native literature and theater at the end of the 19th century: "In Japan, the authors of fiction and dramas always pursue the idea of encouraging good and punishing evil. Therefore our fictional characters...always suffer their due penalty or receive their deserved reward, and the authors' first aim is to impress this upon their readers or spectators by using the idea's implementation. They hit their goal almost every time... In short, Japanese theater is indeed a school for educating the national moral" (Nikolaev, 1905). Says Nikolai Bernstein: "In Japan, music and theater function as mentors; they advocate morality, loyalty and honesty in vivid language" (Bernstein, 1905, as quoted in Anarina, 1984). The famous Japanese scientist Yaichi Haga also noted the simplicity of the Japanese attitude to life and literature: "There is scarcely any inclination in the mind of the Japanese to go to extremes in getting angry with the world, in deploring, in being cynical or in being snobbish. That is the reason why the literature of our country is simple" (Nakamura, 1960).

The simple plot and expressed didacticism of Japanese art enabled Dmitry Pozdneev to make an eloquent remark in 1925 about the Japanese attitude toward serious literature: "Russian literature is too abstract, sophisticated and of quite a different worldview, and is unclear and strange to the practical world perception of a modern

Japanese person whose taste in literature is confined to following a storyline" (Pozdneev, 1925).

Material Things and Immaterial Thoughts

The Japanese have always been more indifferent to fancies and fiction than to the real facts and phenomena of the world around them. Simple notions are more attractive to them, as they are easier to comprehend and more convenient to use than sophisticated ideas. The Japanese dislike for abstract thoughts and categories has longstanding roots. The Chinese scientist Sorai Ogyu (1666–1728) wrote: "The great sage kings of the past taught by means of 'things' and not by means of 'principles.' Those who teach by means of 'things' always have a work to which they devote themselves; those who teach by means of 'principles' merely expatiate with words. In 'things' all 'principles' are brought together; hence, all who have long devoted themselves to work come to have a genuine intuitive under-standing of them" (Nakamura, 1967).

The Japanese scholar Atsutane Hirata (1776–1843) shared this opinion. He stated that true knowledge was hidden in the particular things and phenomena of the world rather than in scientific literature. As soon as a phenomenon becomes clear to a scholar, it supersedes any abstract concepts in his mind. Thus, ideas are always secondary to substantial objects.

Hajime Nakamura, who devoted many years to studies of the Japanese national character, admitted that specifics have priority over general conclusions. He believed that Japanese thinkers have always aimed at the realities of life, trying to perceive and to analyze them discretely (Nakamura, 1967).

The prevalence of specifics and the lack of abstract thinking, typical for Japanese scholars of the past, impeded them from differ-entiating many fundamental notions like the multiple and the single or the general and the particular. The subject was touched upon by some Buddhist philosophers, but it has never been of primary impor-tance. The word *kobutsu*, which denotes a single object, came into the

Japanese language only after the Japanese became familiar with Western philosophy.

The situation has been gradually changing, especially in the field of research. However, this is a slow process and many traditional features of the Japanese perception of the world are still apparent. Yasuo Takeuchi stated that the "Japanese tend to simplify any abstract categories and notions. If *A* is different from *B* but the difference has no particular practical use, the Japanese would consider both to be identical" (Takeuchi, 2000). Hideo Kishimoto noted that "immediate perception plays a very important role for the Japanese. It is introspective and extremely specific. If any discourse starts to go too far into abstraction, the Japanese will soon find it uninteresting" (Kishimoto, 1967). Hideki Yukawa remarked that the "Japanese mentality is distinguished by a lack of abstract thinking. Only objects immediately perceivable can be of true interest to the Japanese. This is the reason for the incredible talent of the nation for arts and crafts... I don't think abstract thinking will soon be eagerly adopted by the Japanese mentality. It can be attractive for the Japanese as a matter of exoticism only, capable of satisfying the purely intellectual needs of someone's inquisitive mind" (Yukawa, 1967). Masamitsu Kawakami wrote that "due to well-established tradition, our country has never appreciated distinctiveness, especially originality of thinking" (Kawakami, 1989).

The Japanese tendency to simplify complicated notions and their dislike for abstract categories has shaped the Japanese language. Tokyo Imperial University professor Hesse–Wartegg (1851–1918) wrote that the "vocabulary [of the Japanese language] is extremely material and is poor in abstract expressions that are necessary for denoting ideas. As a result, the Japanese can easily comprehend fundamentals of science and engineering, but stop short of the noetic spheres of knowledge such as higher mathematics, or the theory of law or philosophy. As soon as they come against any abstract notion, their imperfect language gives out, and they are not able to compose an accurate phrase" (Hesse–Wartegg, 1904).

Once brought into Japan, Chinese Buddhist and Confucian manuscripts containing sophisticated notions of religion and philosophy remained untranslated until the 14th and 15th centuries. For many more years after that, translated tracts were considered as marginal apocryphal works, secondary to Chinese classics. As for the Confucian texts, these were translated even later, during the Tokugawa Period (17th to 19th centuries). To avoid any deviation from the canons, Japanese translators preferred to leave Chinese terms as they were and avoided the creation of new words for borrowed notions. In modern Japanese writing, abstract notions are expressed by words of the so-called Chinese vocabulary (*kango*). The original Japanese vocabulary (*wago*) is used to denote more concrete categories, such as common objects, human feelings and relations.

All of the great religious educators of Japan, both Buddhist and Confucian, were poets and all of their texts were influenced by poetry. The conceptual structure and principles of religion and philosophy that were borrowed from India and China were simplified and made specific in order to be assimilated within the Japanese mentality. For instance, an abstract Buddhist principle, "three worlds in one mind," was rendered in comprehensible terms to the Japanese: "The dew falls on thousands of leaves of grass in every field, but it is the same dew of the same autumn" (Nakamura, 1960). Modern Japanese still believe that their native tongue is "excellent for expressing personal feelings and emotions but unsuitable for conveying logical notions" (Kanayama, 1988).

The Japanese acquired writing systems very early on and managed to preserve a large number of remarkable literary works. Unlike the ancients, who viewed grammar studies as essential, Japanese scholars limited themselves to studying the language of classics and did not pay much attention to grammar patterns. The well-known Japanese linguist Shinkichi Hashimoto (1882–1945) wrote that "achievements in text studies deserved commendation, while, conceptually, the discipline dealt mostly with practical aspects of the language, notwithstanding a modern scientific approach" (Hashimoto, 1983).

Before the Japanese became acquainted with Western science, they had no systematic description of native grammar, nor had they learned grammar in schools. Language textbooks provided only examples of letters accompanied by lists of useful words and phrases. Students had to learn them by heart and to remember the rules of their application. In spite of the difficulty that the Japanese language posed to foreign linguists, Western scholars were the first to provide a systematic description of Japanese grammar in the late 19th century (Aston, 1871; Hoffman, 1876; Chamberlain, 1886).

As for Japanese linguists, until the second half of the 20th century, even the most outstanding were affected to a great extent by applied thinking. For instance, the greatest Japanese linguist, Motoki Tokieda (1900–1967), treated language as a mere neurophysiologic process of speech production. He was strongly against the common thesis of world linguistics, which proposes that a language is a system of conventional and therefore abstract signs (Tokieda, 1983). In his effort to describe the grammatical system of his native tongue, Tokieda faced the problem of correlation between lexical and grammatical elements of a word, phrase and sentence. He proposed a simple and demonstrative scheme, which he called the "box-in-box pattern structure" (*irekogata kozo*) as a solution to this complicated issue (Tokieda, 1978). Tokieda's theory exemplifies the peculiarity of scientific knowledge typical of the Japanese mentality. This is probably why the theory was incredibly popular in Japan. Tokieda's main work *Kokugaku genron* (*Principles of Japanese Linguistics*) underwent 28 editions in 32 years from 1941 to 1973 (Alpatov, 2003).

Japanese scholars have contributed to global linguistics in a specific practical field where they have always been successful. The Japanese (obviously influenced by Tokieda's work) invented the research method called "linguistic life" (*gengo seikatsu*). Without going into abstract linguistic patterns, Japanese scholars used technical aids to continually record the entire speech flow produced by an average speaker around the clock for weeks at a time. They then carefully analyzed the records to determine how and why people were talking to each other and what they were talking about. This "first principles" method of continuous sampling for linguistic study is absolutely consistent with the traditional scope of national creativity and with Japanese attitudes towards investigation of the world.

All of these examples lead to the conclusion that the Japanese perception of the world is distinguished by hyposensitivity to common, universal and abstract notions and hypersensitivity to material, particular and tangible things. A consistent priority for material things over immaterial thoughts and for real facts over intangible theories predetermine the desire to understand and to explain complicated phenomena by using simple ones. Popular science texts and oral presentations, where more-or-less complicated categories are employed, are the most vivid manifestation of this trend. The following abstract from a book by professor emeritus Masamitsu Kawakami, former president of Tokyo Technical University and Nagaoka Technical University and winner of several awards in his research field, is quite typical. Here the author explains the need for dedicated service:

"Now I would like to mention what dedication means for a researcher. Honda-sensei studied alloys for all his life. In 1931, he was lucky to obtain a new chromium-cobalt alloy and then improved it considerably and earned an academic award in 1937. He was a wonderful person and was dedicated to research. Once I heard about an incident after his graduation from Tokyo University. Terada, a young colleague of Honda, had miscellaneous interests and many hobbies. On a fine Sunday morning Terada decided to visit an art exhibition in Ueno Park in Tokyo. On the way he met Honda who said: 'Terada, look what wonderful weather we are having today, come to the laboratory.' There was nothing for it and Terada had to work on his day off... When Honda was asked about what he normally did when he was tired of his experiments, he answered: 'I go on experimenting, naturally.' I think all of us must develop the same approach that Honda-sensei had" (Kawakami, 1989).

The abstract has three prominent features. First, it is abundant in minor details. Second, stories by third persons about the main character seem to be relied on as the unreliable basis for the argument. Third, the conclusion that a researcher must work hard is obvious. What might be expressed in a few succinct phrases is presented by the author with many minor details and intensifiers. He must be appealing to his readers' feelings rather than to their minds.

In his argument feelings and mood predominate over logic and persuasion. This style of delivery over substantive content is inherent in most Japanese books.

The reports of Japanese scholars and experts are similarly typical. Regardless of the audience's background, the presenters' reports are always elaborately and perfectly arranged. Each listener would be given a summary of the report and other explanatory materials (*shiryo*). A speaker chooses clear and simple words to carefully explain every term, which may seem difficult, sometimes using specially prepared illustrations for this purpose. All of the illustrations and materials are carefully designed and professionally delivered. Rather than the meticulous preparation and measured details of the report's presentation, one might wish the presenter could have provided more food for thought by putting greater emphasis on the report's contents. The strongest merit of such presentations is probably the effect of the execution itself: the speaker is diligent and focused, the audience is attentive and agreeable and the applause at the end of the talk is sincere and appreciative. This congenial experience, together with the general modesty of the environment, can somehow compensate for any shortcomings in content, as is frequently the case at such events.

Some years ago, a central newspaper published an article by Japanese writer Setouchi Jakucho. As the author of several popular novels and a famous cultural figure, she explored the lack of imagination (*sozo*) in Japanese youth. She saw this phenomenon as a specific ethical aspect of practical behavior. Such a vision of imagination seems to be the most conceivable for Japanese readers.

She stated that the financially sound modern Japanese society is witnessing a remarkable reduction in imaginative children. There are too many kids who are absolutely incapable of imagining what the other person wants and why. A person sitting next to such a child may change color, but the child will notice nothing until he or she is asked for help. The child is oblivious to the condition of his friend whose father has lost his job. Many awful crimes committed recently by Japanese children can be explained by a lack of imagination (*Nihon Keizai Shimbun*: 30 June 2001).

On the other hand, the Japanese are excellent in dealing with simple concepts and categories. Not many can explain a sequence of actions, the significance and objectives of each operation better than can the Japanese. One can actually enjoy reading Japanese manuals and instructions for some product or device. The language is clear and simple and the text is illustrated by graphics that are sufficiently instructive for an illiterate person to be able to understand their meaning.

The Japanese attitude toward presentation, comprehension and argumentation is quite different from the Western orientation. Claude Lévi-Strauss, who understood Japanese culture well, suggested a differentiation between the scientific mind and the mythical mind. According to the anthropologist, the scientific (Western) mind operates mostly on concepts whereas the mythical (Japanese) mind operates by using symbols (Lévi-Strauss, 1976). Western scientific literature often calls the Japanese world view anti-intellectual, irrational or intuitively sensuous. Robert March (1996) says that the "Japanese are convinced that logic has little place in discussion when something deeply cherished is threatened. When there is a sense of threat and strong emotionality, the Japanese disdain neat, logical structures as unfeeling, unfriendly and cold... The Japanese are also weak in conceptual arguments and the use of analogy, not because they are intellectually inferior, but because they use them so infrequently... When Japanese or foreigners do try to use concepts, analogies and systematic logic, they find that they merely antagonize Japanese listeners by portraying themselves as cold, unfeeling and inhuman." For the Japanese, harmony of logic, a just proportion of conclusions and the elegance of thought are devoid of the beauty attributed to them by the Westerners since ancient times.

Japanese sociologists reinforce this. Hajime Nakamura stated that Japanese expressions focus a person's thought and perspective on the immediate and concrete details of life. This tendency is quite unique to the Japanese. This is why the Japanese way of thinking habitually avoids summations of separate facts into broad statements about whole categories of things, although such abstraction is necessary for logical and scientific thinking (Nakamura, 1967b). These features must be the basis of the accepted truth that where a Westerner would think and analyze, a Japanese would feel and endure.

Worldviews and mindsets are progressively swept along by the swell of globalization. Here, as in many other spheres, the Japanese are borrowing much and learning quickly. In recent research papers Japanese scholars have demonstrated a growing level of logical analysis and abstract thinking while preserving their national peculiarity toward the subject matter.

Chapter 3

Everything Has Its Own *Kata*

Addiction to Algorithms

Many people associate Japan with an almost militaristic conformity to order. Japanese lawns are cut, streets are swept clean, buildings are kept neat and workers are well-trained and well-disciplined. This impression is strengthened by the people's commonality of greetings and speech responses to recurrent situations, by their adherence to moderation and self-control, and by their drive for accuracy and attention to small details. Robert March's observation that "they learn…how to obey and follow the commands of superiors" (March, 1996) also suggests military order and discipline.

Despite all of the variety and diversity of modern Japanese life, the tendency toward uniformity is still unmistakable. Foreign journalists have often described the sea of Japanese employees, dressed in identical grey or blue suits and with identically concentrated expressions on their faces, sweeping into and out of Tokyo office buildings daily. Thousands of neat adjoining houses flicker past the windows of the *Shinkansen* (Japanese Bullet Train), showcasing an elaborate diversity that mysteriously fades into a single exemplar called a "typical Japanese house".

According to travelers' notes, uniformity was clearly apparent in Japanese life in the past as well.

"Common clothes are worn by both genders and all of the social classes wear similar garments; the only difference is the value and color of the fabric. The rich wear exactly the same shoes as do the poor" (Zibold *et al.*, 1999).

"I have never seen such uniformity in both cut and color of clothing as in Japan. In any other country it [the populace] should be called ... a 'gray crowd.' I would rather call it 'blue' here, as all of them, young and old, regardless of gender, age and title, wear gowns as they would a uniform, colored in every imaginable blurred tincture of indigo" (Mechnikov, 1992).

"The estates of the Japanese...do not show any of the sharp differences that are so evident in our [Russian] people... Habits, inclinations and household patterns are absolutely the same for every estate of Japanese society. Officers, governmental clerks, merchants, farmers and workers all live in the same way and arrange their houses and household effects similarly. Wealth means a difference in quality and quantity only, while the main features are still the same. The governor's floor mat is as clean as the farmer's, although the former is more expensive and beautiful. Everyone wears clothing of the same cut, although of different value. Even the comfort level is not very different between rich and poor houses" (Bartoshevsky, 1999).

The public behavior and communication styles of the Japanese reveal a high level of unification. In many situations, the Japanese will address each other by position or title rather than by name or surname. The best-known honorific is probably sensei, which has gained international recognition. There are, however, many more such honorifics that are not as well known outside Japan. For instance, it is not customary to call superiors by surname (and even less customary to do so by personal name); they are addressed by their position only: a department manager is addressed as *bucho*, the director of a center as *sentacho* and a company president as *shacho*. Rank alone, without a polite suffix attached, is used to address any official: a store director as *tencho*, the rector of a university as *gakucho*, an ambassador as *taishi* and a minister as *daijin*. Addressing by family name with the polite suffix –*san*, the most common honorific and a title of respect similar to "Mr." or "Ms." is considered unsuitable because in formal situations it can point to informal relations, which is a violation of the conformity principle. Students in different years of study do not call each other by name or by surname either. Regardless of their personal relations, a junior would call a senior *sempai* while a senior would use *kohai* to address a junior. These words express nothing other than seniority of age. Generally, Japanese call each other by name less frequently than do people of other cultures. Even siblings only rarely address one another by name, usually using their position in a family hierarchy: elder brother (*ani*), younger sister (*imoto*), for example.

In Japanese society, people feel comforted by the conditions of formalized public communication, where a speech pattern or a stereotypical behavior model is followed for any situation that might occur (Dybovsky, 2007). These *pro forma* elements are distinguished by high quality and courtly ways. A "socially mature" Japanese adult must be faultlessly proficient in the art of communication. Traditional etiquette was formed in the Tokugawa Age (1603–1867), as described by Bogdanovich: "An overwhelming proportion of the complicated etiquette requirements that we can still admire in Japan originates from that age. Thousands of bows, token gestures, cut-and-dry smiles had to accompany every meeting between people, especially between a subordinate and a superior" (Bogdanovich, 2002).

The commonality of Japanese speech behaviors have been noted by everyone familiar with the Japanese language. The language has a standard phrase ready for every recurrent situation. There is a phrase for leaving and returning home and a different phrase for starting and leaving work. There are phrases specific to treating a guest, for giving a present to someone, for entering and leaving somebody else's house, for meeting somebody else's child, for seeing an acquaintance after a long time and many others. Having found himself in a certain situation, a Japanese man must say a certain phrase prescribed for that situation by speech etiquette. Such phrases are called *kimari monku* in Japanese. For instance, when presenting someone with a gift one must say *hon no tsumaranai mono desu ga...* (literally, this gift is nothing, but...). When entertaining guests at home, notwithstanding the abundance of dishes, one must say *nani mo arimasen ga...* ([we] have nothing, but...). The full list of prescribed phrases is quite long.

Many modern Japanese guide books state the standard phrases and how to say them, sometimes with the admonition: "When you fall back upon standard etiquette phrases, it is important to remember that you should speak them confidently and without any hesitation...You must use the patterns, not just study them. At first you might feel uncomfortable and uneasy, but this feeling will go away with time... The main thing is to learn the phrases by heart" (Muraoka, 2006).

It is impossible to list all of the situations throughout one's life that require standard etiquette phrases. On a hot day, etiquette pre-scribes that you tell everyone that you are very hot. On a cold day, you must tell everyone that you are cold. Foreigners often remark that the Japanese like to repeat things that are evident. The reply to this is that doing so makes communication easier. Such "conversation" seems to be more ritual than informative. It is like an exchange of token gestures used by a speaker to inform the listener that he is ready to follow the given norms. This conveys a multiple-fold message: I respond to the situation in the same way as everyone/I am not a stranger/I am predictable/there will be no unexpectedness in com-munication with me. In other words, partners in a dialogue are continuously proving their readiness to follow common speech behavior patterns. In a culture aiming at harmony and cooperation in interactions, the interplay between speaker and listener is essential. "In Japan members of any group are actors in a play. The target of the play is to demonstrate to the members of the group that it is a pleas-ure for me to discuss the topics at hand. Although this might, in fact, be far from the truth" (Miyamoto, 1994).

From an ethno-cultural point of view Japanese society is extremely homogeneous. This facilitates and contributes to the dis-semination of many clichés. You can hardly distinguish a road construction company worker from a university professor, or a clerk at the beginning of his career from a company president based on their behavior in standard situations. This is because all of them know exactly where and how to stand, walk, laugh, what to say, how to say it and when to keep silent. This is not an exaggeration. In almost every Japanese company, newly hired employees have to take basic training for several weeks or even several months. During the train-ing, they must comprehend communication and behavioral norms, dress code and other things necessary for work. Everything is explained in great detail in the provided course materials. This is why a newcomer to a company, having met a guest and accompanying him to the meeting place, would walk one-half step behind and to the right of the guest. When moving alone in a corridor, the worker would try to avoid the central portion of the corridor. He would arrive five minutes before the appointed meeting with a client, and knock on the door lightly as soon as the minute and second hands come together. If he receives no answer, he would wait for about ten seconds and then knock a bit louder. When "come in" is heard, he would not open the door immediately; instead he would call out his name and his company in a loud voice; then open the door slightly to ask permission to enter. He will be taught all of these norms before he will be given his first task.

The formation of moral uniformity on the national scale in Japan began after 1868, when the government proceeded to educate its people in ideology. In the previous three centuries, social codes and everyday norms were developed for the four main estates. Each person was guaranteed lifelong estate immunity, but it was almost impossible to change one's attribution to a certain estate. In Tokugawa Japan, the well-known principle of *kanson mimpi* (revere the government, despise the people) was in force. It drew a clear line between those assigned to make decisions and to govern and those who were expected only to listen and to obey.

In the middle of the 19th century, foreigners observing the life in the Japanese capital noted that "Edo is mostly a city of vast dimensions, and the Japanese people have learned and are strictly following the traffic rules, which is so hard to set in our own streets in spite of all the police efforts" (Humbert, 1870). In the Japanese schools of those times, students learned educational chants (*shitsuke no uta*) that reinforced major life habits and behavior stereotypes. To make the chants easier to remember, they were arranged according to Japanese prosody rules: "Get up, wash up, do your hair and bow to your parents." Each day began with reciting the procedure.

No one, including the ruling elite, was discharged from the common rules and prescriptions. Foreign observers reported that "a traveling Japanese lord was a slave to custom and etiquette. The smallest details of his clothing, escort, luggage, marks of distinction, stops on the route, his lunches and even stops for the night were determined by permanent rules. That is why the lord's position is very boring, hard and even dangerous in Japan." (Ziebold, 1999).

After 1945, *shitsuke* lost its significance as the primary method of ideological education, and the term itself became associated with Japan's militaristic past. However, this method is still attractive to Japanese teachers. In one popular book, several professors from leading Japanese universities proposed a return to the time-honored traditions and to strengthen basic skills training in the educational process. "What should the new education look like? It should be up-to-date. It should teach the students how to deal with information and traffic rules. It should habituate the student to taking care of records, because the loss of any records results in the loss of information. It should habituate the student to putting a date on each page of a record because this is very important... The telephone is used mechanically now. Education should give confidence in the correct handling of telephone calls, in speaking over the phone, in using a computer, in using a multichannel TV etc... There is much to be learned of traffic laws as well; how to cross the road correctly, how to walk around a standing vehicle, how to behave in an accident... These are the issues of basic, rather than moral, skills training. If these skills are incorporated into the content of school training, then both adults and children will eagerly attend such schools" (Umesao and Kato, 1993). As a matter of fact, these are the schools that the Japanese attend, as they have no other.

As is apparent from the above discussion, the Japanese live according to rules. Before proceeding to any more or less complicated action, a Japanese person needs to be familiar with the nature and sequence of the process. The set of rules for proceeding in various situations is called a *kata*, which can be translated as "form, sample, matrix or algorithm." There is nothing of an exclusively Japanese nature in this notion; however, there are not so many countries where this notion is as much respected as in Japan. If written instructions are not found, a Japanese person might seek an explanation from a competent person who would automatically turn into a sensei in such a case, regardless of age or social position. The word sensei can be

Figure 3.1:   Young lady as sensei.

applied in Japan equally to an honored professor, a famous politician or a young lady teaching aerobics in a fitness club.

A *kata* and its implementation are important for the production and the quality of Japanese commodities. In most developed countries the price of commodities depends greatly on their quality. This is true as well in Japan, where the more expensive the goods, the higher the quality. As for the reverse, this rule can work only to a certain degree, as quality will never go below some average standard level that is high compared to the rest of the world. For example, it is difficult to purchase a pair of shoes, no matter how cheap, that will fall apart in a couple of weeks. All Japanese-manufactured goods, be they refrigerators or automobiles, are held in high regard in the four most industrialized countries — the United States, Great Britain, Germany and France — where consumers demand high quality commodities. However, Japanese manufacturers are surpassed by foreign competitors as to a product's appearance, performance and ingenuity of design. This is the reverse side of standardization (Takahashi, 2003).

A production *kata* is a set of technological operations. As a rule, a *kata* is well elaborated and strictly observed. Where all of the processes are automated, quality is assured by technical means. Where everything depends on a person, accuracy, punctuality and focus are crucial. Centuries before the age of automated production, Japanese culture began developing the mindset of the future production environment, almost as if it had known that these skills would one day be useful. More correctly, the skills acquired by the Japanese allowed them to excel once these skills could be used to competitive advantage. In either case, by the beginning of the mechanized age, Japanese managers had an army of competent and disciplined employees at their disposal. These employees naturally perceived any public activity, including labor, as performing tasks according to the rules of one *kata* or another and were able to transfer rules from one *kata* to another. Supported by the latest technology, this ability has become one of the vital pillars of the "postwar economic miracle" of Japan.

In order for workers to adhere to the algorithm, it is first necessary to train them. In Japan they do this carefully and consistently.

A standard sheet of paper is attached to the staffroom door at a Japanese school. It reads:

For pupils entering the staffroom.
Instructions.

Knock on the door carefully.
Having received permission from the teacher to come in, enter the room while saying shitsurei itashimasu (excuse me for being rude).
Briefly describe your purpose.
After the conversation, apologize properly.
Leave the room, carefully closing the door behind you.

This is just one example of a *kata*, albeit a small one but one regularly repeated in everyday life. Many more exist, if not in actuality, then in intention and practice. There is a special *kata* to cross the road safely. Every child knows that, at a pedestrian crossing, he must first look around, take a bright-yellow flag in his hand, raise it above his head to start walking. The flags are kept in special cases on both sides of the street on the main roads. If no flags are available, the child should cross the road with his or her arm either raised or extended forward. This habit has been so deeply engrained that, in small cities, elderly pedestrians still cross roads with their arms raised even if no vehicle is in sight.

A *kata* has even been developed to instruct the elderly on how to age properly. In many polyclinics, you can see the *kata* printed on a poster. If you catch a cold, you must wear a mask. This is why many people wear masks during winter in Japan. If it rains, you should open an umbrella, even if you have to walk for only 10 meters

Figure 3.2:   Crossing the road in the right way.

Source: Website of Hiroshima City, accessed from [http://www.city.hiroshima.jp.]

and the rain is light. If you cut your finger, you should bandage it at once; otherwise everyone will take note and concern themselves with it. All of the actions are simple, absolutely correct and unobjectionable. It is the total adherence to them that is amazing. Perhaps the strict observation of this *kata* accounts for why the Japanese live longer on average than people of other nationalities. In 2006, one-fifth of the Japanese population lived to beyond 65 years, and one out of every 10 Japanese over 75 years (Somusho, 2006).

Archery is a popular sport in Japan. To an unsuspecting observer, the process of hitting the target might seem to be something between a ritual dance and a Shinto ceremony. To earn full marks, the archer must master the precision of setting up the shot besides scoring a bullseye. Japanese archers believe that one cannot possibly shoot poorly after the proper preparatory process. The procedure predetermines the outcome. Spectators come to archery competitions primarily to enjoy the beauty of the presentation.

Like everything in Japan, the love of orderliness has a long tradition. Vasily Golovnin, captured by the Japanese in 1811, noticed that

Figure 3.3:   Art of archery.

Source: Website of Kyoto Karaku Ryokan, accessed from [http://www.karaku.com].

Figure 3.4:   Art of tying criminals.

"the Japanese are quite skillful at tying, and it seemed that their law told them how to tie, because all of us were tied by different people but in absolutely the same manner, with the same number of loops, knots, at the same distance and so on" (Golovnin, 2004). "Japanese policemen are...skilled at tying captured criminals. Some time ago...there even existed a special class of policemen whose specialty was the art of tying criminals" (Shreider, 1999). Japanese policemen checked the reliability of each tying technique on noted contortionists who could escape from the most complicated of traps.

A love for algorithms, matrixes and instructions is endemic in modern Japanese society. I once bought a simple screwdriver with instructions in two paragraphs; one on the screwdriver's use and the other on eye safety. Amazed, I returned home. In the bathroom I turned on the hot water tap to wash my hands and a bright sticker of a red X over a hand and the words "Caution! Do not touch to avoid burns!" caught my eye.

Figure 3.5:   Manual for a screwdriver.

It can be argued that these instructions are included to protect the manufacturer from liability rather than to satisfy an ancient compulsion to develop a *kata* for everyday activities. The user may hurt his eye with the screwdriver, and make a million-dollar claim against the manufacturer who will use the enclosed safety instructions for his defence. Alexander Meshcheryakov, however, states that such *kata* are very ancient. He says:

"Even the privy could not moderate the Japanese passion for writing instructions. Here for example, is direction by Dogen, one of the heads of Zen Buddhism, addressed to monks in the 13th century. "When you go to a privy, take a towel with you. Put it on a hanger in front of the entrance. In case you are wearing a long frock, put it on the same hanger. Then pour water into a bowl up to the ninth mark and hold the bowl in your right hand. Change your shoes before coming in. Close the door with your left hand. Rinse the basin with water and put the bowl in front of the entrance. Step on the mat with both feet; relieve yourself in the squatting position. Do not fool around! Do not laugh, do not sing songs. Do not write on the walls. Having relieved yourself, wipe your bottom with paper or a bamboo plate. Then take the bowl into your right hand and pour water into your left hand, wash the basin with your left hand carefully. After that leave the privy and wash your hands. Wash your hands seven times: three times with ash, three times with soil, one time with seedpods (black locust seedpods were used instead of soap due to their bactericidal properties). After that, rinse your hands with water one more time" (Meshcheryakov, 2004).

It appears that the Japanese changed their shoes before entering a toilet as early as in the 13th century. That is why in every Japanese house, you will see snow-white slippers in every toilet. The requirement to close the door with the left hand is also remarkable. It is obvious that if the bowl is held in the right hand, the door can only be closed by using the left hand. But instructions are instructions — do not waste your time on thinking, just do as you were told.

Still, the Japanese love for instructions seems to reveal more than simply a fear of litigation. My final doubts disappeared completely in an elevator where I noticed what I had missed before coming across the screwdriver's manual: "Having entered the lift, push the button

Figure 3.6:   In the world of manuals.

of the desired floor." Well, what can I say? Just one thing: Thank you for the reminder.

There are more behavioral matrixes which are distributed more widely in Japanese culture than in European culture. Moreover, the Japanese are inclined to unify elements of behavior that belong to personal choice in other countries. This is the reason for many of the misunderstandings between the Japanese and foreigners. R. Miller, an expert in Japanese classics, "complained that the Japanese paid him compliments on his translations of their classics into English and then apologized immediately for having business cards only in Japanese, without English" (Miller, 1982, as cited in Alpatov, 2003). An American would reason that if a foreigner knows Japanese, then it is not necessary to give him a business card in English. The Japanese do not use such logic, especially during ceremonial procedures; his *kata* mandates that a foreigner must be given a business card in the visitor's native language. Knowledge of the Japanese language is not addressed by the *kata*, so from the Japanese's point of view an apology is mandatory.

As with everything, the Japanese love for algorithms has its positives and negatives. The positives have been described above, but the negatives emerge when you find yourself in an unusual situation that requires an unconventional solution. There are many such situations in life, and everyone can make a list of his own. I hope you will not find yourself in such a situation in Japan.

The Principle of Conformity and Sense of Humor

The Japanese love for algorithms and matrixes, for standardization and unification of actions and elements can be explained to some extent by a drive for perfection, which is sometimes called Japanese perfectionism or aestheticism. This drive is also concerned with adherence to traditions and a deep respect for precedent (*zenrei jushishugi*). According to Japanese ideas, anything that has been tried and tested is given priority over new ideas. If an entire algorithm has been tested and proven, it becomes essential.

With all of the many and diverse *kata* providing instructions for almost every aspect of a Japanese person's life, the overall effect is one of conformity; for the most part, all Japanese seem to appear and to act identically to one another. According to Japanese rules, the clothing, appearance and mood of any person must conform with what he or she is doing at a particular moment. This extends from proper work attire to sports equipment and even mountain hiking gear. As we shall see, *kata* permeates Japanese society, from art to food to dress to recreation, for a homogeneity that is unparalleled anywhere else.

One important element of the Japanese drive for perfection is the attention paid to appearance. Japanese artists have claimed top honors at the World Packing Art Exhibition since the exhibition's inception. Japanese industrial and art design that has been internationally recognized in recent decades originates from the same attention to appearance. Any tourist guide would point out the tiny portions and inimitable taste of Japanese cuisine. Whether or not the diner appreciates the taste, he or she will certainly enjoy the presentation. This is probably why seven of every 10 visitors to Japan cite Japanese cuisine as the main incentive for a trip there (*Yomiuri*: 19 *December*, 2007).

One manifestation of the conformity principle is harmony between a person's appearance and his occupation or more simply, a love of uniformity in dress. From a Japanese perspective, membership in a group must be signalled through visual cues. Although Japanese school children might receive some elements of their uniforms, such as schoolbags and hats, as early as primary school, most Japanese students wear a complete uniform by the age of 12 when they enter secondary school, and wear it for six years until graduation. Those who are subsequently enrolled at university might have a four-year break before wearing a corporate uniform until retirement.

The climate of Japan is not severe; temperature differences cannot be compared with those of Russia or Canada. Nevertheless, the Japanese, who are used to carefully adapting their surroundings — their nearest space — to the environment, have a list of dishes corresponding to each season of the year. The appetite languishes on hot days, so chilled dishes with a sour sauce are preferred to stimulate the appetite (for instance, Chinese noodles or *hiyashi chuka*). On cold days, hot dishes are better. The conformity principle does not permit the consumption of ice-cream in winter months, although the temperature never falls below zero in most of the country. This is why the sight of locals gulping down ice cream in subzero temperatures leaves an unforgettable impression on Japanese visitors to Russia.

The same conformity principle underlies the famous Japanese seriousness at work. A Japanese man spends most of his life at work and therefore working habits gradually become second nature. The businesslike demeanor of the Japanese can be either true or affected, but it is not customary in Japan to mix work and pleasure, including jokes and laughter. Business always comes before pleasure. Foreign visitors who only interact with the Japanese in a business environment often return home believing that the Japanese do not laugh at all but just smile politely.

Two important issues should be noted here.

First, in Japanese culture, laughter does not always mean what it does in Western culture. Riotous laughter is seen as an expression of emotions that are inconsistent with the principle of public self-control. When laughing, a woman would cover her mouth with her hand as if she were suppressing her feelings and hiding them. This gesture is still a common feature of well-educated woman today. While in Western culture, a smile is as necessary as shaking hands when saying hello, people bow to each other respectfully in Japan. This is changing in our increasingly globalized world, and the Japanese have begun to smile more frequently when greeting people.

In Western culture, laughter is a purely emotional and mostly uncontrolled reaction, while in Japan, it is an element of public behavior. Its reasons and meaning are sometimes unclear to people from other cultures. There is a remark in Nikolai Bartoshevsky's notes on the European perception of Japanese laughter: "They [the Japanese] laugh quite often, but most of the time they smile in a foolish way, repeating their inevitable *hai, hai*, meaning *yes, yes*" (Bartoshevsky, 1999). This "hai, hai" describes the Japanese's restrained laughter that seemed foolish to the Russian observer. The Japanese do indeed laugh in such a manner, especially when they find themselves in an awkward situation or the focus of attention. The person would hide his confusion and embarrassment with laughter. This is called *terekakushi* in Japanese (*tere*: confusion, *kakushi*: hiding). The Japanese laugh in the same way when they happen to witness irrelevant actions or utterances by other people. Foreigners may find such a reaction unnatural or even insulting, but in fact it has the same intention: to hide the confusion of involuntarily witnessing somebody's misstep. You often hear such laughter during sportscasts when the reporters react to various sporting manoeuvres, including losses. Publicly, the Japanese use gentle and restrained laughter to cover a large range of undesirable feelings and emotional responses according to the rules of etiquette (dissatisfaction, irritation, etc.). For instance, a group of people would respond with such laughter to the announcement that a colleague is late with a necessary document and that everyone will have to wait for some time. In such cases, laughter helps to deflect negative reactions and ease the tension. A. Nikolaev made an accurate observation that Japanese laughter is "not so much an expression of joy as much as a result of long-imparted etiquette and carefully cultivated self-control" (Nikolaev, 1905).

Second, laughter, as an uncontrolled emotional response to something funny and witty, is more restricted in Japanese culture than it is in Western culture. The Japanese try to avoid jokes, humor and laughter in a working environment and often separate humor from serious matters. It is not customary to joke at business meetings, in interactions between service personnel and clients (though clients may do so), and teachers do not play jokes in class. There are, as in everything, some exceptions, but the rule is normally observed. Someone who does otherwise runs the risk of gaining a reputation as a poorly educated person.

A restrained attitude toward laughter directly influences laughter in everyday life. Some foreign authors write that the Japanese have no sense of humor at all, which is not true. Unlike other cultures, Japanese culture does not consider a sense of humor to be of special virtue. Such an attitude can be explained by the fact that a witty joke or an original remark is a demonstration of personal taste or individual ability that conflicts with the expected norms of behavior.

In their pursuit of conformity the Japanese laugh often and without constraint in what is considered the right time and place at various comic shows, informal youth gatherings, entertainment events and other such occasions. Japanese television broadcasts a comedy program called *You May Laugh* (*Waratte ii tomo*). The name itself seems to suggest that the norms of public self-suppression are disregarded, and viewers are free to laugh as they wish. Dramatic genres full of laughter and humor (*manzai, rakugo*) have existed in Japan since ancient times and have always been very popular.

The Japanese and the Western cultures of laughter overlap in this rather large sphere. However, the Japanese segment has specific restrictions unique to itself. For instance, the Japanese do not joke about disease, death, physical and mental disabilities, nationality or race. On the grounds of etiquette, older or superior persons cannot be the subject of jokes. Jokes and anecdotes of a "dark humor" are also prohibited.

Although laughter and humor are of lesser importance in Japanese culture as compared with Western culture, it was the Japanese who first invented a device for measuring laughter. The device is, naturally, compact in size. There is nothing surprising here for those who are familiar with the peculiarities of Japanese national art. The inventors claim that when the device is connected to a computer, the device can measure the intensity of laughter and can even determine whether a person is laughing sincerely or just out of courtesy. The device analyzes the electromagnetic changes (up to three thousand per second) that occur during the contraction of facial muscles during laughter. The device was intended to measure whether or not laughter is beneficial to the human nervous system.

Returning to the principle of conformity, we need to mention Japanese greetings. There are about 40 courtly Japanese statements that are used in everyday situations as often as "thank you" or "would you please". Being so numerous, it seems that the meanings would inevitably overlap, but in reality each statement is used only in certain situations. Generally, the choice of greeting depends on three

(a)

(b)

(c)

Figure 3.7(a), (b), (c):   Funny mimics of *rakugo* storytellers.

factors: place, time and the conditions of the meeting. The combination of the three factors makes possible the diversity of Japanese etiquette clichés. For instance, the standard "hello" would not be enough when meeting an acquaintance who is busy with an important task. His efforts should be noted in a special greeting that expresses gratefulness and an appraisal of the work (*o-tsukare-sama*). If you cross the invisible border and invade a person's personal space, you

Figure 3.8:   Memorial Stone: "Harmony is to be valued."
Source: Website of Asplan Co. Ltd, accessed from [http://www.asplan.jp].

must apologize by using a special form of apology (*shitsurei itashimasu* or *o-jama shimasu*). There are etiquette clichés for numerous other daily situations everywhere and all of these simply cannot be listed. It would require a separate text book just to explain the rules for the most popular greetings. Therefore, by studying the Japanese language, every student automatically becomes familiar with the Confucian concept of relations between people and the role of greetings in the harmonization of relations. This discussion brings us to our next topic, figures of speech.

Patterns of Speech

The Japanese believe that agreement between people is the most important element of global harmony (*wa*). At the beginning of the seventh century, prince Shotoku Taishi prepared the first legislative procedure in Japanese history, where the number one principle was that "[c]oncord should be appreciated; absence of the rebel spirit must form the basis... When the upper echelons demonstrate concord and the lower echelons are friendly, there is always mutual understanding in matters discussed, and they move on smoothly" (*Nihon Shoki*, 1997). Haruhiko Kindaichi (1913–2004) wrote that the "Japanese try not to express their opinion directly; they prefer to support the ideas of their interlocutors by providing the verbal form for the process" (Minami, 1994).

Numerous communicative norms and schemes have been developed by the Japanese to maintain external agreement, such as non-categorical statements, indirect questions, disguised rejections and others.

Non-categorical assertions are used most often in everyday communication. These are related to the expression of one's own feelings and thoughts. For instance, it is not customary to voice a negative opinion of anything or anybody, except among intimates. In such cases a more neutral figure of speech *do kana* (I wonder if it's OK) is used instead of the categorical "I don't think so" or "I don't like it". A non-categorical form is given to statements of absolutely certain facts as well. For example, an employee who sent written notices of a meeting to all of his colleagues the day before will not say "Notices were sent to everyone, so..." The standard version of the phrase must include an assumption: "You might have received these notices, so..."

Indirect questions are also heard frequently. They are used to spare the interlocutor from having to answer. For this purpose a question is reshaped into an uncertain assumption, which can either be confirmed or ignored. Japanese speech etiquette was formed over centuries and it had quite a modern appearance as early as two hundred years ago: "The Japanese consider arguing with fervency to be the extreme of indecency and rudeness; they always deliver their opinions in a respectful manner with many apologies and with a sign of distrustfulness toward their own judgment. They never object directly but instead give gentle hints, mostly by using examples and comparisons" (Golovnin, 2004).

A disguised rejection, which does not look like a rejection at all, is somewhat perplexing to Westerners, who are accustomed to an unambiguous "yes" or "no." Indeed, to a Japanese person a direct negative reply is a violation of harmonious communication (between equal interlocutors) because to reject means to abuse. Even the structure of some phrases is consistent with this rule. Like many other languages, Japanese uses general questions in a negative form, such as "Don't you want to take a walk with me?" In many European languages a negative reply is "No, I don't." The Japanese answer is "Yes, I don't." In European languages, a double negative is aimed both at the action itself and at the interlocutor's suggestion. In Japanese, only the action is rejected, while the suggestion of the interlocutor is affirmed.

That is why foreign experts in Japanese culture warn their countrymen that if a Japanese person tells you "yes", this does not necessarily mean that he agrees with you; most probably this means that he understands you. If he nods his head extensively during your speech as if agreeing with you, this means that your arguments and the meaning of your words are clear to him, and nothing else. However, if he says "OK, let me think," then this is "no" for sure.

In the Japanese language, there are many figures of speech that include half-tones and nuances between "yes," which often means nothing, and "let me think," which means "no." There exists a full complement of other tricks to avoid saying the word "no." Speech behavior norms prescribe not only what to say and when to say it but also when and how to remain silent. The "silence area" in Japanese public behavior is much wider than it is in other cultures. For instance, in communication with a superior or an older person, one should not ask unnecessary questions, express one's beliefs or take the initiative in general; it is sufficient to listen and to remember. Even if a Japanese person has not understood his partner in a conversation, he will not ask his partner to clarify, hoping that he will be able to get the point from the context and from further statements. Objections in a conversation with a superior represent a lack of tact and of good manners. This is a remnant of an ancient Confucian postulate that was later assimilated by samurai code. "A good vassal is the vassal who obeys his master implicitly. We can call him an ideal vassal... You should be careful when talking to older or powerful persons and not speak much about such issues as learning, morals and traditions. Such statements sound impolite" (*Hagakure,* 2000).

A respectful attitude to the superior underlies another Japanese rule that is inconsistent with European etiquette: not to look your listener in the eye when speaking to him. In previous ages, a direct look was considered to be a challenge. That is why today many Japanese prefer to look somewhere else, such as at the tip of their interlocutor's nose, and try not to make eye contact with a stranger.

One Australian residing in Japan decided to uncover how keen the Japanese were on observing the norms of communication. When asked about his ancestors he used to answer, with a straight face, that his great-grandmother was a kangaroo or a koala. To his astonishment, the Japanese seldom expressed doubt or laughed in a way that indicated that they thought he was joking. In most cases they behaved as if his answers were serious and did not comment on them (March, 1996). Regardless of what the Japanese were thinking, they could not object directly, voice doubt or make fun of the foreigner without breaching the golden rule that true thoughts and feelings are secondary to outward decency.

Chapter 4

How They Do It

Formalism and Self-Suppression

The Japanese became acquainted with Confucianism quite early in the first few centuries AD. This teaching is not as much a religion as it is a code of social behavior. It describes the proper relations between a superior and an inferior, between parents and children, between a husband and a wife, between brothers and sisters, and between friends. These five sections cover the majority of relationships in society. The Japanese learned these prescriptions and subsequently made them the basis of public relations, and these are reflected in their language and mentality as well. These are the roots of the Japanese drive for the accurate positioning of each person onto a certain social rank and for applying behavior rules accordingly. A superior must be careful and wise, inferiors must be loyal and obedient, a father must be fair, children must be respectful, friends must be reliable and so on.

Any foreigner immediately notices that relationships between people in Japan are somewhat different from those seen in other countries. The well-known Japanese politeness is based on this tendency to maintain well-balanced and harmonious relations. The formalization and standardization of interpersonal communication plays a crucial role in the process. The classification of society into numerous groups and a unified code of behavior make it easy to observe a common set of rules.

Survey results demonstrate the importance of etiquette and of the external aspects of behavior. At the height of the so-called Japanese economic miracle, the observance of common norms was the third most important human characteristic after a kind heart and being strong (*Nihonjin no kachikan*, 1970).

Relations between people are somewhat formalized in any society due to the modern pace of life. In Japan, the rate of formalization is extremely high compared with other countries. When two Japanese people engage in a conversation, each person treats his or her partner as a representative of a certain group that has a certain status, upon which they choose the correct manner of speech. The unusual love for business cards can also be explained by overwhelming formalization. The name of the group (company) to which the card giver belongs and his status (position) in the group gives the receiver a key to the proper behavior to adopt towards the person. If the difference in the status of the two partners differs by too large a degree, a search for delicate ways out of the situation is actuated. Most likely the inter-locutors will take polite leave of each other and avoid any direct contact in the future. The cultural homogeneity of Japanese society, the unification of ethical and moral principles and commonly shared ideas of proper behavior ensure effective communication in a variety of situations.

Communication with foreigners is much more difficult because they come from another social system where people live under different rules. Their status in the Japanese system is not necessarily clear, even if the visitors present a business card. This results in uncertainty as to which behavior strategies and tactics to use, especially at the begin-ning of the interaction. The many unwritten but strictly maintained rules are one of the main reasons that Japanese society remains rela-tively closed and incomprehensible in the eyes of strangers. Foreigners' unawareness of these rules has always caused anxiety. According to polls, the Japanese see the rapid process of globalization as a violation of social stability, an essential value for them. This con-cern is shared by almost eight out of every 10 Japanese (79 percent) (Takahashi, 2003).

Another specific feature is the pursuit of moderation, self-suppression and studiousness in every external activity. The samurai code of behavior stated that "the golden mean is a reference for all things" (Yamamoto, 2004). In the 19th century, Aime Humbert noted how self-contained the Japanese can be in expressing their admiration: "Stormy applause is not typical for Japanese. They would hold their fans folded in the right hands and hit them on the left palms rather slowly, screaming in a restrained manner to express their pleasure" (Humbert, 1870). Under the influence of Western culture, the Japanese now shower athletes or artists with enthusiastic applause, but it is not customary to whistle loudly, as do the Americans, or to beat drums and toot on trumpets as they do in Europe. Japanese fans prefer light plastic balloons that can barely be heard when hit against each other, but that can be seen clearly from a long distance.

According to the same polls, the majority of the Japanese are eager to find themselves in the "golden mean"; ordinary people with typical needs and an average quality of life. In other words they want to belong to what sociologists call "the middle class." In 2003 about 80 percent of Japanese considered themselves to be in the middle class, 10 percent more than in the United States and Europe where the middle class originated (Takahashi, 2003). According to other sources, more than 90 percent of the Japanese feel that they belong to the average majority (Kanayama, 1988).

In Japan, eccentric behavior and excessively emotional speech are regarded as being insincere or lacking in common sense. Japanese youth are allowed some latitude and occasional bouts of outrageous behavior are permitted. Otherwise, Japanese etiquette requirements are strict and cover the entire range of external behaviors. The rules dictate a reserved and practical mode of dress, a suppression of feelings, that speakers use the minimum number of gestures and that they do not touch a partner in conversation. Even popular artists, sportsmen and public figures must follow the rules strictly in order to maintain their status.

The use of plain and practical clothing influences both the fashion styles and the concepts of Japanese designers. Japanese fashion designers, such as Issei Miyake, Yoji Yamamoto and Rei Kawakubo, were at the height of their fame in the West in the 1980s. Since then, however, the Japanese fashion world has focused on more practical and utilitarian designs. "Modern young designers reflect the new social reality where functionality is more important than glamour, and where modesty means morality. It does not even matter today whether your clothing is attractive. Unlike their European and American colleagues, most Japanese designers reject the idea of glamour or even elegance" (Beals, 2001). This observation can be confirmed by a walk through a Japanese city. Says John Beck, dean of the business school at Globis University in Tokyo and a prominent Japanese business watcher: "A lot of (Japanese) people say things like 'Oh no, we just make minor, little changes. We are not really creative.' But to stay competitive, Japan must come up with a new strategy for growth by focusing on creative industries, including fashion and design" (Terada, 2008).

Physical contact during communication is related to emotional expression and is therefore minimized. According to the Japanese ideal, adult interlocutors must not touch each other. Etiquette does not allow for any patting on the shoulder or even simple handshakes. That is why TV reports from the Soviet Union where CPSU leaders enthusiastically hugged and kissed representatives of "brotherly communist parties" greatly impressed the Japanese. In Japan, one may hug and caress children only until they are seven years old. This dates back to an ancient belief, which has its roots in the high child mortality of the day, that until the age of seven years, a child was in the world of the gods and therefore not subject to adult rules. If a child died before age seven, his or her body was not buried but simply abandoned somewhere near the village. After turning seven years old, a child joined the human world and the touching stopped. This is why Japanese mothers do not embrace their own children when meeting or parting, but instead bow politely to the astonishment of foreigners.

The Japanese, who do not hug one another when meeting or parting, find a certain exotic charm in the European gesture. After traveling abroad, Japanese youth are sometimes enthusiastic about Free Hugs, the popular trend of hugging unfamiliar people that emerged several years ago. Groups of Free Hug enthusiasts sometimes appear in Japanese cities offering people the warmth of a friendly gesture that helps to overcome everyday stresses. Sanae Ohno, after returning from abroad, confessed: "I was surprised how easy and straightforward people are there [abroad] in expressing their feelings. When speaking to each other, they shake hands and hold each other by shoulders. This is not done in Japan, where email is the main means of communication" (*Yomiuri*: January 22, 2008). However, despite the enthusiasm of its young promoters, this practice is unlikely to become widespread in Japan. Fortunately, however, one cannot be prosecuted for hugging in Japan, unlike in China where people caught hugging had to answer to the police when the custom was first introduced.

Self-control and self-suppression are essential elements of group and public behavior in Japan. Moreover, the habitual discipline and suppression of feelings contribute to the formation of certain rules of behavior at public events and ceremonies. These events are normally presided over by a master of ceremonies (emcee). The emcee opens the ceremony, makes explanations, gives the floor to speakers and officially closes the event. If the official event is followed by an informal continuation, then another appointed person serves as the emcee for this portion. This second emcee is a toastmaster whose task is to build upon the mood of the crowd and to direct it so that everyone enjoys the occasion. He is permitted to, and indeed must, make jokes, energize the audience and help them to have fun. Such ceremonies are often attended by people who know each other well, so the atmosphere can be quite informal. However, because the event is public, the participants are not expected to make merry or to express their emotions in a straightforward manner. The emcee is like the special personnel (*oshiya*, train pushers) in Tokyo subways who push people onto the coaches during the rush hours so that the doors can close. In both cases, the Japanese rely more on the self-discipline and diligence of special staff rather than on the initiative and improvisation of the participants on passengers.

The pursuit of discipline and order is also evidenced by the strict time limits of any public event, however informal and merry it is. Oral or written notices, such as "The party starts at seven and finishes at nine," are provided to all participants of public events. The belief that every process must have its time limit is inherent in the Japanese perception of the world.

Discipline, self-control and self-suppression are the elements of samurai behavior. Medieval moral rule books outlined very strict requirements for the military estate. Although not always observed, they still influence the look and the behavior of the Japanese. The following is a sample of some of the commandments.

"All samurais must be respectful and modest." "It is ugly and careless to appear untidy before other people." "Be straightforward and flexible, honest and law-abiding." "Never speak a lie or half-truth." "Take things as they are; you have what you have, you don't have what you don't have." "Appear before your master only when you are called. Listen to what he says respectfully. Then go away quickly, do what you were told to do, come back and report on what you've done honestly and frankly" (Sato, 1999).

For many centuries the arts in Japan were, with rare exception (poetry, calligraphy, tea ceremony), considered as crafts and entertainment for the city gutter. Samurais were not permitted to sing, dance or perform on the stage. "It is the role of people of art to deal with arts, not a role of the samurai. If we believe that involvement in the arts is harmful for a samurai, then all of the arts become useless" (Yamamoto, 2000). This is why Japanese men do not like to dance and therefore usually do not. Russian folk dances, with all their acrobatics, dexterity and power, astonish the Japanese by the physical ability, boldness, range and expression required for the movements.

What about originality, individuality, self-expression and other personal features? It would be wrong to say that Japanese culture discourages these ideas altogether. Although not forbidden, a separate space, more narrow and more restricted than in other cultures, is allocated for them. In Japan there is a proper time and place for such displays. Individual initiative, fantasy and genuine creativity are welcome in authorized group activities and in deeply private settings.

Authorized group activities include all types of group discussions and the search for solutions. These include the well-known "quality clubs" in production enterprises and discussions of the *nemawashi* style, which are mandatory for any institution or organization. Participants in such discussions might propose the most incredible ideas or ask the most ridiculous questions without being afraid of ridicule. In private life, people are allowed to pursue various hobbies and leisure activities in spheres where contact with others is minor. Within these spheres, the Japanese show numerous interests and preferences almost completely free from public restraints.

One's unique identity and personal creativity are treated by the Japanese in the same way they treat the enjoyment and delights of life; people love them, cultivate them and keep them out of the eye of strangers. Ruth Benedict was on target when she said that the "Japanese do not condemn self-gratification. They are not Puritans. They consider physical pleasures good and worthy of cultivation. They are sought and valued. Nevertheless, they have to be kept in their place. They must not intrude upon the serious affairs of life" (Benedict, 1994).

However, the greatest portion of a Japanese person's life goes on in the sphere of official public relations, where manifestations of individuality are prohibited. Naturally, the behaviors developed by public life become second nature to the Japanese. The major characteristics include emotional restraint, self-suppression in thoughts and in deeds, priority to group interests, conformity to group norms, accuracy, promptness in obedience and persistence in achieving a goal. When the ability to express originality is necessary, Japanese companies send their employees abroad for training. To observe a Japanese person in a foreign country is quite interesting. In general, the person adapts rather quickly and adjusts to the new communication style, but upon his return to Japan, he soon resumes his former habits.

Japanese etiquette discourages straightforwardness and the expression of opinions, thoughts and deeds. What is there behind the polite mask of the Japanese? It is difficult to provide a definite answer to this question. It is true, to be sure, that the mask is not meant to cover the dark intentions of evil-minded and malicious persons. The people behind the masks are all different; some of them are sensitive and kindhearted while some of them are passive and cautious. I can tell you from my personal experience that explicit aggressiveness and malicious acts for selfish ends are not typical of the Japanese. The observation is supported to some extent by comparative research. One international poll included a question regarding whether or not one should trust the people around them. On this question Japan scored 9th internationally (among 74 countries), with 40 percent of the respondents replying in the affirmative. This result suggests a positive self-evaluation of national morals. By comparison, Russians were twice as cautious as the Japanese, placing 39th with 23 percent of the respondents answering in the affirmative (Takahashi, 2003). Similar characteristics of the main Japanese national features were noted by renowned linguist Yasushi Haga: "Japanese society consists of people distinguished by moderation of all kinds, increased attention to small details, emotional sensitivity, even gentleness, and striving for small scopes" (Haga, 1979 as cited in Minami, 1994).

The Aesthetics of Silence

The Japanese proverb *chimmoku wa kin, yuben wa gin* (eloquence is silver, silence is gold) means that an unexpressed feeling is closer to the truth and therefore more refined. This is the key principle of Japanese poetry, where words are used to construct a visual sequence that helps to convey only the person's mood. This feature of Japanese poetry has often been the subject of analysis and literary criticism. The well-known Japanese philologist Haruhiko Kindaichi (1913–2004) stated that the trend for silence is the most important feature of Japan's national style of expression. "Where oral or written text is necessary, [the Japanese] try to make it as laconic as possible" (Minami, 1994).

This love for understatement and the happiness that comes from comprehension of a concealed meaning is, of course, not unique to the Japanese. If you try to tell your favorite anecdote and must take the time to explain which parts are funny, the anecdote will no longer be funny. Obviously, the desire to understand and to be understood by using a minimum level of expressiveness is universal. It is a special contact between reader and writer on a profound level.

For centuries, the aesthetics of silence has been the dominant Japanese attitude to oratory, public discussions and many other aspects of expression. The Japanese have always preferred the persuasiveness of deeds to the persuasiveness of words. This preference is notable in myths. For instance, when Amaterasu Omikami (the Sun Goddess) had to be lured out of the heavenly cave, no one tried to persuade her by giving an ardent speech. Instead, the gods organized a celebration and Amaterasu became curious and came out on her own accord. Some modern events, such as the Japanese victory at Port Arthur in December 1904, are also the subject of myths and legends. One such legend says that after several attacks failed, and as the Russians fought for the fortress with what was left of their strength, the Japanese commander Maresuke Nogi (1849–1912) organized his soldiers and cut down his own son in front of the line. The fortress was defeated on the same day. In actuality, Nogi's son was killed on the battlefield, but the author's point was that the fort was taken by virtue of Nogi's actions, in the manner of bushido code, rather than by his oratorical skills.

There are many phrases in the Japanese language that can be translated as "to speak well and skillfully," and most of them have a negative connotation. There are also many proverbs that caution against verbosity: *kuchi tassya no shigoto heta* (smart in words, weak in deeds), *akidaru wa oto ga takai* (an empty drum thunders loudly), *naku neko nezumi torazu* (a mewing cat will not catch a mouse), and others. Unlike the Euro-American tradition where oratory is associated with a well-developed intellect, the Japanese believe that verbal moderation is evidence of a deep and integral personality. "[The Japanese] are suspicious about skillful public speakers" (Kanayama, 1988). In the Japanese perception, public argumentation means thrusting one's opinion upon the audience. Sociolinguist Takeshi Naruse states that the "mood of a partner in conversation is more important to the Japanese than is the topic of the conversation or the accuracy of the verbal delivery of thoughts... Verbosity kills aesthetics; it is vulgar to say aloud what can be clear without words..." (Naruse, as cited in Minami, 1994).

In the early 1870s which saw the beginning of Westernization in Japan, discussion clubs came into fashion. These clubs were based upon the Western model, and two outstanding educators of that time, Yukichi Fukuzawa (1834–1901) and Arinori Mori (1847–1889) had a debate on the need for the clubs. Mori spoke against public discussions and gave demonstrative arguments. He said the Japanese language was not intended to be used for public speeches aimed at convincing somebody of something. Such speeches had never been made in Japan and the language simply lacked the appropriate oratory techniques. Up to that time, public speech was used only for the interpretation of classical texts, where the speaker is not speaking on his own behalf and is neither trying to persuade anyone nor appealing to an audience. Therefore the audience's role is to listen and to remember, but not to discuss the speech. Mori even proposed, at a later date, to drop the Japanese language altogether and to replace it with English.

Mori was a well-educated person, but he was not the first to notice the Japanese dislike for public speeches and discussions. A century earlier, Norinaga Motoori (1730–1801), an ardent supporter of the pureness of Japanese culture, stated that "in ancient times, we had no talk at all even about the Way. Not to argue means not to expatiate or have much talk, as is the custom in foreign countries." Renowned Japanese poet Hitomaro Kakinomoto declared in the seventh century "that in our land covered with reed and rice-ears, they haven't argued since the time of gods "(Nakamura, 1960). Therefore, this is obviously quite an old tradition.

Having recognized this tradition, the samurais could not help mentioning women. After coming to power, the military estate put everyone where they should be, and a woman was given a proper place: "two steps behind her husband." Soon the samurai issued a series of moral instructions (*kakun*) describing "the three types of obedience" (to father, husband and elder son) and seven female evils, of which talkativeness was one. Any of these evils entitled a husband to send his wife away from the house. Thus, verbosity was once again declared a vice.

In the Meiji period (1868–1912) the notion of public speech began penetrating the public's consciousness due a revival of political life. Members of the civil movement for freedom and public rights (*jiyu minken undo*) and members of Parliament gave public speeches. This form of public speech flourished in the first decades of the 20th century and rhetoric was introduced as a school discipline.

Figure 4.1:   Walking two steps behind her husband.

As the national political situation changed in the 1930s, the traditional attitudes toward public speech regained favor. The word *enzetsu* as a translation for the English word 'speech' was superseded by *koen* with the same meaning. In contemporary Japan, public speeches as they are thought of in the West take a back seat in public life. Speeches given in Parliament and business situations resemble reports with an analysis, a problem description and proposed solutions to the problems. The habit of public oratory, despite its popularity one hundred years ago, did not catch on.

In Japan, all decisions are made and implemented by a group. This process begins with preliminary discussions known as *nemawashi*, which is the name of the technique used for the transplantation of an adult tree. Indeed, *nemawashi* means "digging around the roots." The metaphor is apt, as during such discussions, ideas are clipped, pruned, moved to a new area and then reinforced. *Nemawashi* is a way to reach compromise and consent.

Ardent speeches are not delivered during a *nemawashi*. Such meetings are a quiet and careful exchange of opinions. Proposals might be made in the form of a rhetorical question or of an assumption. Since nothing is proposed directly, objections are seldom voiced and are indirect when they are. Everyone seems to be trying to avoid any sharp corners and is waiting for the exchange of opinions to generate a natural approach or a point of view that will be acceptable to the majority. A newcomer to a *nemawashi* might find it difficult to catch the meaning of the issue or what the participants are discussing. If a consensus cannot be reached, the meeting will be adjourned. The participants will meet again, and again if necessary, until a consensus is reached. Reaching a resolution by majority vote is not very popular and is used as a last resort. The reason is the same: there may be dissatisfied participants whose views were not taken into account.

There are no programs on Japanese TV with only one hostess, except for the news programs. Normally there are five or six persons in the studio discussing the given topic. The TV audience is not addressed directly; the members of the panel converse with each other. Certainly, there are no objections, even veiled, and the general trend and conclusions are unambiguous.

In Pursuit of Excellence: Tidiness, Cleanliness and Punctuality

Japanese culture was formed by, and is well adapted to, a restrained space. People living in such a space divide the world around them into segments and then skillfully organize them using their imagination, wit, aesthetics and rationality. The process of improving each segment is endless.

From kindergarten age, Japanese children are taught healthy habits, neatness and proper hygiene. They are taught how to hold a tooth brush, the correct movements for brushing the teeth and how to gargle. Gargling is generally the main preventive measure against cold-related diseases. If some children catch an acute respiratory disease in a primary school, the whole class is told to stay home. Children are told that they must brush their teeth three times a day, take a bath and wash their heads with shampoo every day. Japanese pupils do not use ball-point or fountain pens, just pencils. Any corrections must be erased easily and must not spoil the notebook's appearance. These habits survive into the higher grades. At the beginning of the lesson, university students usually put several beautifully sharpened pencils in front of them, and of course the appearance of the pencils also matters.

A famous Japanese tradition is to take off one's shoes at the entrance to any room, which, of course, concerns cleanliness. The floor is usually raised 20 to 30 centimeters to mark the border between the inside and the outside space. In spite of the fact that Japanese bathrooms are very clean, they can only be entered while wearing special slippers that are placed in front of the door.

The Japanese love for accuracy, punctuality and cleanliness was noticed by many Europeans in the 18th and 19th centuries by such comments as: "The Japanese are extremely clean and neat" (Shreider, 1999); "The Japanese like cleanliness, and the amazing cleanliness of mats, the most widely used piece of furniture, can prove that" (Bartoshevsky, 1999); and "The Japanese are very much like Englishmen in keeping order of different kinds. Like Englishmen, they love cleanliness and absolute punctuality" (Golovnin, 2004).

The love for cleanliness and punctuality can explain the increased sensitivity and disgust towards anything that can be considered dirty, unhealthy or polluted. This feature pertains to all people to some extent, but it is accentuated in the Japanese. The last shogun Yoshinobu Tokugawa (1837–1913) lived quietly and modestly after abdicating his power. In 1897, two young thieves entered his house and stole some valuables from his storeroom. The thieves were soon caught and the valuables were returned to the owner. But Tokugawa, a samurai by birth, could not live in the desecrated house and moved to another place (Shiba, 2000). Robert March states two interesting facts: "The National Institute for Cancer Research wipes with alcohol all of the pages of books lent to patients, even though cancer is not contagious... One amusing incident occurred in 1982 when a Yokohama woman found one million yen [more than USD 8,000] in notes in a discarded trunk. Prior to taking the money to the local police station, she laundered and then ironed every note" (March, 1996).

Numerous Japanese TV programs are devoted to cleanliness, hygiene and a healthy lifestyle. In one program, the people in the studio were discussing means for improving the national fight against contamination of every kind. One of the participants was anxious to say that something is wrong with the toilets in Japan. She stated that although the bathrooms are very clean, the taps are not arranged properly. If a person comes out of a stall and then pushes a tap to wash her hands, she will have to push the tap again to turn it off. Her hands are now clean but she must touch the same tap again. This happens every time a visitor uses a public washroom. Is this proper hygiene? The audience agreed with the lady that something needed to be done.

In this way the public attitude toward cleanliness is formed. Before the public pressure became too great, Japanese manufacturers anticipated the national inclination to sterility and began to install noncontact washstands in public places. These washstands are operated by a motion sensor that turns the taps on and off; no contact is required. Every public canteen in Japan must have these devices installed if it wants to have any clients, even if the meals are delicious and the prices are acceptable. Before accepting guests in her house, a typical Japanese housewife will prepare the house to give it a museum-quality appearance and the sterility of a surgical wing. This is one of the reasons why the Japanese seldom visit each other at home.

Accuracy and punctuality are another two features of Japanese perfectionism. The Japanese like to act according to an elaborated plan where they know for sure where to start, how to continue and where to finish each particular stage as well as the entire process. The ability to make a decision on the spot and to improvise as you go through the procedure is not considered to be meritorious and is not encouraged, while the consecutive and accurate performance of the scheduled steps is an essential element of any activity. Most Japanese employees work according to ready-made plans where the duties are prescribed several weeks in advance. Millions of calendars, notebooks and pads of all formats find their new owners every New Year. Careful planning and performance of the plan's points is typical in both the business and private lives of the Japanese. Unlike in many countries where people live in a happy-go-lucky fashion, most Japanese prefer to have a more-or-less clear vision of what they are going to do during each period of their lives.

Time is another essential element of the Japanese perception of the world. A common school pupil may be unaware of the various polite forms and patterns of speech, but he knows for sure that he must arrive at every meeting five minutes before it starts. For an adult, being late for an appointment is a gross impropriety. "International surveys have shown that the Japanese are the most precise, timetable-driven people in the world" (March, 1996).

Modern technology has attached new features to Japanese punctuality. The congruence and concurrency of actions depend on the accuracy of watches. That is why as early as 1940 standard time signals were broadcast in Japan so that people could synchronize their watches. On 10 June 1999, a modern system of standard time was commissioned based on a radio signal generator which broadcasts the time. The signals are transmitted on a low-frequency band and serve the entire country. The accuracy of the signals is guaranteed by using a nuclear clock that deviates by one second every thirty thousand years. Most of the watches presently manufactured are equipped with receivers and automatically adjust the time according to the radio signals. The number of hand watches with this automatic adjustment function is growing as well. Japan has only one time zone, so the entire country can be synchronized.

The drive for punctuality has many aspects and can result in some unexpected outcomes. For instance, it influences such thing as gratuities, which seem to have nothing in common with time. Anyone who has taken a taxi in Japan knows that the drivers wear suits, ties and white gloves. There is a beautiful plate on the instrument panel displaying the driver's surname and a company telephone number. Taxi services offer several payment options, but one of the most popular is a fare of 600 yen for the first 1.5 kilometers, then 80 yen per each distance of 326 meters. Not 300 or 350, but 326 meters exactly.

In many countries, there is a custom to thank service staff by giving them small coins, formally called a "gratuity" but commonly referred to as a "tip." In the United States, for example, the amount of the tip is determined by the client depending on the quality of the service. In some US restaurants, the tip is added to the bill as a fixed percentage of the total bill. Japan has borrowed many practices from abroad, but tips are not one of them. Why is this so?

There are several reasons. First and foremost a Japanese taxi driver, waiter, porter or other service person works on behalf of a group and not as an individual. Belonging to the group is a key factor that determines the rules of their interactions with clients. While an American manager tells a taxi driver or a waiter: "You can earn a guaranteed minimum wage and unrestricted extras depending on your personal abilities; work hard and earn your tips" a Japanese manager says: "Your salary will depend on how you perform your duties; if you work hard we will raise it."

The second reason is that, like any service cost, the taxi fare is very carefully verified and fixed. Because tips can change the fare, sometimes considerably, and because the tip amount can be determined by many factors, tipping is beyond the control of the company and is therefore not allowed.

The third reason is related to a very strict distribution of the roles played in the public service sphere. According to the Japanese ideal, all of the responsibility and all of the authority in a service transaction shall be borne by the service provider. A client is an extremely passive participant in the process. The only thing that he is to do is to relax and to enjoy the service. This is why he is released from even the need to open and close the door of a taxi cab — the taxi driver will do that for him by using a special switch. If you decide, even with the best of motives, to help a salesperson in a store by holding a package for him to put with your purchases, he will most likely get confused and begin apologizing. Your assistance can be seen as interference with his duties and an invasion of his area of responsibility. In the worst case, and this happens quite often, he may understand your generous impulse as disapproval of his sluggishness. With such an approach to role distribution, a client's participation in determining the tip amount becomes a difficult task. Therefore the Japanese believe that it is better to release clients from the trouble.

The pursuit of external propriety and of harmonious relations between people is the next manifestation of Japanese perfectionism. A person must not be suddenly surprised, hurt or be confused by something. This requirement is mandatory and covers various spheres of life in Japan. For instance, despite the popularity of modern media, the Japanese press never show any candid shots of traffic accidents, terrorist acts or disasters, nor do they show any wounded or dead. They try to avoid anything that might shock a reader or a spectator. This might be the reason why violent scenes in Japanese TV dramas are shot in such a way that even a child can easily understand that the fight being shown is a production, and not a very skillful one at that, and that the blood shown is either tomato juice or a red paint. Westerners watching Japanese dramas therefore see such programs as farcical, not understanding that visual realism is not the point.

The hypersensitivity to external correctness and propriety was clearly manifested when the national image of Japan and the people's attitude toward their own history were formed. The main role was played here by the idea of the permanence of the rule of the imperial family, which has provided its citizens with perpetual protection since ancient times, when the gods were creating the Japan Archipelago. Another important aspect is an elevated attitude toward national history. The Japanese would like to treat their history as a continuous ascent from the romantic "age of gods" to modern scientific and technical perfection and social prosperity, free from collapse. They would like to treat it as a large and beautiful *tatemae* (outward stance) on a national scale. The country that is first to welcome the morning sun has never been conquered by a foreign force, the imperial power has always been legitimate and its culture has always been integral and genuine. Any problems that the nation faced on its historical route were overcome gradually, consistent with the general rate of development and in agreement with traditional values. As history shows, some of these attitudes are more patriotic sentiment than they are historical fact.

Celebration and Gift-Giving

The groupism, interdependency and mutual responsibilities of the Japanese are amazing. Takao Suzuki writes that "Japanese culture is a culture of mutual understanding and interaction; the Japanese rely on their partners and are ready for a similar attitude on their part" (Minami, 1994). The effort required to maintain relationships seem to be a heavy burden to many foreigners. Exchanging gifts and messages play an important role in relationships and are an integral part of Japanese culture and enjoy a long and rich history. During the period of the military estate, the rules of gift-giving and the presentation ceremony were studied in *hanko*, the high-level samurai schools.

There are more than enough occasions for gift-giving in modern Japanese life. If you visit someone in his office and intend to ask the person for a favor, a small gift will be appropriate. People leaving for a business trip return with gifts from the city they have visited. A traveler being seen off will also be given a present. Generally, a gift should be the response to any favor you receive. Presentation may be done immediately or in the official gift-giving season, which comes twice a year, once in June (*chugen*) and again in December (*seibo*). Opponents of Japanese traditions say that this is a legalized excuse for bribery.

The boundary between a gift and a bribe is very thin and sometimes elusive; in Japanese culture it is transparent and intangible almost all of the time. In combination with the traditional behavioral roles that attribute unlimited respect to "the inferior", and attribute protection and generosity to "the superior", gift-giving often crosses this vague border. There is nothing better for a Japanese taxi driver than to receive an officer of the government body as a passenger; that is why the taxis gather every evening at the Kasumigaseki, the area of the capital district that houses the governmental buildings. By law Japanese government officials can return home by taxi only after the last train has left. This happens quite often, and the central departments allocate a portion of the national budget for employee transportation. For instance, in 2007, the allowance amounted to 5 billion yen (USD 41,667,000). No holds are barred in the competition for passengers, some of whom pay US$100 per trip. Most taxi companies provide their drivers with compact mini bars to make the way home more pleasant for the fortunate passenger, treating him to free beer, soft drinks and snacks. The agency that regulates the taxpayers' money conducted a poll and found that 520 officers of 13 governmental institutions received gifts, gift certificates and sometimes money from grateful taxi drivers. Government officials have their own cast-iron logic: "When I work until midnight, why shouldn't I have a bottle of beer on my way home or a sandwich at the taxi company's expense, if the fare does not change anyway?" (*Yomiuri*: 6 *June* 2008). Department managers must decide how to combine traditional conduct and the modern ethics of government employees.

Needless to say, in private life, many activities are accompanied by gift-giving. Having moved to a new place of residence, a newcomer usually pays visits to his neighbors and presents them with symbolic and inexpensive gifts, most often bath or kitchen towels in beautiful packs. A housewarming, the birth of a child and other remarkable events are also celebrated by gift-giving. On such occasions, the celebrant of the day always receives a gift from the group to which he belongs. This is an essential element of a group ritual that acknowledges the participation of each of its members. The higher the group's status the more substantial the gift can be. Money for the gift is taken from a joint fund formed by participation fees.

If a Japanese man wishes to repair his house, he will certainly visit his neighbors in advance, apologize for any future disturbance and present them with symbolic gifts similar to those presented at a housewarming. He will do the same before moving to a new place. This ritual is practiced even if the neighbors have no personal relationship with the family.

This tradition was born in the Tokugawa Age (1603–1867) with its solidarity, group responsibility and neighbors keeping an eye on each other. Foreign observers mentioned that "with such a system of mutual observation, the right to choose one's neighbors should be permitted. That is why nobody can move to a new house without a favorable reference from his former neighbors and without the formal consent of his new neighbors" (Ziebold, 1999).

According to Asian tradition, a gift cannot be received without reciprocation from the receiver. An equal status of the giver and receiver implies that equivalent gifts must be exchanged, but when the giver and receiver are not, an ancient rule states that the higher up the social ladder a person is, the more expensive the gift should be. For solemn occasions accompanied by the receiving of gifts or money, gifts might be sent in reply. The reciprocal gifts must be more modest than the original gifts. For instance, after a wedding ceremony, newlyweds can reciprocate their guests by giving them summer caps, tee shirts with their photographs or any other wedding symbol. Alternately, guests are sometimes given souvenirs right away at the end of the ceremony. A funeral in Japan includes a funeral feast and money is presented to the relatives of the deceased. In this case, all those who presented gifts or money will receive thank you letters from the deceased's family.

What do people give each other as gifts in Japan? Almost anything, including some items that would seem odd to a foreigner. This can be a loaf of ham or a smoked fish, a bottle of sake, a pack of beer or a fruit basket. The main point is that the gift must be very nicely wrapped. The appearance, packaging and the place of purchase often mean as much as the gift itself. The tradition of giving common items as presents is very old. In the Middle Ages, parents requesting a teacher to accept their son as an apprentice normally gave the teacher a simple fan or a brush as a gift. The gift had a symbolic, rather than practical, value.

Modern Japanese do not hesitate to pass along an unwanted or useless gift to other people, an idea recently called "regifting" in the United States. Those who do not drink give beer and whiskey to their friends, nonsmokers do the same with packs of cigarettes and vegetarians dispose of the ham. Although looked upon as a lack of gratitude in the West, to the Japanese there is nothing shameful about the practice and the gift's origin is not concealed. A lot of gifts change hands accompanied by notes such as "I was given this as a gift, but I do not need it." Famous people receive so many gifts that they are not able to present all of them to others. In large Japanese cities, there are special shops that buy unwanted gifts. This is a remarkable combination of symbolic aesthetics and pragmatism.

In its march around the world, Saint Valentine's Day has called in on Japan. In many countries, lovers give each other presents on 14 February. In Japan, this festive tradition has been modified, like all of the other borrowings, and adjusted to meet local conditions. First, gifts are given by the women to the men, and not the other way round. Second, these gifts can only be made of chocolate. Third, to avoid confusion, the chocolate is called an "etiquette bar" (*giri choko*). The name makes it clear that the gift is not related to any romantic interest but symbolizes only a friendly empathy or gratitude. One Japanese man surveyed 30 of his male friends regarding their attitudes toward *giri choko*. Eighteen of them said that they were glad to receive the gift, but almost all of the respondents gave the chocolate bars to their friends or family members. An unwritten rule and the principle of conformity discourage a love for sweets in men, and this rule cannot be broken.

Letters and cards follow gifts on the courtesy scale. Nowhere in the world do people send as many cards and greetings as in Japan, and it does not appear that the tradition is being affected by the growing prevalence of email and other up-to-date means of communication.

Messages are sent on special occasions and are written on special forms. Entire study guides have been written on proper message sending. The text must contain obligatory components including a seasonal greeting, an opening greeting, the main content, links and finally a parting salutation. The messages are extremely formalized and contain phrases that are rarely, if ever, heard in conversation. This tradition, like most others, was borrowed from China. A classic book of the 13th century, *Junigetsu orai* (*Twelve-Month Letter-Writing Manual*) prescribed that an aristocrat must write a letter and reply to a friend or an acquaintance at least once every month. Five of the 12 messages were timed to coincide with remarkable events, the other seven were sent "to maintain the friendly relationship." Over nine centuries, the Japanese have written more than seven thousand epistolary manuals, all of which were always in demand. From the notes of foreign observers in the nineteenth century: "Japanese of the higher circles are proficient in all their customs of refined politeness. They never mix up those whom they must pay a personal visit with those for whom a personal card will be sufficient. They also know those to whom the card must be delivered in person and those for whom sending the card through a servant will do. Each card has a special format and decorations depending on the title and position of the potential receiver" (Humbert, 1870).

The Japanese might no longer write letters every month but three or four seasonal cards per year is the norm now. The peak season is the New Year. Exchanging New Year greetings could be considered a national pastime but for the serious attitude toward the procedure. According to reports in the Japanese media, the most disciplined people spend several hours daily writing hundreds of greetings as the New Year approaches. It is simply impossible to remember all of the people who have greeted you and to whom you must respond. Therefore the Japanese usually store the cards they have received and then write their cards according to this list. Certainly, this method of writing postcards and letters gives less individual pleasure to the addressees, but no one is offended. The principle of reciprocity is automatically maintained, although with a one-year delay. For instance, if a person greets you for the first time this year, then you return the respect within the next year. It is not customary to reply to courtesies in January — everything must be done in time. If a greeting from an old friend fails to come in a certain year, he will be automatically deleted from your list of addressees.

Convenient rules were developed in order not to mix joy and sorrow. For instance, if someone's close relative dies this year, the person should not exchange greetings. In this case, he will send letters of apology to those he exchanges greetings with and explain everything in detail. Phrases in such letters are strictly formalized; they don't require any individual creativity.

Generally, the drive for formalization is one of the main reasons for the popularity of written communication in Japan. It is easier to write a letter according to all of the etiquette rules than it is to communicate orally. Besides, written text has always been more important in Japanese culture. This is explained first of all by the peculiarities of the written characters and by the material form of the communication. A written text can be stored and read again, whereas sounds vanish in time and in space. That is why visual images are primary and aural representations are secondary. This trend is also evidenced by the fact that the Japanese seldom dub foreign feature films and instead provide them with subtitles. The number of TV programs where all of the speech is provided in subtitles running at the bottom of the screen is growing every year. Japanese viewers are more used to seeing the words than they are to listening to them.

Chapter 5

Cultural Rituality and Group Behavior

Touching Eternity

Sociologists distinguish between two types of groups — open and closed. The latter group includes people who are truly committed to the group and who consider the group's common goals as their own. In cases where personal interests do not coincide with group objectives, priority is given to the group. Such an approach is reflected in the well-known concept of *messhi hoko* (sacrifice of self in service to the public), which was partially formed under the influence of the samurai code of honor. "Being a vassal is nothing else but following your master, entrusting him to make decisions as to what is right or wrong and sacrificing your personal needs." This is one of the postulates from *Hagakure* (*Hidden by the Leaves*), a well-known practical and spiritual guide for warriors.

The idols of devoted and selfless service changed over time; until 1868 it was the shogun, the regional lord (*daimyo*) or his direct vassal, and then the Emperor. After World War II, most Japanese people chose to stick to their companies as their closest life-supporting group, regarding them as objects worthy of loyalty. In everyday communication the Japanese add the polite suffix -*san* when they mention companies' names (Toyota-*san*, Toshiba-*san*), regardless of the companies' size and status, thereby attributing to companies a private and personalized character.

Japanese society consists of numerous family-style groups organized on a hierarchical basis. The state, with its laws, tops the pyramid. Moreover, the entire nation, to some extent, feels like a big family where peace and harmony should prevail. Japanese scholar Yaichi Haga (1867–1927) wrote the following about this trend: "Individuals or groups of individuals make up the main constituents of Western society. In Japan, sets of families make up the state and this is a crucial difference" (Nakamura, 1960). Closed groups bear such a character when the relationships between members of the group are more important than external links and when intra-group rules are a priority. If the interests of the group require the breaking of outside norms, then it should be done.

In 2007–2008, several medical universities in Japan were rocked by scandals in which candidates seeking degrees had bribed the universities' leading professors. At the Yokohama Municipal Medical University (*Yokohama shiritsu ika daigaku*) two-thirds of all of the scientific researchers — including professors and degree-seekers — were involved in illegal payments. Potential degree holders were not experienced criminals but were simply forced to follow a long-established tradition. Former inspector Norio Munakata, who headed the official investigation of the case, said that "they didn't necessarily give cash gifts because they wanted to be treated favorably in degree screenings. They didn't think it was good [to give gifts] but they did it because it was a customary practice. They were trapped in a group mentality of considering that if everybody crosses against the red light, then there's nothing to be afraid of." The final report that was released by the university internal committee tasked with investigating the gift scandal noted the danger to each medical department of acting as a closed organization (*Yomiuri*: 7 August 2008).

The cult of ancestors was cemented in Japan from an early century. In ancient Shinto rituals, a central place was given to family altars designed for worshiping *ujigami* (family gods), who were believed to link the living with their ancestors. Family members tried to maintain the family's honor and dignity in pristine condition in order to ensure the continuity of the generations.

At the beginning of the 20th century, A. Nikolaev wrote: "The whole family structure is determined...by the cult of ancestors, which forms the very basis of all the religious beliefs of the Japanese nation. The integrity of the family, its continuity in the distant future and its deep commitment to the past compose the foundation of family relations. These principles are so strong that the interests of individual members of the family are sacrificed for their sake. Indeed, in many cases, the state regards a family as a clan and does not see the individual as a constituent of society; this principle...is implemented with such consistency and rigidity that it astonishes representatives of Western individualistic culture" (Nikolaev, 1905). The Japanese, who were interrogating Russian sailors commanded by Lieutenant Commander Vasily Golovnin, initially could not believe that the crew members serving on one ship came from different cities (Golovnin, 2004). According to Japanese concepts, such a situation could hardly happen.

In the Middle Ages, the family, and not the individual, bore a socially accepted status. But unlike Chinese or Indian families which were solely based on consanguinity, the Japanese family was reinforced by a social agreement. Family members of lineal consanguinity could be expelled from the clan while people without any consanguinity could be accepted into it. The head of the clan had the right to deprive any of his children of his inheritance or of the family profession, both of which were a type of expulsion from the clan. If the expelled person failed to be adopted by another family, he was then an outcast.

The head of the family could also skip his own child and nominate a foster son, such as a committed pupil, as his successor. Two conditions were required for adoption: the adopting person must be of age and he must be older than the adoptee by at least one day. Thus, families with high social status usually did not count on nature and preferred to invite pupils into their homes, choosing them from among distant relatives or sometimes from complete strangers. This practice served as a guarantee that the family business would be continued, even in case of death or the inability of the blood heirs. The list of family clans that "supplied" potential successors was kept secret and it was a great honor to be adopted by an influential family. This peculiarity of the Japanese family pattern was described by Vasily Golovnin (1776–1831), who had lived in Japan for two years as a captive: "It often happens that the lord, seeing the incapability of his own children, deprives them of their inheritance and adopts the brightest of the junior sons of some other lord, of his relatives or even of a complete stranger, and he himself brings up the adopted boy and then passes to him the title and all of his possessions. This practice has the result that influential lords in Japan are almost always smart people who have great talents for state affairs" (Golovnin, 2004).

The Tokugawa clan, which provided the shoguns that ruled Japan from 1603 to 1867, was no exception. The clan regularly accepted boys from three related aristocratic houses — Kishu, Owari and Mito — into the family for education. There are many cases in the history of Japan when foster sons glorified the families that had adopted them. For example, the last shogun Yoshinobu Tokugawa (1837–1913) originally came from the Mito clan, an offshoot of the Tokugawa clan, but he became heir to the supreme sovereign as a foster son in the Hitotsubashi family.

In Japan, the head of the family performed important social functions and enjoyed as much respect as the general manager of any of today's enterprises. Like any executive, he had his term of service and could not leave until he turned 60 years old. Only a court ruling could remove the head of the family from his position of duty. All of these norms were written into the civil code of that time. In most cases, patriarchs regarded their family responsibilities as work and many of them looked forward to the day when they could retire and pass on the duties and powers to a successor. The head of the clan, like an heir to the throne, was appointed in advance and his name was solemnly announced in public. The candidacy of a would-be successor in the Tokugawa clan had to be formally approved by the Emperor.

The management and representative functions of the family head determined the rules of his behavior in public and at home with his family. The Western tradition of "showing in public" with a spouse or inviting other couples to celebrate family events is completely alien to Japanese culture. Even today the joint participation of both spouses in public events is a rare practice. Unwritten but long-established rules forbid them from even working at the same enterprise. In most cases the husband and the wife have completely different life styles and only share common interests at home. But, even here, their duties are strictly divided; the husband earns money and takes his family for walks during weekends while his wife takes care of everything else. Family duties wholly and fully determine the type of relations and the behavior of married people. Takao Suzuki writes: "In Japan spouses do not act like a husband and a wife but like a father and a mother. They won't demonstrate love and affection. It is a sphere of private relations that should not be shown in public. When in public, spouses behave as if they do not know each other" (Minami, 1994).

For centuries, the Japanese authorities considered as "an operating unit" not only a family with blood ties but also any organized group, regardless of its activities. The main requirement was that the group had its inner hierarchy and a working set of rules.

At the beginning of the 20th century, the blind clearly stood apart from many other social classes and groups in Japan. Organized like a military unit, this group had a monopoly on one certain type of activity: massage. Some foreigners who were surprised by this fact thought that it was caused by Japanese aestheticism: "canons of decent behavior require that touching and patting should be performed by people who cannot see" (Humbert, 1870). However, moral norms could hardly be a true reason for this fact. Most probably, it was for practical purposes and common sense. For a masseur, the sensitivity of his hands is more important than his sight and it is widely known that the hands of the blind person, according to the law of compensation, are more sensitive to touch than are the hands of people who are able to see. "When it gets dark," G. Veilerze writes, "a blind masseur would take his pipe and...wander along the city's streets and the sounds of his pipe would let the residents know that he is ready to provide his services." Like all other groups of that time, the Japanese society of blind people was closed and, according to Vasily Golovnin's definition, a "strange institution." "The blind people are absolutely out of the attention of the city's authorities even when they may face a death penalty for criminal actions" (Nikolaev, 1905). The authorities were sure that the society, which had its own system of rules, punishment and rewards, was able to cope with any case. This smooth functioning

Figure 5.1:   Blind masseur.

of the "mechanism of group life" has deep roots and forms the foundation of the distinctiveness of Japanese society.

Not only minor social groups but also many state institutions in Japan were organized like military units. After 1886, pedagogical colleges had a squadron platoon detachment structure. Each unit had its number of members and its appointed commander, the curriculum included military-style physical training and the entire regime of future teachers was in line with a set of strict college charter rules. Teachers who had graduated from such colleges were referred to as "military men in a civilian uniform."

The understanding of the family's role and place in Japanese society is mainly determined by the special attitude of the Japanese toward time, which is expressed in the proverb *keizoku wa chikara nari* (literally, "continuance is strength"). Only those things that have passed the test of time are considered truly strong, viable and worthy of respect. Partially influenced by the ideals of Shinto, the Japanese believe that the main purpose of life is to continue the business that was started by ancestors. It is good if business can be developed and taken to a higher level but it is more important not to let it collapse.

Family is the closest knit of all human groups and therefore all of the above mentioned characteristics apply to it fully. "Members of the family come and go, but the family itself is eternal." This point of view has hardly changed over the centuries. Be it today or many years ago, for a Japanese man to become a member of an organized group is to touch eternity and to leave his mark in it; such a goal is worth sacrificing his life for.

The art of the tea ceremony (*chanoyu*) came to Japan from Chinese monasteries. Initially only major medieval warlords held such ceremonies. Their example was followed by low-ranking samurais and then the ceremony spread across the whole nation. A famous master Sen Rikyu (1522–1591, whose social name was Yoshiro Tanaka) is the developer of the Japanese philosophy of *chanoyu*. His successors later divided the ceremony into three forms, which currently represent the three major schools of the tea ceremony: *Omote-senke*, *Ura-senke* and *Mushyanokoji-senke*.

There is a school of the tea ceremony Ura-senke at Moscow University. An Internet site presents it in the following way: "The Ura-senke Fund, like any tea society, has a hierarchical structure. The head of the organization and the spiritual leader of all interested people practicing the tea ceremony is a Great Master of the 16th generation Sen Genshitsu Zabosai Iemoto who is also the director of the school 'Tea Way' and is the head of the research center of tea culture. His successor (the eldest son in his family) traditionally holds a significant position in the tea society as the Wakasosho, or 'young master.' One of the key positions in the hierarchy is held by 'masters of upper rank' (*Gyotei-sensei*), and they are masters of the highest level who devote their lives to studying, practicing and teaching the whole system of knowledge about the tea ceremony. They are the main assistants to the head of the house, custodians of traditions" (Chanoyu, 2008).

Even more schools and trends can be found in the art of ikebana. There are about 10 rather large groups but the most popular among them are *Ikenobo*, *Ohara* and *Sogetsu*. The older the school, the more reputable it is; the more effort it has invested into its development and the more authority it has. The *Ikenobo* school was established in the 15th century and its current head, Sen'ei Ikenobo, comes from the 45th generation of the clan's founders. The *Ohara* school was founded in the 19th century and has more than 130,000 followers, while the *Sogetsu* school, despite its relatively recent founding at the beginning of the 20th century, has already won the attention of almost one million adherents worldwide. All Japanese schools and trends, regardless of the type of activities they conduct, have their own structures, hierarchy, cult leaders, certification and promotion systems and list of followers.

In Japan, there are many industrial, trade and craft dynasties represented by tens of generations. For example, in the city of Osaka, there is a sushi restaurant that was opened more than 350 years ago. The Japanese believe that arts and crafts are not the only spheres that require a serious dynastic approach. In the Tokugawa Age (1603–1867) the family clan of Kasai, which originated in the 12th century, was well known in Japan. In the suburbs of Kamakura is a place called Kasaigayatsu that is supposedly the place of origin of this clan. At the beginning of the 17th century this clan was given a monopoly (a great honor) to clean the sewage pits of the huge castle Edo, the residence of the powerful Tokugawa shoguns. Two ships used to leave Kamakura for Edo in the morning to bring fresh vegetables to the capital and in the evening the ships returned loaded with barrels of excrement. Some gossips say that because of this, the residents of the capital never ate fresh vegetables without thermal treatment (Furukawa, 2008). It is difficult to confirm that this is the main reason, but the contemporary habit of frying or boiling fresh vegetables is notable. Thus, not only have generations of noble aristocrats entered into the records of history but also generations of sewage cleaners.

Such an attitude toward group activity can be seen in modern Japan in many spheres, including household activities. The Japanese tend to form groups of many kinds and keenly support their activities. They spare no small amount of personal time, effort and money on them. Termination of the group's activities and its collapse is a very painful process. Even if a group has worked to its full potential, all possible efforts are usually applied to prolong its existence. When a well-established group is threatened with termination, the situation captures national attention.

Several years ago, a large Japanese corporation operating in the stock market went bankrupt. The announcement of the bankruptcy was performed according to all of the traditions of Confucian ritual. The corporation management publicly admitted responsibility for the bankruptcy and then asked their subordinates who had lost their jobs to forgive them. During a ritual bow, they all had tears in their eyes, seemingly quite genuine.

In many industries there are funds for mutual support built by the collection of financial contributions from the members of the organization. Despite fierce competition in their professional fields, all organizations are united by the concept of professional community. For example, all private universities in Japan are members of the same association. These universities are currently experiencing the largest enrolment declines since World War II. Ruthless competition for students will eventually lead to the closure of some of the universities. Therefore the association has created an insurance fund that will be used to support those who lose their jobs as a result of a closure. Although they are competitors, the members of the association collect money for their rivals.

Masks and Rituals

The relationship between group members and outsiders has a remarkably ritualistic character. In the process of such communication, the Japanese put on imaginary masks that are appropriate in certain situations. Such masks help to hide entirely the person's true face, leaving no place for personal emotions. In any society, people perform different roles and consequently they have to wear certain masks from time to time. The peculiarity of the Japanese people is that they use a great variety of masks and the masks always fit perfectly. "In general we can say that an ordinary Japanese man seems to be kind, well bred and polite in everyday life but to find out whether these emotions are sincere is possible only in separate cases since the art of public behavior...has been mastered by the Japanese to a state of perfection, and this is common not only for the upper classes of the society but for all Japanese without any exceptions" (Pozdneev, 1925).

During road repairs, a regime of one-way traffic is often introduced on narrow Japanese streets and road workers must regulate the traffic. In this situation, workers give a military-style salute to every passing car, touching their hats with a slight bow to apologize for the inconvenience. These gestures greet every motorist and there is nothing personal about it. Communication is performed between two groups: one group (the road repair company) addresses another group (the drivers). The Japanese man communicates in such a way for most of his life.

Every aspect of group life is highly ritualized, from admittance to behavior inside the group and when leaving the group. The more prestigious the group, the more emphatic are its rituals. If a person decides to play several sets of tennis with a new group of people, it will be sufficient to be first recommended by one of the regular members and to briefly introduce himself. However, if you are accepted into a well-established group for a more or less considerable period of time, you will have to address the group members by giving a short speech. It is necessary to mention who you are, where you are from and your reasons for joining the group. Being a novice, you can also ask for support or advice and promise to apply all of your efforts to achieve the desired results. Applause usually ends the official part of the ritual, after which follows an informal part; traditionally a welcome drinking party (*kangeikai*) at which the newly accepted member heads the table and becomes the center of the party's attention. At the party, he will have to get acquainted with everybody by mingling around the table, having a couple of drinks and having friendly conversations with everyone. Once he has accomplished the actions mentioned above, the formal ritual of acceptance can be considered complete.

Leaving a group is ritualized in the same way. The group members receive advance notification and, during an informal gathering, the person who wants to leave explains his motives, outwardly proper but

Figure 5.2: Saluting on the roads.

not necessarily true. The induction ritual is then repeated. The person has to address the members with a farewell speech at the last meeting and to attend a relatively solemn party (*sobetsukai*). This ritual is obligatory and only minor deviations are permitted.

Complete adherence to rituals and etiquette might involve not only kindness, courtesy and other pleasant things; it can press, humiliate and sometimes even kill. Pozdneev wrote that "the Japanese are undoubtedly extremely polite people, but it is not a personal quality of every Japanese man but an obligation of his lifestyle. When it is necessary to display superiority, to humiliate another person, it well might be that no other people can be so artful in tormenting a victim and being so immensely arrogant and mean as the Japanese" (Pozdneev, 1925). In the time of the warlords, a samurai had the right to kill immediately any commoner if the latter dared welcome him in an inappropriate way, specifically without bowing to the ground or falling on his knees. The first shogun Ieyasu Tokugawa (1543–1616) left clear instruction in his testament: "In case any person from three lower groups causes offence to a samurai, the latter has rights to punish the offender himself...and in case the inferior is not respectful to the superior and insults him, then the latter can treat him like a merchant." Apart from outcasts, the merchants were the lowest class in Tokugawa society and decisions concerning their fate were quick. The most common type of samurai "punishment" for low class people had its own name: *kirisute*. It is quite easy to guess its meaning — the word *kirisute* is formed with the root forms of two verbs: *kiru* (stab) and *suteru* (throw away). The first shogun, at least, tried to put some order into relations between samurais and commoners by introducing punishment for those who did not hesitate to take out their swords. Up to 1602, some warriors, upon receiving a new sword from a swordsmith, used to go out and try it on the first passerby just to see if the sword cut as well as the artisan had assured. It was called "stabbing on the sidewalk" (*tsujigiri*).

Figure 5.3:   Stabbing on the sidewalk — a samurai and his random victim.

However, a set of rules regulating the behavior of samurais, the only armed class in the Tokugawa Period, remained relatively unclear for a long time. What can we assume about the behavior of adult samurais if children regularly fought with swords?

In 1672, 70 years after the order of Ieyasu Tokugawa, the nine-year-old Tokunosuke Hayashi and the 11-year-old Sampei Kawaguchi had a harsh quarrel in which both took out their swords. The boys fatally wounded each other and died some days later. The following year, two 14-year-olds killed each other in the same way. There are many such examples in the historical records of the first half of the Tokugawa Period (1603–1867). Japan is indeed a surprising country. Here the understanding of the value of human life was also formed in an unusual way. In 1682 the fifth shogun Tsunayoshi Tokugawa (1646–1709), who was an ardent adherent of Buddhism, introduced a law ordering the death penalty in cases concerning the cruel treatment of dogs. Several other laws followed, all known under the common name "Law to protect all living beings" (*Shorui awaremi no rei*). Tormentors of animals and those who incidentally caused their deaths were strictly punished. The number of dogs in the capital quickly grew to 100,000, and about 44,000 of these animals were kept with care in an official dog shelter (Furukawa, 2008). Only after the adoption of laws for animal protection did the Japanese notice that a man's life was not as well protected by the law as those of dogs. The next series of laws prohibited abandoning children, the elderly, the disabled and the sick, which were quite common practices at that time. There then appeared a law prescribing punishment for any actions that disturbed the peace and comfort of people in one's vicinity. Punishment was severe and it might have partially resulted in the Japanese politeness and thoughtfulness that we observe today. After Tsunayoshi's death, his laws concerning animals were repealed but the laws concerning people were retained and the number of non-motivated crimes began to diminish.

The peculiar relationships among the different classes in Japanese society and their rigorous observance provoked many conflicts with "foreign barbarians," as the Japanese called them. After Japan allowed foreigners to enter the country, misunderstandings of the rules of honor and etiquette caused numerous international scandals.

On 14 September 1862, four travelers on horses were headed for the Japanese capital. They were traders, nationals of Great Britain and the Queen's servants, three men and a woman. They were approached by Hisamitsu Shimazu, a powerful lord of Satsuma Province and one of the most influential samurais of that time. Shimazu was traveling in the opposite direction with about a thousand of his servants. The Japanese met the English travelers near the village of Namamugi (in what are now the suburbs of Yokohama). The lord's watchmen stopped the Englishmen, demanded that they get off their horses and give right of way. The latter did not show appropriate obedience and respect, resulting in an attack. One of the travelers, Charles Richardson, was stabbed on the spot; the other two men were wounded, but the woman was unharmed. This incident stirred intense reaction among foreigners, who considered the attack unmotivated and barbaric. Great Britain demanded £100,000 compensation from the Japanese government, official apologies and punishment of those who were guilty. The Satsuma clan rejected the demands. Eleven months after the incident, seven English warships arrived bearing an ultimatum from the Queen. The Satsuma lord responded that he could not understand why the Queen of such a powerful country as Great Britain should be concerned with the fate of a lowly merchant who had been punished for insulting a Japanese samurai. Eventually, they failed to reach an agreement. The incident caused a sea battle in the bay of Kagoshima in which 70 people were killed and about 500 houses as well as three ships recently bought by Satsuma lords were burned. The battle intensified the coming civil war in Japan and turned the Satsuma lords into the bitterest enemies of the shogun and all foreigners.

According to witnesses, similar conflicts between samurais, who rigorously stuck to their traditions, and foreigners took place regularly in the suburbs of the capital: "Bloody punishments executed by arrogant samurais over intended or unintended offenders went on and on, each time causing diplomatic incidents and the threat of diplomatic interference" (Mechnikov, 1992).

Behavior Categories

The scrupulous attention that the Japanese pay to interpersonal relationships and fundamental categories is mainly explained by the influence of Confucianism. Buddhist postulates were also often adapted for use in everyday life. According to the Japanese perception, all surrounding material objects should have their own names and places. The same approach is applied when they think about concepts and categories reflecting the understanding of rules for human behavior. None of the concepts originated in Japan; all of them can be found in other cultures. They are universal and typical of any situation in which people communicate. Japanese culture is unique not because it has concepts unknown in other cultures but because it treats them in a special way, filling them with new meanings and systemizing them by using different criteria. These concepts do not have firm equivalents in other languages and therefore they are often used without translation, such as ikebana, kimono, and others. The main Japanese ideas regulating the relationships between people include *tatemae, honne, hikae (enryo), amae, giri,* and *sekentei.*

Tatemae and *honne*: there is no established origin of these terms. In ancient times, the word *tatemae* described a ceremony that was held after the establishment of a building's foundation. As for *honne*, some believe that the word originates from a combination of *honto no neiro* (real sound, true timbre). *Tatemae* and *honne* were frequently used in speech and gradually acquired completely contrasting meanings. In modern language they can represent a wide spectrum of notions.

Tatemae can have the following meanings: (1) things that are pronounced publicly, (2) things that coincide with group interests, (3) a common wish or goal, (4) a systemized theory and practice, (5) in religion it is an orthodox belief or one of its versions, (6) a father, paternal line or position and (7) a tradition or precedent.

Honne can have the following meanings: (1) things that are kept inside one's heart, (2) things of personal interest, (3) personal wishes and goals, (4) a non-systemized theory and practice, (5) in religion it is a secret, apocryphal theory or doctrine, (6) a mother, maternal line or position and (7) an innovation or reform (Shibata, 1986).

Any idea, deduction or reasoning can be used as an external formally demonstrative attribute (*tatemae*) if it is difficult to oppose such an idea in public. It can be a line or scheme of behavior and thoughts admitted by the majority of people, an undisputable virtue or any prioritized thing or idea. For example, it is difficult to oppose postulates for which every person is striving, such as happiness, or the idea that a strong person should not offend a weak person, etc. Therefore, such attributes are often used in official public argumentation.

Anything connected with a person's heart and senses can be seen as a true, hidden essence (*honne*) but these things should not be discussed in public. The reasons for reticence can be alternately appropriate or lame. Such a dichotomy can be found in Western culture as well but the elements are opposed to each other by using different criteria. Westerners see lame reticence as hypocrisy or duplicity while appropriate reticence is referred to as tact or prudence. Here we can find the hidden Christian habit of judging all people and actions as either blessed or cursed. For example, if a person thinks badly about someone but speaks complimentarily of him, then he is seen as two-faced and his behavior is condemned. However if he thinks badly about a deceased person but speaks only good things about him or keeps silent, then he is seen as behaving with great tact and such behavior is appreciated. The only difference is whether the person being discussed is dead or alive.

The Japanese do not divide reticence into good and bad. It can surely help or hinder the achievement of personal goals, but generally this reticence is intended to smooth things over and to deal appropriately with delicate situations.

According to Japanese etiquette, it is preferable to solve a difficult situation by using the appropriate external formal attributes instead of voicing the facts that can disgrace the participants, even if these formal attributes completely differ from reality and even if everybody knows it. *Tatemae* is used to help the participants to maintain their honor in the situation and to avoid a direct clash of interests. This principle dominates the sphere of formal and official relations and forms the foundation of Japanese self-control. "A Japanese man who has been bred according to old traditions is a polite, tactful and fairly cultured man. If a Japanese man with such an education is a pretentious and proud person by nature, then he will artfully hide these qualities, displaying modesty and prudence in public" (Vollan, 1906). "A Japanese man always tries to be polite, calm and emotionless. To share grief publicly is considered non-esthetic and thus unacceptable in Japanese society" (Nikolaev, 1905).

The sphere of influence of the *tatemae* principle is very broad. In many Japanese hospitals, a patient undergoing diagnostic tests for a serious illness will be offered a choice in how the results are announced. The patient's choices are: (1) to be told all of the information and the full details concerning the illness, (2) to have the patient's relatives informed about the illness and methods of treatment but to not inform the patient and (3) to perform treatment without informing the patient or his relatives about his condition. Here, the second and third variants are based on the principle of *tatemae*, having the form of reticence by mutual agreement.

Tatemae is often used even in informal, friendly and family relations. This specific feature of the Japanese character is seen by foreigners as emotional isolation and insincerity, even towards people with whom they should be close.

One foreigner who married a Japanese woman stated that "once the honeymoon period ended, I spent the next 10 years trying to understand where my wife had come from. Part of the problem was that she, like so many Japanese, refuses to communicate what she is thinking or feeling, or, which is hardly any better, she gives me a *tatemae* explanation that explains nothing. It has been a very painful process for me and for her too. I'm surprised that we are still together" (March, 1996). A German researcher says about the salutations of Japanese girls: "Why are these salutations so irritating? Because they are artificial and not genuine and extra-expressive signs of friendship that do not reflect true feelings. On the contrary, when a Japanese girl meets with a person whom she dearly loves, she would hide her feelings and never show them in public" (Noiman, 2001).

In Western traditions, profound and fair friendships without restraints and limitations are of high value. People who are blessed to have such friendship are considered fortunate. The Japanese stress personal loyalty accompanied by the strict observance of etiquette. The following well-known Japanese proverbs *shitashiki ni mo reigi ari* (etiquette should be observed in friendship) and *shitashiki ni mo kaki wo seyo* (limits should be put on friendship as well) demonstrate this fact. From the point of view of the Japanese, the relationships between close friends in Russia often cross the line of basic politeness, while the Russians, in their turn, can hardly distinguish between Japanese friendship and basic politeness. For example, if a Japanese man works in a store and his wife's closest friend is a regular customer there, then the man's wife will always find a formal way of thanking her friend for her patronage; the fact that her girlfriend is related to the organization where her husband works will necessarily influence the woman's relationship with her friend.

Regardless of a person's attitude toward the principle of *tatemae*, the habit of concealing feelings and thoughts has deep roots in the Japanese subconscious. Instructions from the Middle Ages instructed samurais to "always watch what you say. One word is enough for people to guess what you think" (Sato, 1999). According to the Japanese ideal, the expression of feelings is unfavorable. Here we can find an explanation for why the Japanese culture is described as a culture of self-control, self-restriction and reticence.

Amae and *hikae*. Self-control and self-restriction in relations with other people play a key role in the understanding of these two categories. The two terms have the opposite meaning. *Hikae* (or *enryo*) can be translated as self-control, self-restriction or restraint, preventing a person from taking actions that are beyond the accepted norms. *Amae* has the opposite meaning: the absence of these qualities when communicating with another person. The *Kojien* dictionary gives the following definitions of the verb *amaeru*: "The use of kindness and gentleness by another person toward you without any restraint" (Shinmura, 1998). A descriptive translation of this word means that the category *amae* does not have a direct analog in foreign languages. Socio-linguists point out that "such categories can be found in other, non-Japanese cultures; however, other languages do not have terms that would encompass all of the meanings and uses of the word *amae*" (Bower, 2004).

The category of *amae* caught the attention of foreign researchers after the Pacific Scientific Conference was held in Hawaii in 1961. The Japanese psychologist Takeo Doi became the first scientist to deliver research results on this category at the conference. He stressed that *amae* is not an exclusively Japanese phenomenon and that it is quite possible to study the psychology of human relations in any culture by using this category (Doi, 2001). However, the idea is best known in Japan, and in 1967 the Japanese Psychological Society (*Nihon seishin bunseki gakkai*) made *amae* the subject of an annual scientific symposium.

In Japanese culture, it is appropriate for a senior (strong) person to show generosity toward a junior (weak) person. Such a principle is in operation on the roads, where drivers represent a more powerful group than do pedestrians. If a pedestrian starts to cross the street a few seconds before the lights changes from green to red, he then continues walking against the red light without any haste while the drivers turning left wait patiently for him to reach the other side, regardless of the fact that the motorist might be pressed for time and that they have the legal right to move. It is not customary to hurry a "vulnerable" pedestrian or to ask him to obey the regulations because such behavior contradicts the principle of *amae*. Sometimes pedestrians cross the road against a red light without paying any attention to the vehicles at all. Of course, this is not seen in modern megapolises, but in provincial towns with little traffic, it occurs quite often. People everywhere violate some minor rules, but you will not easily find any other country where "vulnerable pedestrians" are so confident that drivers as a "strong side" will yield the way. Such pedestrians are hardly aware of the fact that their behavior perfectly reflects the category of *amae*, and if they were told this they would probably be surprised. "A car is made of iron and a pedestrian is not," they would think, "so the vehicle is supposed to yield, that is all; there is no need for any categories."

Courteous relationships between equal partners go by the name *omoiyari* (understanding and valuing another's feelings or thinking). Motorists can say that such a category also exists in their relations, although it is not always followed. It does show a clear division of all partners into three categories — lower, equal or higher classes — which are obligatory for Japanese ethics and interpersonal relations.

Giri is a set of moral principles and obligations toward other people. It is a very broad category, Confucian in its nature. It has different levels of imperatives: debt of gratitude, debt of protection, loyalty duties, filial responsibilities and others. "No Japanese can talk about motivations or good repute or the dilemmas that confront men and women in his home country without constantly speaking of *giri*" (Benedict, 1994). An old Japanese proverb *oya no on yori giri no on* (*giri* is even more important than filial responsibilities) shows that moral duties are obligatory.

Today *giri* has lost the extensive and undisputed power it had in previous times, but it still significantly influences the actions and the perceptions of the Japanese people.

Once while visiting a doctor in Japan for a slight cold, I was surprised when I did not receive a bill for the consultation. I later found that while the Japanese doctor was studying medicine abroad, he had seen a doctor for a minor medical condition. The case was not complicated and the foreign doctor did not charge any fee for his services. Although this charity conferred no obligations upon the young Japanese doctor, upon returning to Japan he made it a practice not to charge foreign visitors for consultations. By doing so he repays a debt of gratitude (*giri no on*) for the service that was once freely granted to him. It is one of many examples of how the principle of *giri* works in life.

Sekentei (literally, social appearance, reputation or dignity in the community or in public): this notion is often used to refer to the attention paid to the estimates, evaluations and opinions of other people, especially toward you. It can be translated as a consciousness of others, dependence on other people's opinions, reflection or conformity. It might be used either as a factor of reprimand or, on the other hand, as an appraisal of a person's actions from the point of view of accepted norms and traditions. This category is not used solely in Japan and can of course be found in any society.

The category *sekentei* was defined and described by Japanese researchers in the 1960s and 1970s (Inoue, 1977). The word is formed by the combination of two roots, *tei* (appearance, face, honor) and *seken* (human society, local commune). The latter was used in the Japanese language until the middle of the 19th century instead of the modern word *shakai* (society). The word *shakai* appeared in the early period of Meiji modernization and replaced the word *seken*, which nevertheless can be found in many sayings and proverbs. One such proverb is *seken wa hiroi yo de semai* (the world is not as big as it seems to be). The meaning of the proverb is that the world is small because a man is always being watched by other people, a fact that he should not forget. The category *sekentei* was formed in the Tokugawa Period and reflects the psychological behavior of small social groups that made up Japanese society at that time. In the past and in the present it is widely used in teaching (do not do it or you will be laughed at), in social rituals like weddings (we will have a wedding worthy of everybody's attention) and in many other aspects of life.

In any society, people try to avoid public condemnation or dishonor, but the Japanese take such dishonor so seriously that they sometimes commit suicide in such situations. This is caused by the high level of unification in public life, by the rituality of public behavior and etiquette and by the increased sense of responsibility for one's actions. After the 1946 publication of the book *The Chrysanthemum and the Sword* by Ruth Benedict, Japanese culture received the name "culture of shame." This intensified the interest of Japanese researchers in regulating the function of *sekentei*. The Japanese believe that the opinions of others, especially those close to them, are of great importance. Many actions are performed simply in compliance with the "I do it because everybody does it" principle. Such actions include entering a university, purchasing of foreign goods, travelling abroad and many others. The same principle restrains most Japanese people from developing the bad habits so widespread in other countries. According to a recent survey, 68 percent of the Japanese try to avoid public condemnation and think that this factor heavily influences their behavior (*Nihonjin no kachikan*, 2005).

Concern for public opinion and dependence upon it has developed into a habit by which the Japanese search for and find the hidden meaning of spoken words. Sometimes this is good and

Figure 5.4

sometimes it is definitely bad. It is good when your sincerity towards a delicate situation is easily understood without the need for extra words. For example, when you start reflecting upon someone's suggestion, they will immediately tell you that it is a preliminary suggestion and you are not obliged to take it. It is harmful when your words are interpreted in the wrong way. For example, suppose one of your subordinates has fallen ill and has asked to take sick leave. You might answer, with the best of intentions, that he should not worry and that his work will be completed by other employees. If you do not express any concern regarding his absence and his importance to the team's work, he might interpret a hidden disapproval of his performance; he might think that you are suggesting that the company is as well off without him. These rules, though unwritten, are nevertheless well known.

Chapter 6

Japanese Service: Simply the Best

It's Not About Money

From the 17th to the 19th centuries, life in Japan was based on the so-called rice economy, and the samurai estate lived according to a code of honor. A vassal had to serve his overlord for his entire life and not overly worry himself about the fee for his services. For an overlord, the financial welfare of the vassal and his family was a point of honor as well. Livelihood was provided in kind, and livelihood was guaranteed by rice. The richer a suzerain and the higher his vassal's rank, the larger was his annual rice allowance.

Money was not of special value at first. However, with time, tradesmen dealing exclusively with goods and money appeared and gained influence. As we saw above, the samurai treated merchants according to the samurai code of honor: "calculating people are worthy of contempt" (Yamamoto, 2004). As usual, the entire society imitated the elite and emulated its moral values. Until 1868, the social status of tradesmen remained the lowest in Japanese society in spite of the fortunes they had accumulated by that time. Even when the government turned to the mercantile guild for occasional help, it did not influence the guild's status very much. Golovnin (2004) mentioned that "in Japan the merchant class is very large in number and rich, however it is not respected there." Many noble people found it disgraceful to communicate with tradesmen and assigned shopping tasks to their aides. In their turn, tradesmen did not dare to call their clients by name and used the respectful *uesama* (Your Excellency), regardless of their origin and status, to address them.

Figure 6.1: A commoner before a samurai.

It was not customary for a respected person to count money or to pay for his purchases in a shop or restaurant. An ability to add up figures was considered plebeian and unworthy of a true warrior; arithmetic was not among the samurai school subjects for a long time. However, since trade and monetary relations became essential, people had to get used to them somehow.

In order to separate the lofty process of beneficial consumption from the lower tasks of calculation, tradesmen postponed payment for their service until the next day or the day after that. They world visit their client's house, bow low, profusely expressing thanks for the honor given to them before receiving their money from the house-keepers. According to Aime Humbert: "In all affairs where a merchant had to contact a samurai, the former must bow down to the latter. A merchant entering a nobleman's house must kneel, bend his head to the ground and stay in such a position until he is ordered to get up. Even after that, he must talk to the master with his arms at his side and while leaning forward" (Humbert, 1870).

Figure 6.2: How merchants are paid.

There were no prices posted in places where food and drinks were served. The owner had to skillfully draw a bill that would be consistent both with the food's quality and the client's financial status. Therefore the same meal could be priced differently for different clients. A rich and noble client could and was expected to pay more in order to maintain his status. Thus the service was based on financial consideration and on the observance of certain principles by both parties.

In the second half of the Tokugawa Age, money became the equivalent of goods and services. Nevertheless, it was not the custom to speak or to act openly with respect to money. Golovnin noted that "although magnates and officials seem to be majestic in their relations with tradesmen and do not appear to pay any attention to the mercantile class, they do deal with rich merchants privately, make friends with them and are even often obliged to them" (Golovnin, 2004).

Many things have changed in today's Japan, but traces of the old traditions can still be found in some trade and service spheres. Mostly, these are the old-fashioned trades such as geisha services, kimono tailoring and tea houses. Sometimes hereditary craftsman (carpenters, stone carvers and others) do not quote the price when receiving orders from their clients. As a rule, the skilled craftsmen are proud of their trade and guarantee the quality with their name and reputation. They avoid speaking about money and leave it up to their client; the craftsmen believe that a worthy man can recognize true art and accurately estimate its true worth. You can still find sushi restaurants in Japan where the menu does not specify prices. In such places, the owner normally knows everyone and everyone knows the owner. Long-term relationships and mutual trust play a key role. Although most Japanese restaurants have adopted modern payment systems, it is still considered inappropriate to examine the bill; it is all the more inappropriate to check it openly. If it is necessary to check the bill, one should check it without appearing to do so.

For more than two and a half centuries, the estate of urban merchants and servicemen were pegged at the bottom of the social hierarchy. This means that several generations were strictly allocated to certain ranks and were obliged to do what they were expected to do. The habits, way of life and thinking, moral values and code of behavior of the tradesmen were inherited by several generations and engraved on the collective memory of their descendants. As time passed, these ideas turned into one of many national traditions. The roots of refinement of Japanese service might be found in the character of the Edo Period. Initially, the ruling samurai estate was the main consumer of various services, so merchants and craftsmen had to adjust to their rules. The rules were severe even for the samurais themselves, let alone for their subordinates and servants. In a time when a commoner could be legally killed for breaching etiquette rules, being able to dispose of a fraudulent tradesman was a sacred duty for every self-respecting samurai. It goes without saying that samurais did not lack self-esteem. For all who have been lucky enough to enjoy incredible Japanese service and the famous Japanese courtesy, it would be good to remember the price that was paid in the past.

Figure 6.3: A poster listing violations by a tradesman for all to see in front of his shop.

The Customer is Always Right — The Japanese Version

One can encounter genuine Japanese service in any place — in a store, in a restaurant or on the subway. A foreigner can feel it at once everywhere. In a restaurant, a waitress will do her best to find a proper place where she can be positioned lower than the customer and talk to him from below. If the client is sitting on a high chair, she will sit on a lower one. If the client's chair is not high, she will squat. In a Japanese restaurant where patrons are sitting on *tatami*, waitresses crawl into the room in order to be lower than the clients' heads. This manner seems to indicate overwhelming service etiquette, and recently it has been borrowed by employees of some of the other service spheres.

A patron is spoken to in such a tone and with such an expression on the service staff's face as if the patron was not an ordinary man, but a messenger from the heavens. Refined politeness, careful consideration of the smallest detail and absolute competence distinguish a Japanese service staff who knows exactly what he must do in every possible situation at his workplace.

Figure 6.4:   The higher service quality, the lower the service staff's position.

There was once a program on Japanese TV about a tradesmen's life. One of the newly employed women could not greet clients properly. To be more exact, she could do it, but the greeting was considered not warm and sincere enough. She was given a task to practice in front of a mirror at home. While all of the other participants in the program worked on the trade floor, she was still studying hard and being guided by her supervisor. Finally, after several days of dramatic and psychological training, her face was lit up by the required smile and she came out to greet her first clients, proud of the victory over herself. The woman's progress throughout the program was gradual and natural and created the illusion of true reality. There was no doubt that the participants were ordinary salespersons and not actors.

Everyone who has spent a long time in Japan can certainly remember situations that would spoil this idyllic picture. To be fair, such situations are quite rare, so they stick in the memory for a long time.

The same service attitude toward a client is evident in business as well. Marketing experts have noted that "in Japan, as in other countries, the 'buyer is king,' only here he or she is 'the greater king'. Here, the seller, beyond meeting pricing, delivery, special specifications, and the other usual conditions, must do as much as possible to meet a buyer's wishes... Many companies doing business in Japan make it a practice to deliver more than what is called for under the terms of their contracts" (MIPRO, 1980).

There is a Japanese phrase: *kyakusama wa kamisama*. It is usually translated as "a client is always right," but the literal translation is more complimentary to the client: "His Majesty the client is god". To a casual observer, it might seem that this is the key principle of Japanese service. Salespersons communicate to their clients by using a set of clichés in which every word has been verified. This is also a *kata*, and one for a special purpose at that. A typical set of remarks and gestures at a cashier's counter is as follows:

Seller (Bowing slightly): "Welcome. Sorry to keep you waiting. Could I have you member's card, please? No card? Sorry for my tactlessness." (Having counted the purchase amount): "Sorry to keep you waiting. This item costs this much." (Having received the money): "The amount received from you is this much. Your change is this much." (Counts the change twice, turns every banknote diagonally and checks them on both sides). "Here is your change, would you check it, please." (Gives the money to the client by using both hands and bows slightly). "Thank you for the purchase. We will be happy to see you again." (To the next client): "Sorry to keep you waiting..." and so on, according to the same pattern.

If a five-year-old child appears in front of the cashier's counter with a toy in his hands, the exact same pattern will be used. Generally, children in Japan are spoken to in other, less polite, forms than those used for adults. This is not so different from some European languages such as French and Spanish which have formal and familiar verb tenses. However, the status of a child customer is momentarily more important than his age, and this might cause some pretense. It is often the case when a single norm covers the entire communication space and inconsistency or blank spots emerge in some circumstances. For instance, the Soviets coined the term *comrade* after the October Revolution as a gender-neutral form of address to replace the "bourgeois" terms *gospodin* (sir) and *gospozha* (madam). Meant to fill a blank spot in the language, the term never caught on and the previous terms were revived in 1991. English has a similar blank spot with its lack of a gender-neutral singular pronoun to replace "him" and "her," although in conversation "they" is commonly, but incorrectly, used. Japanese service etiquette has no provisions for addressing children, so the "heavy" adult forms are used.

In expensive Western stores, the attitude toward the client is impeccably polite as well. The difference is that Western service staff remain equal to their customers, although they are extremely attentive, professionally polite and friendly. They may be permitted personal digressions to a certain extent such as idle chitchat. In Japan a professional service staff must be lower than his client both visually and subjectively in any situation; he may never be superior or even equal to his client. No personal digressions, jokes or irrelevant remarks are permitted at any time. The super-polite automation and formalism of Japanese service communication is unique indeed.

Several centuries and the special lifestyle of the Tokugawa Period (1603–1867) were required for the algorithm to take root in the public consciousness. A competitive mechanism was then activated: those who wanted to succeed in the service trades had to accept the rules of the game and add something new to excel against their rivals. The customers were raised to a higher and higher level until it became a regular practice for service staff to thank a customer of any sex, age and social status. Today, a barber shop client would be thanked for coming to have his hair cut and a reader in a library would be thanked for checking out a book. Moreover, clients anywhere would be thanked several times, once for every separate action.

The overwhelming courtesy of staff could be rife with awkwardness but for the diversity and specificity of polite Japanese phrases. As we have already discussed, Japanese etiquette phrases are plentiful and extremely specific. For instance, a patient who is discharged from a hospital where the doctors have saved his life might be seen as a client who must be thanked according to the rules, however illogical that might be. But in reality, the medical staff would wish the recovering patient good health (*odaijini*), and it would be the patient, not the doctors, who would express his gratitude for their help and care.

Hey, I'm a JR Passenger!

Speaking of Japanese service, we cannot but mention public transport. This is where the service staff's gracious attitudes toward customers are in full bloom.

Most commuters in Japan travel by trains, on the subways and buses. The cabins of public buses are equipped with turn and stop signal transponders. Every time a driver slows down or turns, corresponding red or green signals light up above his seat. Then, a recorded female voice announces to which side the bus is turning so that the passengers can adjust their body position accordingly. Also, the passengers are constantly reminded that the driver sometimes has to push the brake pedal and that they should be aware of this fact. Requests not to get up until the bus has completely stopped are printed on plates which are fixed above each passenger seat and the same request is repeated verbally by a recorded voice. The passengers' safety is the main goal. The bus schedules are verified and correct to within a minute in its two versions: one for weekdays and one for weekends. The schedule is posted at each station and on Internet sites. In spite of all of the drivers' efforts, the schedule is inevitably disrupted during rush hours but the buses continue according to the "passenger's comfort and safety as a top priority" principle. Every station on the route is announced twice. An automatic guide also announces what useful places are located in the vicinity of each station. Some urban routes provide video displays of oncoming buses for the passengers awaiting them. Visual information is reinforced by announcements from a speaker. The additional conveniences are costly and reduce transportation profits, but the general trend of urban life is to enhance these conveniences gradually and steadily. It is true, however, that fares are growing steadily as well. In 2008 it cost US$3 on average for a 5–10 km intra-urban trip. This price might vary slightly in different cities.

The high quality of Japanese service has an interesting effect on the clients. Having found themselves cared for by service personnel, the Japanese relax immediately and become children, looking like true copies of adults. This is typified by an obedient look, a hesitation in movements and a readiness to follow the person who will lead them to where they need to go and to have everything explained to them. On one hand, this is beneficial, as Japanese service and trade reach higher peaks in the endless pursuit of perfection. On the other hand, the effect is detrimental as more and more fraudsters can take advantage of the total trust of clients. Professor Sadao Asami, who investigated the problem of fraud, called the Japanese "the most gullible" nation in the world. According to him, Japanese salesmen cheat their country-men 10 to 20 times more often than do salesmen in other countries (March, 1996). Reports of fraud are rather frequent in Japanese newspapers.

A lonely elderly woman lived in her own house but did not know how to repair it. Over the course of several years, 11 agents from different construction companies cheated her out of 55 million yen (about US$450,000) for mostly useless preventive repairs. The woman had to pay again to remove the previous repairs when another fraudu-lent contractor convinced her that the repairs were not necessary.

The tendency of the Japanese in letting down their guard in their interaction with their service providers and the sacred belief in their permanent protection has sometimes taken curious forms.

One evening on a Japan Railways (JR) community train, two men, one younger and one older, began to have a heated argument. The younger of the two men suggested that they get off the train at the next platform and settle the matter with a fist fight. His opponent was less aggressive and did not feel like getting off the train. When the younger man started to pull the older man towards the exit, the older one delivers the last deadly argument: "Leave me alone! Don't you see that I am a JR passenger?" The younger man continued to blus-ter but eventually calmed down. The quarrel continued for a time, but the JR passenger argument proved to be effective and the two passengers parted without further incident. Indeed, the Japanese belief in domestic service is a source of true power.

What kind of interaction must there be between the railroad service and the passengers if even an angry combatant is made to change his mind at the bare mention of the service? The relationships are very interesting indeed, although they are not innovative from the point of view of the "His Majesty the client is god" concept. Japanese railroad workers are similar to other service providers in these terms; they observe the same rules of service and perpetual politeness.

During a rail commute in Japan, the following is sure to be seen. A train conductor makes a round of the train. He enters a coach, closes the door behind him and then stops. He takes off his service cap, bows and then addresses the passengers: "Sorry to trouble you," he says. Then he puts on his cap, goes through the coach and then stops at the opposite door. He turns round to the passengers again, bows slightly, repeats the "Sorry to trouble you" mantra and then goes to the next coach. In the next coach the scenario is repeated. According to the rules, he must take off his cap when leaving the coach as well, and all the newcomers do so too. Older people can sometimes neglect the ritual. The ritual character of the conductor's behavior is demonstrated by the fact that he does not actually bother anyone; he was taught to make the rounds in such a way when he was hired.

The Japanese public transportation system is one of the most developed in the world. Its daily capacity is tens of millions of passengers, and it expects the proper fare payment. Like anywhere else, there are free riders in Japan, and Japanese service is unique in its attitude toward them. A conductor goes through the coach to let those passengers who have not paid their fare, or who have paid only part of it, to cover the short payment. In some cases, passengers simply did not have time to purchase the ticket. The passengers state the boarding point and their destination and then get their tickets on the spot. Not everyone does so, therefore railway personnel occasionally check the tickets, speaking politely and apologizing all of the time. If free loaders are detected, what is the result?

Based on what has been discussed so far, you can easily guess. The conductor asks the rider where he boarded the train (which the conductor, of course, cannot know without seeing the ticket) and where he is going to get off (the destination can be the subject of a later check) and then sells a ticket for the trip described by the passenger. The conductor does not ask the dodger why he did not buy a ticket and, surely, the conductor does not doubt the information received. There are, of course, no fines on intercity public transportation; at least not in the cities that I have visited.

From where does such liberalism come?

Generally, it comes from two sources, one of which will be discussed shortly and one that has already been addressed in this chapter: the drive for conflict-free relationships in general and for smooth relations between the service sphere and clients in particular. Japanese service just never gets into conflict with a client.

Does this mean that financial profit should be sacrificed for the sake of harmonious relations? "No, it should not," answer the Japanese railroads. To cope with the problem of non-paying passengers the railways have installed pay gate turnstiles. Every station has them, even on platforms where passenger flow is light. In true Japanese fashion, every detail has been perfected: the machines are a lovely sight, are state-of-the-art and are very expensive. Some models are provided with displays on which an animated woman bows politely, greets passengers and then invites them to proceed to the platform. Of course, a nimble free rider can easily jump over the pay gate. For this reason the railroads have installed security cameras over the pay gates but nobody knows for sure whether the camera is real or simply a dummy. Installation of the complicated monitoring equipment costs a lot of money, and it appears that Japanese public transportation goes to great lengths for the sake of harmonious relationships with its passengers.

Such technology is not only used by the railroads. Speed radar-equipped cameras are becoming common on the motorways. A driver who dares to push the throttle will receive by mail photos of his vehicle with the vehicle plate clearly visible. As with the cameras in the railway stations, nobody is certain if any particular camera is operating at the moment. It is conceivable that in the near future road traffic and railway passenger flow will be controlled exclusively by automated devices. The idea of totally controlled social space where everything is elaborated, convenient and safe is congenial to the Japanese soul. This is the kind of society that the Japanese have been building for years and why the transportation industry is ready to invest money in up-to-date monitoring devices.

The main difference between the Japanese rail system and that used in Canada is the fate of free loaders. In Canada, a fine of C$200 is imposed on those who ride but do not pay. Given the fact that the regular fare is 2 dollars for a trip to any point, the fine is 100 times higher. Unlike the Japanese, North Americans do not worry about social harmony; effectiveness is the only goal.

However, a balance must be met between the upfront cost of controlling admittance and the prosecution of those who violate the law. This is why it is still debatable which method works best — the Japanese (high upfront costs) or the North American (high prosecution costs). The ideology of the Japanese people allows a system by which passengers are highly controlled. It does not sound very romantic, but it works well in Japan and would be very unlikely to work in the United States or Canada. As of February 2005, relatively peaceful and trouble-free Canada had twice as many prisoners, and the United States, 12 times as many prisoners per 100,000 population as Japan (Walmsley, 2007). Of course these prisoners are not all fare dodgers, but the Japanese willingness to be controlled at every step, including in subway ticket purchases, contributes to this statistic.

The Most Punctual Trains in the World

Railroads are the main form of both intercity and cross-city public transport in Japan. They are also the most punctual transportation network in the world. According to the East Japan Railway Company, in 1999 the super-expresses of the *Shinkansen* (literally, New Trunk Line) were a mere 20 seconds late on average for each trip while ordinary trains and commuter trains were one minute late on average. Arriving at a destination up to one minute late is considered to be on schedule in Japan, but being late by more than a minute constitutes a delay. By this definition 95 percent of all bullet trains and 98 percent of ordinary trains run on time and have done so since the late 1980s.

Japan is the only country in the world where a one-minute threshold is considered the criterion of being late. In the most punctual of the European countries, Germany and Switzerland, a late arrival is defined as an arrival five minutes or more after the scheduled time. In England, the threshold is 10 minutes, and in Italy and France, it is 15 minutes. According to European standards, 90 percent of all trains in England, France and Italy run on schedule, and the French super express TGV reached the 92 percent level. But let us not forget about the 15-minute delay criterion. At the main railway station in Tokyo, 15 minutes is sufficient for the *Shinkansen* express to arrive, to take on passengers and to be dispatched to its next destination. During these 15 minutes, the passengers disembark, the entire train undergoes a general cleaning, all of the seats are changed to face the direction of the train's motion with special devices and the new passengers embark.

In order to close the gap, German and Swiss engineers have regularly visited Japan to observe the logistical techniques, but these visits have not yet produced results. The German railroads admit that it is impossible to implement the Japanese achievements into European practice (Mito, 2001). Therefore Japan has maintained its leadership in railroad punctuality since 1930s.

Outside the Japanese megalopolises, many suburban trains are still cruising on single-track lines because of dense development, land deficiency and as a money-saving measure. Trains moving on a single track can cross each other only at the big stations. Under such conditions, maintaining a by-the-minute schedule requires incredible accuracy by the traffic superintendents and diligence by the engine drivers. Frequent earthquakes, strong monsoon winds and snowfall in the northeastern part of the country contribute to efforts to increase transportation safety. As soon as the winds reach a certain speed, all of the trains stop at the nearest station until the weather improves. Once traffic is renewed, the trains are manually guided by traffic superintendents until the entire process returns to its standard schedule.

However, Japanese passengers, accustomed to comfort, are indifferent to railroad staff problems. They get downright angry with any deviations in the schedule. A five-minute delay of a commuter train drives some of them, polite and humble in other situations, to raise hell and sometimes attack the railroad staff. I have witnessed some unpleasant scenes.

One weekday afternoon at a railroad station in a town with a population of half a million, I saw one of the passengers waiting for a commuter train. He seemed to be an ordinary white collar worker in outward appearance, but he was nervously glancing at his watch and pacing the platform. The railroad man on duty announced through the speaker that, for technical reasons, the commuter train was six minutes late and he apologized for the inconvenience. The passenger fell into a rage and started shouting loudly at the duty man sitting in his booth. The irate passenger felt that the railroad should have informed him of the delay beforehand. He could have taken a taxi, but because they did not inform him, he was now late. Having heard the yelling, the man on duty left his service booth and stopped on the platform opposite the passenger. The duty man took off his service cap, bowed and apologized. The passenger went on yelling. People began to look out of the windows of the nearby houses. The railroad man stood still and apologized again and again for several minutes until the late train finally appeared. The man on duty held his cap in his hand and stayed on the platform until the train departed with the unruly passenger on it. He then put on his cap and went back to his booth.

In some countries, people use lofty good humor to relieve the tension associated with transportation problems. They sometimes treat them like mistaken weather forecasts: "There you go! Late again." But not the Japanese; when the high-speed express schedule is broken due to weather conditions, all of the national TV channels broadcast text announcements indicating the delay duration. As soon as the schedule is restored, this news is broadcast nationwide.

Winter 1998 was a record in Japan for the number of snowfalls and the number of delays of the *Shinkansen* super express. Vulnerability to snow is probably the weakest point of the bullet train's operation. The situation is aggravated by a number of faults in equipment installed as early as the 1960s. The expresses, which are considered the source of national pride, set the whole country in turmoil when

Figure 6.5:   Apologizing for a delayed train.

they are delayed. Criticism in the mass media, moderately self-critical reports by the railroads, plans and measures for crisis management soon normalized the situation.

To all appearances, the Japanese will soon surpass the French in terms of rail traffic speed. In July 2007, the Eastern Japan Railways declared its intention to commission a 100-kilometer long track on the Tokyo to Aomori route in 2010, where the *Shinkansen* would drive at 320 km/hour, as fast as the French super express TGV. Presently Japanese trains drive at a top speed of 300 km/hour only on the Tokaido route between Osaka and Fukuoka.

Transportation network development and ongoing improvement have taken top positions in the list of Japanese priorities. The first hybrid automobiles, where battery packs are used along with gasoline engines, were followed in Japan by the world's first hybrid locomotive. The electro-diesel locomotive is environmentally friendly as it

Figure 6.6: New model of a bullet train.

Source: Website of Dankai Hiroba.

uses the kinetic energy of the train to charge the batteries when braking, as it does in hybrid automobiles. In 2007, a new series of high-speed expresses, N700, was commissioned on the Tokaido and Sanyo lines. Japanese designers used up-to-date materials and technology to reduce the coach weight by 30 percent and thus lighten the entire train by eight tons. The innovation resulted in electric power savings as well as increased passenger comfort and transportation speed. In 1964, the first super expresses cruising on the Tokyo to Osaka route covered the distance of 552 km in 3 hours and 10 minutes, while modern N700 bullet trains manage to do it in 2 hours 25 minutes. The pace of life in Japan is being matched by the speed at which it travels.

At the end of 2008, the Japanese decommissioned the 0 Series *Shinkansen*, the original model that debuted with the opening of the *Shinkansen* network in 1964. The trains of this series were retired from service, having traveled a combined total distance equivalent to

Figure 6.7: Farewell ceremony for 0 series *Shinkansen*.

30,000 times the circumference of the Earth. The Japanese retire their bullet trains in the same way they retire their loved ones: they were scheduled to run for a final three days in mid-December 2008 so that passengers and the people who worked on them could say their last goodbyes to the engineering landmark.

Chapter 7

Motives and Consequences
of Incredible Service

Bakufu as a Driving Force of Progress

What are the roots of the Japanese railroad men's drive for punctuality? Generally speaking, all Japanese are very punctual, not only railway personnel. Besides, there are some historical reasons for this phenomenon which was quite evident as early as 1872, when the first railroad line connected Tokyo to Yokohama. In order to understand the nature of their motives we will have to turn again to the Tokugawa Period.

There was a remarkable turning point in the life of the Japanese capital then: the capital received and dispatched caravans from each and every appanage principality on a regular basis. Appanage lords (*daimyo*) arrived at the shogun's court with their caravans to serve their military service (*sankin kotai*), which was normally to last for one year at a time. Most of them used to come in April and, after having performed the duty of loyal vassals, returned to their sovereign's court the next April. While the lords went home, their family members were held hostage in the capital.

The tradition originated long ago. In the 13th century, the Kamakura shogunate assembled its vassals in the sovereign's castle. Hideyoshi Toyotomi (1537–1598) did the same some time later. In 1635, the third shogun Iemitsu Tokugawa (1604–1651) made the assemblies mandatory and universal. The system remained unchanged for 227 years and became one of the distinguishing features of the Tokugawa Period.

There were both allies of the ruling family and distant clans among the appanage lords so the terms and intervals of service differed considerably. Lords were called to the capital for many reasons, but mostly for them to be reminded who was ruling the country. The feudal lords had to be in touch with current state affairs as well. They spent a year in their domains and another year in the capital, and some of them arrived twice a year for a shorter stay. The most loyal and the most reliable lords were permitted to appear in the shogun's court only once every several years. The system made no exceptions, even for foreigners. The Dutch trade mission also had to make regular journeys from Nagasaki to the capital to deliver its gifts and affirmations of loyalty to the shogun.

By the end of the Tokugawa Period, there were 273 fiefs in Japan. The lords' caravans entered the capital and left it almost every day. Along with government officials and liaison officers, they formed the main body of travelers. At that time the samurais alone were allowed to ride horses, whereas common people were required to walk. "Before foreigners came here, a huge number of Japanese had always traveled on foot. There existed neither cabs nor even simple carts, and the right to ride horses had been vested exclusively in privileged representatives of the military estate" (Mechnikov, 1992).

The treacheries and plots of the "warring provinces" period (*Sengoku jidai*, 1467–1568) were still fresh in the national memory, so the government kept an eye on the groups of people approaching the capital. They did not try to enlarge the roads, leaving natural obstacles such as rivers and mountains as additional protection from any painful surprises. There was no stock rearing in Japan, and plow cattle were used only in the capital. Therefore, cargoes were delivered mostly by sea, as the surrounding waters provided for a cheap and convenient method of transportation.

Appanage lords arrived in the capital with a solemn escort that was consistent with their status. The escort consisted of relatives, vassals, journey organizers and servants, all numbering between 150 and 300 persons, although the caravan of the then-largest Kaga Principality (the territory of modern Ishikawa and Toyama Prefectures), ruled by the Maeda clan, consisted of 4,000 people. Engelbert Kempfer

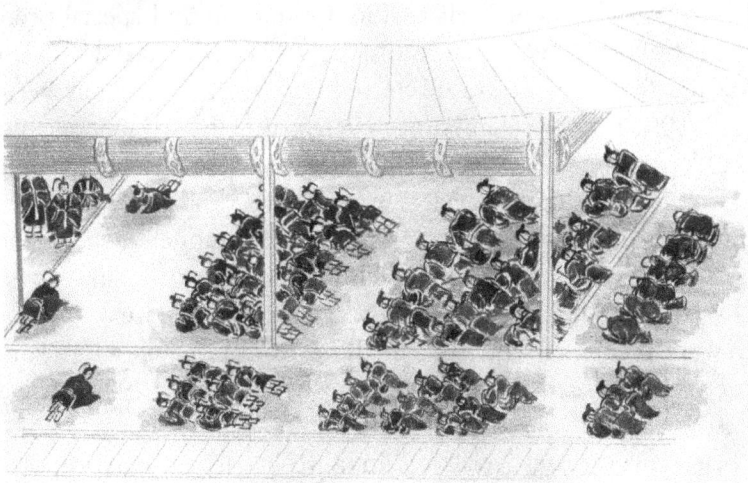

Figure 7.1: Reception at the shogun's residence.

(1651–1716) witnessed in the beginning of the 18th century that "the lords and magnates of the empire, with their enormous escorts and governors of the empire cities and lands owned by the treasury, take the first place among travelers… Escorts of some of the greatest lords of the empire can be large enough to spread across a several days-long path" (Ziebold, 1999).

In Edo, many lords had special residences in which their families could stay. Generally, the cost of trips to the capital and for escort maintenance was quite high; some principalities could spend from 25 to 80 percent of their annual revenue on the journey. The government was certainly aware of the expenses and did not mind the financial exhaustion of its vassals. One modern history textbook explains to Japanese school children that a visit by Lord Maeda to the capital could cost up to US$3 million in current prices. Such financial exhaustion likely limited the lords' ability to make war on the capital.

The journeys were very carefully prepared. Long before the trip, detailed lists of the delegations, side arms, fire arms, horses and other important items were submitted to government officials for approval.

The caravan movement itself required attention and special preparations as the trips covered large distances over several days. Requests for staying for a night were submitted beforehand, normally between 50 and 100 days but sometimes even a year in advance. A month before departure, the requests were checked again. When passing by another lord's lands, the travelers were to pay compliments to the master, notify him in advance of the arrival date, arrange for the changing of horses and other formalities. The most influential and powerful lords were welcomed in a tea house according to a ritual. Obviously, there were plenty of requests and things for approval, and a smooth journey required careful consideration (Maruyama, 1992). "It is very interesting and amazing to watch the endless escort of people wearing black silk dresses...walking in a strict order with importance and so silently that only the rustle of their clothing and the patter of hoofs and feet can be heard, inseparable from any movement" (Ziebold, 1999).

Trips to the capital were undertaken regularly, and with time the principalities developed certain rules for the trips. The Kaga Principality, then the richest in Japan, introduced two permanent traffic schedules from Kanazawa to Nihonbashi in the center of the capital. One of the routes was 12 days and 11 nights long while the

Figure 7.2:   Traveling procession of the lord's household (*daimyo gyoretsu*).

other was 10 days and nine nights long. The schedules, made by a confidant of Lord Maeda, Nagasada Arisawa by name, were the first valid schedules and appeared long before the first railroad was constructed.

The regular military duty of the lords in the shogun's court established the main rules for the journeys. These rules were preserved and consolidated under new circumstances when public transportation came into use. This process was well demonstrated in Yuko Mito's book devoted to the current status of Japan Railways (Mito, 2001). Curiously, Japanese employees today calculate the exact number of days and nights that they will have to spend on a business trip; Japanese accounting and personnel offices do the same. Is this because of tradition or a habitual punctuality?

In 1830, the English opened the era of railroad communication by launching a passenger train on the Manchester to Liverpool line. Japanese rail lines were first laid in Tokyo, Kyoto and Osaka. In 1872 the 29-km long Tokyo to Yokohama railroad was commissioned. The Osaka to Kobe line was put into operation in 1874 and the Osaka to Kyoto railroad started in 1877. Over the course of 20 years, from 1872 to 1891, Japan constructed 2760 km of railways.

The first lines were supervised by English engineers, Japanese personnel did not operate the trains until 1879. However, by the end of the 1890s, all Japanese rail lines were operated by the Japanese and the English had been thanked, well paid for their service and replaced in typical Japanese fashion. Also in typical Japanese fashion, the new technology and the skills necessary to use it were mastered and verified, the personnel were trained and whatever could be improved was improved.

The railway industry in Japan was unique from the very beginning. First, there were a large number of stations and stops. In the Tokugawa Period, when common people traveled on foot, hostels were located in the provinces at a one-day walking distance (about 30 km) from each another. In the central districts, they were even closer to each other so that the travelers could reach them before dark. The hostels grew and developed, surrounded by the homes of those who helped to welcome the travelers. Thus, the numerous

Japanese towns that now form a continuous line along railroad rights-of-way have existed for decades or even centuries.

Who were the first railroad passengers? They were mostly government officials, the revived court nobility, former feudal lords and their relatives and liaison officers. They were accompanied by members of the recently established parliament who were going to their regular sessions, rich merchants from Tokyo and Osaka and other honorable persons who lived in any of the three largest cities or those who visited these cities regularly.

The code of honor was officially cancelled by that time, but traditions cannot be changed all at once. How could the first railroad men relax with such a contingent of passengers? Many organizational patterns of the *sankin kotai* times were successfully followed under the new conditions. An attentive attitude toward passengers was one of these patterns. Frequent and convenient stops, the desire to deliver a passenger to his destination strictly according to the schedule and the attentiveness and politeness of the service distinguished the Japanese railroads. The railroad's operation was initially controlled by the central government but was later assigned to *Nihon Tetsudo* (Japan Railways), a private company that still exists today. The project was supervised by the government long after the transfer and, as a result, the company received a lot of benefits and preferences.

Lev Mechnikov, who lived in Japan at this time, wrote: "A railroad between Yokohama and the capital was new then, but traffic on the road was really amazing, because of the extremely dense population of the area and the exceptionally mobile nature of the people... No other country could demonstrate the ability to create the movement peculiar of [*sic*] the railroads" (Mechnikov, 1992).

Not least of all, the high standards of the transportation service can be attributed to the railroad's public nature. Any public idea or action was traditionally held in great esteem in Japan. In the Tokugawa Period, even the most powerful lords had to give way for the simple postmen: "Should the greatest and most significant lord of the empire meet a post courier, he must make way for the courier and cause his escort to do the same" (Ziebold, 1999). Some other habits of the past have survived as well. When railways became available to the common people, the passengers were immediately separated into first-, second- and third-class coaches. Without a second thought, train conductors locked the third-class passengers in their coaches and let them out only after the honorable men had completed their boarding and debarkation.

However, it took time to bring Japanese railroad service up to modern standards. For 50 years after their introduction, Japanese trains were often late and only began keeping to their schedules at the beginning of the 1920s. Ten years later, they were the most punctual in the world (Mito, 2001).

Japanese achievements in railroad transportation are strongly mirrored in the Japanese automobile industry. During the postwar occupation of Japan by the United States, Americans routinely made fun of Japanese automobiles, even removing the "Made in Japan" plates from the cars and attaching them to obscene items. This was pretty fair as Japanese cars did not compare in quality to American vehicles. In true Japanese style, the Japanese began studying the American automobile industry and improving on what could be improved.

On 25 April 2007, the business world announced that the Japanese automobile giant Toyota had become the world's largest

Figure 7.3:   First railway steam locomotive.

automobile manufacturer with over 2.3 million cars sold all over the world. For the first time in history, the Americans lost their spot at the top of the world's automobile manufacturers. Generally, many experts believed that General Motors would be defeated by Toyota at some point, but they did not expect it to happen so quickly. The Japanese automobile industry overtook all rivals within 55 years; similar to the 58 years it took the Japanese rail industry to overrun its rivals.

It has been said that appetite comes with eating. In the beginning of June 2007, the government announced its decision to facilitate the manufacture of the first Japanese passenger aircraft. From 2008 to 2012, Mitsubishi engineering plants will receive from the government over US$40 billion as a budget allowance, but the entire project is estimated to run to about US$120 billion. Japan plans to start manufacturing mid-haul liners able to carry 70–90 passengers in 2012. It is not clear if the Japanese aircraft industry will be able to overtake its foreign rivals and how many years it will take to do this.

Side Effects of Perfect Service

Japanese sociologists and publicists are paying increasing attention to gradual and invisible changes occurring in Japanese society. Thirty or 40 years ago, the main topic of publications was the nation's pride in postwar national achievements and the unique features of the Japanese spirit that contributed to these achievements. The concept of "Japanism" (*nihonjinron*) was aimed at proving that the Japanese were a unique people. The concept was treated with usual diligence and energy: according to data from the Nomura Research Institute, more than 700 books and research papers in the *nihonjinron* genre were published in Japan between 1946 and 1978. During these 33 years, nearly two books were published every month. Only seven percent of these books were published by foreign authors, showing the vast amount of pride Japanese writers, and the Japanese readers who purchased the books, took in their culture and in their drive to succeed in the postwar world (Sugimoto and Mouer, 1982).

It is certainly a measure of one's self esteem to persuade oneself and others about the uniqueness of your own nation. As always, the

Japanese were obsessively careful and meticulous in their studies. No point was left unaddressed that related to any topic. An entire and quite thick book could be devoted to any single category recognized as an element of Japanese culture (see Doi, 2001a, for example). The wave of national pride even led to the popularity of the idea that the Japanese have a different brain structure than other peoples (Tsunoda, 1986), which obviously went too far and at about this time the unrestrained patriotism began to subside. From 1983 to 2003, the number of Japanese who thought that "they possess outstanding features as compared to other people" decreased from 71 percent to 51 percent. On the contrary, the share of those who believe that the Japanese can learn a lot from other countries increased from 15 percent to 20 percent (*Gendai nihonjin*, 2004).

Unfortunately, the agitated enthusiasm for Japanism has bequeathed prejudice and suspicion toward any further attempts to write anything new about Japanese culture. Nowadays the common response to any such attempts is usually a disappointed "There you go again!" Some resist the attempts to study Japanese culture as if no other approach except *nihonjinron* ever existed. The rise of Japanism in the last half of the 20th century confirmed that the best is indeed an enemy of the good. Although Japan is a unique civilization, this fact might provoke some authors, such as Tsunoda, to overestimate this quality and to picture it as unique without precedent.

The nation has managed to recover safely from Japanism. Japanese sociologists are currently interested in problems such as public moral decline. This is not to say that the Japanese have corporately turned into louts and rowdies; compared with most other countries, public safety is still higher and overt loutishness is a rare event. According to the Japanese themselves, however, there appears to be more and more such instances. The newspaper *Yomiuri Shimbun* has recently published a debate on this issue. The main assertion is that egoism and detachment from other people are becoming evident in society. These features are mostly attributable to the baby boomers of the 1970s and early 1980s, and especially to those who have been successful in their lives. "Are we a society or a crowd?" asked the newspaper. The 70-year old pianist Izumi Tateno, who returned to his motherland after spending 40 years in Finland, recently shared his impressions. In his opinion the Japanese have changed much for the worse and this can be felt everywhere (*Yomiuri*: 20 May 2007).

One of the points of tension is the relationship between clients and service personnel, where service is always the defendant. Here is a typical everyday situation that illustrates the nature of these relations.

Like anywhere else, subway passengers in Japan sometimes jump into coaches at the last second. Engine drivers follow strict safety regulations and when passengers do this, departure is delayed, which results in the disruption of schedules. The burden of this responsibility can result in nervous breakdowns and other stress-related problems for the engine drivers. On 4 June 2005 at the Tokyo subway station *Kokubunji*, a passenger pushed the closing doors aside and jumped onto the train at the last second. The engine driver saw this and, through the train's speaker, reminded the passengers that the responsibility for any potential mishap will be borne by those who ignore the safety rules. The reprimand was rather tactful, but one of the passengers who heard it felt offended and complained to the East Japan Railroad Administration. The complaint was considered, and the engine driver was warned that any impolite treatment of the passengers should be avoided. The company management found it necessary to notify passengers of the measures taken by placing an announcement in the central newspaper. Actually, the engine driver was right and his reprimand was not rude. But the fact that a serviceman was reminding his client of the latter's responsibility was considered offensive and caused the complaint.

The railroad companies understand that they should not expect any changes in relationship between passengers and service staff, so they started to equip the subways with additional sliding doors on the platforms. These are synchronized with the train doors to prevent passengers from leaving the platform at inappropriate times.

The matter of responsibility takes a central place in the relationship between clients and service providers. Responsibility is generally one of the key ideas in the Japanese mentality. In the most tense and crucial moments of their business and personal life, the Japanese often repeat a mantra to eliminate any doubts and obstacles on their way to achieving something better: *kochira wa sekinin o motte...* (By undertaking all of the responsibility...). The "magic phrase" leaves no doubt about the feelings and intentions of the person who uttered it. The train passenger who complained about the engine driver was offended because he was reminded of the safety precautions that he and the other passengers were responsible for.

It was noted previously that a patron in Japan traditionally bears no responsibilities; he is in charge of only enjoying and paying for the service. If a line appears in a store, restaurant or hairdressing salon, the staff must take appropriate measures according to strict instructions. In a store, the attentive and disciplined salespersons would immediately call their colleagues from throughout the establishment to tend to the cashier counter; in a restaurant or a hairdressing saloon, they would fill out a waiting list (prepared beforehand) and enforce line etiquette. Japanese clients must not do anything themselves, not even to think. In a library, polyclinic or any other institution, a visitor who has forgotten his registration card would either be issued a new one or attended to without the card. No one would ever think of sending the visitor back for his card.

One of my Japanese friends told me about the "lucky beggars" who were hit by a rack of goods in a store or had sauce spilled on them in a restaurant. If the service staff is obviously the guilty party, then the injured client can count on great compensation, far greater than the actual damage. Also, service companies try to settle such issues in a confidential matter and not in the courtroom. This is because, first, public opinion will always support the customer and disclosure of the case will damage the company's reputation. Customer loyalty costs time as well as money. Second, a smooth and warm relationship with its clients, meaning overwhelming satisfaction for the service received, is a fundamental requirement of Japanese service and has nothing to do with legalities. A suit can be resorted to in exceptional circumstances when a client goes hog-wild and loses any sense of proportion. Overestimated claims are normalized by the Japanese's favorite negotiation style (persuasion and apologies) rather than by confrontation in the courtroom.

Many Japanese maintain a feudal attitude of service. They act like celestial beings with ever-present service staff at their beck and call. In 1996, Japanese police registered 1026 incidents involving railway passengers, while in 2000 there were almost twice as many, 1911. Note that these statistics only include serious incidents like fights, attacks on personnel or arson. The situation is worse in air transportation, where the number of harassment incidents toward service staff increased by a factor of five between 1998 and 2002 (Mori, 2005).

Foreigners who are familiar with news reports of an incredibly polite Japan would hardly believe what happens in the evening in Japanese bars and restaurants. The management of such establishments must often call either the police or an ambulance to remove the "knocked out" clientele. While the clientele are conscious, their behavior contrasts sharply with the traditional idea of Japanese self-restraint. Shoot-outs between clients occur less often than they do in other countries, while abusing the helpless staff is quite usual. The owners of private bars protect the interests of their clients and do not disclose these incidents, so there are no statistics on them. Should such records be kept, the picture would be quite shocking.

On 21 March 2004, *Yomiuri Shimbun* wrote that the job of salespersons and hotel officers had become dangerous because young clients, mostly men between the ages of 20 and 35, tend to quarrel with their own shadows. However, disorderly conduct and violence towards service staff is not the only area of worsening public behaviour. Increasing problems with public morals are evidenced by a remarkable growth in the incidence of child abuse. In 2008 the number of cases handled by child consultation centers in Japan reached a record of 42,662, which is 39 times the number seen in 1990 (*Yomiuri*: 15 July 2009).

Shameful client behavior has begun to be seen in public health care institutions which have always been quite safe. In developed countries, scandals often occur when paid medical personnel refuse to assist insolvent patients. In Japan the problem is of another nature. In September 2007, the Kobe Municipal Hospital Association asked for police squads to be stationed at the hospitals. In the previous month alone, municipal hospitals provided emergency services to

12,500 patients. It turned out later that 85 percent of these patients did not need hospitalization at all; they had been picked up by ambulance as they were unconscious or in a state of alcohol intoxication. Some of those who recovered refused to pay for the treatment while others raised hell and offended the hospital staff, and another group did not want to be discharged from the clinics as they liked to be treated there. Kobe, a port city with one and one-half million residents, provides the highest rate of off-hour medical assistance in Japan. Surprisingly, the Japanese, with their love of charters and instructions, have failed to prescribe any measures to deal with such incidents in the hospitals. A large number of medical personnel resigned due to the stress caused by the patients, and now half of the hospitals in Kobe lack on-duty doctors. The Association requested that night patients be accompanied by policemen until the end of their examination and that the patient be escorted out if necessary.

The problem of violent patients has grown to a national scale and has resulted in more problems. A survey conducted in Tokyo showed that in 2006 alone, 273 medical workers resigned due to violence and offenses committed by their patients, and in 2008 a similar problem was reported in the Aichi Prefecture. The actual number is even higher because one-third of the capital's clinics refused to submit data. The immensity of the phenomenon is clear if we remember that the Japanese do not change their jobs easily or lightly. The Tokyo Association of Medical Institutions was the first to begin instructing its staff on how to deal with aggressive patients, providing a checklist to be followed. The Shizuoka Prefecture even held a scientific symposium to discuss the problem.

The mass resignations of medical workers has aggravated the growing problem of providing health care to the fast-aging Japanese population. The number of patients who are dissatisfied with Japanese service is also growing. In 2008, 182 hospitals in the capital received 7,641 complaints of poor medical service (42 complaints per institution on average) and many patients refused to pay for their medical treatment. Japanese experts believe that the main reason is the lack of doctors (*Yomiuri*: 8 June 2008).

It is widely known that the Japanese pay great attention to formal etiquette. Children are accustomed to mandatory greetings from a kindergarten age. A greeting must be loud and enthusiastic; the words must be uttered distinctly and with sincere feeling. In order to obtain the necessary vocal quality, students practice greetings as a group and individually in schools and even in universities. I have many times heard students practicing greetings in unison, taking the task very seriously and devoting themselves entirely to it. Correct arm, body position and posture are given separate training. One of the modern etiquette guides emphasizes the points that demand attention: (1) stand still with your back straightened, (2) keep your arms naturally hanging at your sides, (3) do not move your neck or shoulders, (4) avoid any unnecessary movements (like scratching your head, rubbing your mouth or adjusting your necktie) and (5) look at your conversation partner in an open and kind manner with your chin slightly lowered (Muraoka, 2006). In many Japanese hospitals, greeters are employed with the sole task of bowing to and greeting every incoming person and wishing a quick recovery to every

Figure 7.4:   Volunteer on a "Say hello with a smile" campaign.
Source: Website of Ayabe Ando, accessed from [http://andoayabe.exblog.jp]

departing patient. In some stores, the salespersons greet their first customers in the morning in the same way. Generally, the greeting ritual is a serious matter and needs to be treated appropriately.

In such circumstances, a carelessly uttered greeting can mean a lot. Ignoring a greeting is similar to refusing to shake hands in Europe. Japanese etiquette discourages public confrontation, so this seldom occurs. However, a Japanese person will engage in the minimum greeting necessary toward a man he does not like. While passing by such a person, he will keep his head down and avoid eye contact, and a slight bend of the head can be interpreted either as an unintentional gesture or as an incomplete greeting. These nuances are well known to everyone in Japan, even to children; ignoring greetings is in bad taste and is not condoned.

Imagine, however, that a child sees his parents and other adults ignoring the greetings of the sales staff in stores or the welcome of service staff in restaurants, hotels, and on public transport. The hospitality of service workers can be so sincere that foreigners who are used to more personalized communication cannot help but greet the workers in return, even though customers are not expected to do so. Service workers seem to be the only group of people in Japan who can be ignored in formal communication, quite reasonably and without any repercussions. Having put on his service uniform, a person in Japan immediately turns into something of a second-class citizen or a whipping boy. The contrast with strict Japanese etiquette is really impressive.

Of course, a service staff understands this and does not hold it as a grievance against clients; it is part of the job. But tiny cuts can topple great oaks. In the end, the moral values that the Japanese learn from childhood are distorted. This is of special importance for young people because, unlike adults, they have yet to know another life, another system of etiquette or other relationships.

One Japanese university has, for many years, dispatched its students to Great Britain for internships. Recently, this university began receiving complaints from the students' host families. The hosts say that the Japanese trainees avoid communication with them, take their meals alone and sometimes do not even say "hello" to family members.

The university asked the students to explain their behavior. The students responded that since they had paid for everything in full, including their room and board, they did not understand why they had to meet their hosts' expectations. In short, the students saw themselves as customers and therefore they did not have to return the courtesy of their "service providers." Professor T. Uchida, who studies Japanese youth problems, believes that this is the result of a "consumption psychology" that is quickly becoming prevalent. "I have paid for the service and I don't owe them anything else, including friendliness" (*Yomiuri*: 20 May 2007). If Professor Uchida is right, then the traditionally belittled position of the Japanese service industry and its desire to appease the customer in every possible way has begun to defeat the moral values that have for centuries formed the basis of Japanese virtue.

There are much worse cases. On 1 December 2005, Takeshi Koizumi, a 46-year old unemployed man was crossing a street. An approaching taxi slowed down to let him pass. But after Koizumi stepped onto the sidewalk, he suddenly jumped back onto the road where his foot was run over by the accelerating taxi. Koizumi attacked the driver, banged on the hood of the taxi and demanded compensation for his injuries, which the veteran taxi driver refused to pay. The "victim" then told the driver to kneel and apologize. A string of cars were living up and causing a traffic jam. The passenger in the taxi did not see the details of the incident so the company's reputation was in jeopardy. Eventually the driver knelt before Koizumi and the pedestrian left with his head high, not waiting for the ambulance that had been called. A few days later, the taxi company received a complaint from Koizumi demanding compensation for his medical expenses. A medical referral was enclosed stating that his foot had to be treated for a week. Copies of the documents were sent to the police. During the investigation, the driver swore that there had been no injury. The case should have been settled in a courtroom but never was; the taxi company agreed to pay Koizumi's expenses. Soon Koizumi became a nightmare for the taxi company. Throughout the following year, he continued to go to the hospital, almost every day, at the expense of the taxi company. This example shows the extremes to which the

Japanese service industry will go in trying to avoid conflicts with its customers.

This story has a tragic postscript. In November 2008, Takeshi Koizumi was arrested for killing a retired high-ranking bureaucrat and his wife. The story of his encounter with the taxi company was well documented prior to the murders, and is therefore not apocryphal. Despite obvious mental problems, Koizumi was able to pinpoint and to exploit the weakest link in the relationship between the Japanese service industry and its customers.

Despite the tragic examples that can be given, striving for perfection in customer service is helping the industry to reach new peaks. In 2000 Japan Railways and subways introduced women-only coaches "to protect female passengers from unauthorized touching". According to police reports, in 2004 a record 2201 inappropriate contact complaints were filed by women, a number that was three times higher than it was eight years previously. A survey showed that 64 percent of all Japanese women between the ages of 20 and 40 have been subject to such abuse at least once in their lives. At first, women were provided with only one or two coaches and only during rush hours, but after 2004 the process accelerated and now up to half of the train, at least in densely populated areas, is at the women's disposal. As usual, the innovation originated from another country, in this case, India, but the Japanese were quick to borrow the idea and to improve upon it.

Japanese women were unanimously satisfied with the innovation, whereas Japanese men were divided into two camps. One was grateful to be rid of the potential of being suspected of undue behavior while the other demanded male-only coaches in pursuance of gender equality. As normally happens in Japan, two societies were formed to achieve the two opposite goals; one to fight transport abuses and the other to eliminate separate coaches.

The innovation posed new problems because progress is a process rather than a result. Japanese women passengers immediately began complaining, in writing, to the railway company about the temperature on the women-only coaches. In the first year the railway company in West Japan received 55 written complaints about the coaches being

Figure 7.5: "Women only" carriages.

too cold and 37 complaints about the coaches being too hot. The problem was that the two groups of women were complaining about the same temperature (*Asahi*: 15 May 2003). The 18-vote difference became the motive for further enhancement of the comfort-control settings on short-distance trips.

It is hard to identify the exact reasons for this phenomenon — either service quality or quality of life — that the Japanese are far ahead of the Americans and the Europeans by the number of various appliances that enhance comfort. As early as the 19th century, foreign observers had noted the Japanese lust for all sorts of unusual things that were the boast of people elsewhere: "Like all of the southern people the Japanese are extremely inquisitive and curious, they are keen about everything unusual, new, amazing and catching (they even have an untranslatable word *kembutsu* [local brand or point of interest — A.P.] to denote such things)" (Mechnikov, 1992).

The new model of the Apple iPhone 3G was first offered for sale in Japan on Friday, 11 July 2008. Wishing to overtake its competitors, one of the Tokyo stores in the Shibuya District announced that they would open at 7 a.m. At 6:55 a.m., a line of one thousand five hundred young Japanese was excitedly standing in front of the store. Many of them had come the night before. They could easily buy the desired gadget at other stores merely two or three hours later, but that would not be the same.

The Japanese love for unusual items and commodities has grown stronger. In 2007 only 8 percent of the cars driven in the United States were equipped with navigation systems, compared with 20 percent in Europe and about 40 percent in Japan. The gap in using portable TV sets in automobiles is even greater. In spite of the fact that many doubt the necessity of having a mobile TV in a car, the spoon-fed nature of Japanese consumerism encourages this in every way. I have seen cars with three TV sets in the passenger compartment.

No one seems to be very much surprised by the fact that the newer models of the navigation systems warn drivers in a gentle female voice (in Japan all the announcements are made in gentle female voices) of the nearest traffic lights and turns as well as of round-the-clock stores, filling stations and parking areas the driver is approaching. Every two hours, an invisible guide reminds the driver that it is time to have a rest. The voice also warns of traffic jams ahead and the time the driver will need to navigate through them. Some of the newer Toyota models are equipped with the G-book system including embedded karaoke, Internet access and IPA (intelligent parking assistance), which can park a car in a vacant lot almost without the driver's help. Indeed, if a driver is in a traffic jam and in good spirits, why not sing along with a karaoke?

"A more complete satisfaction of working class needs," as they used to say in the USSR, is an unrestricted and thus extremely promising trend in Japanese service development.

Chapter 8

Wildlife: Natural and Cultivated

Domesticating the Natural World through Imitation

Apologists of the cultural peculiarity of Japan do not miss the opportunity to emphasize the Japanese attitude to nature. They say that nowhere but in the Land of the Rising Sun can such a highly refined appreciation of nature be found. The Japanese delight in flowering *sakura* in spring, melt at the sight of yellow-red maple leaves in autumn and enjoy watching the moon, the first snow and many other natural phenomena.

Is there anything truly peculiar in the Japanese attitude toward wildlife and the amenities of nature? The tendency of people to place themselves at the center of their inner world can be seen in ancient times. The so-called gigantomania of ancient civilizations, evidenced by monuments constructed elsewhere (such as the Egyptian Pyramids, the Roman Coliseum and the Great Wall of China) had a rather short life in Japan. This fact was foreordained by the narrow territory in which Japanese civilization arose and the consequently restricted human resources. For most of their history, the Japanese have been quite happy with monuments and even household objects of modest size. The outward nature and its chaotic glory were too big to fit the tastes of the ancient Japanese well.

Then, they began to improve upon nature. Alexander Meshcheryakov wrote on this topic: "Instead of searching for physical contact with the wild and frightful world by long and tiring travel, Japanese nobles made up their mind to bring the outside world into their houses. It was like they 'drew' a portion of the wildness of nature closer to their dwellings, but at the same time they made it

147

smaller. At this time the famous Japanese ornamental gardens came into being as miniature models of nature" (Meshcheryakov, 2004).

In the course of improvement, the Japanese people were changing as well. They adapted themselves to conditions of their own making and their mentality obtained new traits. This focus on the nearest space is reflected in Japanese folklore. In ancient tales and myths of other nations, the characters time and again set out for distant lands and for a variety of important purposes. In Russia, it was also considered since ancient times that there were many interesting things "beyond seas, mountains, and primeval forests." In fairy tales, the action often happens in a far-flung kingdom. Regardless of the culture of origin, the hero journeys either of his own accord or against his will by using any number of "vehicles"; seven-league boots, a flying carpet or by changing into a swift-winged bird. On his home-coming, the hero narrates that overseas life is magical and wonderful. In short, the folk tales of other nations are always outside-directed. In Japanese folklore, all miracles happen near the areas where the hero was born and lived; if anybody leaves for anywhere, it is not for long distance travel and is usually from the province to the capital.

The Japanese traditionally divided all outward things into two categories. One category contains the natural world, created without human interference and existing independently of mankind. The other category contains things developed by humans and refined by their hands and minds. It is widely known that the Japanese have learned to imitate nature through small-scale reproduction and to bring it into their dwellings. In addition, bonsai (literally, tray planting), the growing of miniature trees, and ikebana (literally, living flowers), the arrangement of flowers, are popular hobbies in Japan and elsewhere. In both cases, the Japanese have created products that cannot be found in nature but are based solely on natural material. It is a pure art of creative imitation.

Of course, people of all cultures have imitated nature since ancient times. A park is an imitation of a forest, and a swimming pool is an imitation of the sea or lakes. With their homeland's unique variety of wildlife and climatic conditions, the Japanese are rapidly increasing their contact with imitations and decreasing their contact with wild and uncultivated nature. During the summer, public swimming pools are overcrowded while only the youngsters swim in the sea. When asked why they do not bathe in the sea, Japanese adults reply that the water is too salty, the beach is too sandy and that there are few shower facilities. Such an attitude toward swimming in the sea was formed a long time ago and apparently caused by the island position of Japan. In 1870 a French diplomat wrote: "At the same time I would like to note a strange fact: as far as I can judge, swimming in the sea among them [the Japanese] isn't done at all" (Humbert, 1870). There are many beautiful places on the coast, but nobody will tan or swim except on established and maintained beaches. The only attraction of a beach is that it is cooler near the sea in hot weather. This is why on a hot day, many people rest and tan on a beach but very few go into the water. Nevertheless, such recreational activities as water skis, wave runners and windsurfing are very popular. It seems that uncultivated nature can be tolerated if it is enjoyed by using the latest technical achievements.

It is curious that the word "ocean" (*kaiyo*) is seldom used in the spoken Japanese language. This seems unusual for the inhabitants of a country in which most of the population faces the Pacific Ocean. You can hear the word *umi* (sea) anywhere, but *kaiyo* is apparently not in the spoken language. The Japanese routinely call any part of the world's oceans as *umi*, and in this regard they do not differ from other nations. The peculiarity is that the word *kaiyo*, never used in everyday conversation, is regarded as a scientific term. Therefore the difference between the expressions "a river flows into the sea" and "a river flows into the ocean" is clear to many foreign schoolchildren but not to the ordinary Japanese; you must first explain the difference between a sea and an ocean.

One day, my Japanese students were shown a documentary film about the life of the ethnic groups of Russia. In the film, an Udegheis hunter was leading a group of journalists and cameramen by following a wheel track left in the snow by another cross-country vehicle. He showed the group a set of tiger tracks which were fresh, and explained that after a heavy snowfall, people and tigers walk in the same rut out of ease, but also try not to come across each other. The episode left a great impression on the Japanese students. In their opinion, a man should not walk on the same path as a tiger; it is dangerous and unnatural. This case demonstrates that the Japanese clearly divide the world into one where things are close and therefore tame, and a distant and strange one where there is no place for a human being.

By actively developing their nearest space, the Japanese skillfully imitate not only natural landscapes but also manmade objects, sometimes even entire countries and their cultures, but in a minimalist way, of course. The Heian custom of drawing separate elements of the outer world to themselves has recently found new life. By using the latest technologies, the Japanese construct theme parks that completely reproduce landscapes and architecture, household furniture and clothes, articles of handicraft and art, ethnic cuisine and many other things for which foreign countries are famous. These parks, constructed with extremely skillful imitation, are called "villages" (*mura*). A German village receives Japanese tourists in Tokyo; there is a Dutch village in Nagasaki, an Italian village in Nagoya, a Spanish village in Shima (Mie Prefecture), a Turkish village in Kashiwazaki (Niigata Prefecture), a Finnish village in Koumi (Nagano Prefecture) and there are two villages (one English and one Canadian) in Izu (Sizuoka Prefecture). A Russian village accommodated visitors in Niigata for five years and an American village opened in 2008 in Misawa (Aomori Prefecture).

Unlike their Heian ancestors, modern Japanese travel all over the world. In 2006, about 17.5 million Japanese visited foreign countries. This means that one out of every seven Japanese, including infants and seniors, went abroad. This proportion has remained at approximately the same level for the last 10 years (IBJ, 2007). The theme parks, which are always crowded, are visited by both Japanese who have visited other countries and those who have never left Japan. For example, 4.35 million tourists visited the Italian village in Nagoya in 2005. The senior manager of the village, Atsushi Fujiwara, emphasized that "people will not go to a park if it does not look absolutely real. The fact that those who had been to Italy find that this park conforms to the original is very important for us" (Kitamura, 2006). Just as the Japanese will brave water sports if the latest technology is involved, Japanese "tourists" will overcome their typically watchful attitude to the outer world if they can experience other cultures in a miniaturized and characteristically Japanese style.

On Environmental Protection

Wilderness activities are slowly but steadily losing favor in Japan. For example, the forests of Japan supply plenty of mushrooms but only a few people in remote villages are used to mushrooming; most modern townspeople have never even heard of such a hobby. As elsewhere, supermarkets in Japan are glutted with cultivated mushrooms that lack both natural aroma and taste, and although the mushrooms are selling well, the Japanese seem completely uninterested in mushrooming, even for fun and recreation. In contrast to Russia, with its long winters and vitamin deficiencies, the Japanese are not used to canned fruits and vegetables. The compotes made with dried fruits, homemade pickled mushrooms, cucumbers or tomatoes so popular in Russia are not even considered palatable in Japan. Japanese cuisine is based on seafood and fresh vegetables and the long-term storage of food is not of primary importance as greenhouse-grown fruits and vegetables are available year-round. A liking for canned fruits and vegetables often seems exotic to the Japanese who have visited other countries. It does not seem to matter to the Japanese that vegetables grown in natural conditions and then canned might be more delicious than fresh greenhouse products.

Similarly, fresh wild berries have not been popular until recently. At the beginning of the 19th century, Vasily Golovnin wondered apropos of this: "Among the berries, the raspberry, the wild strawberry, which are in great esteem in Europe, have no value in the Japanese's opinion; these berries are thought by them to be extremely detrimental to health... The Japanese do not eat any berries that grow on grass [i.e., not on trees]" (Golovnin, 2004). Golovnin might be quite amused today to see how many "harmful" raspberries, strawberries, sweet cherries and other overseas berries the modern Japanese consume. However, these berries are a product of modern greenhouse cultivation, clean and finely packaged; why not use them for food?

The Japanese attitude toward wild plants remains the same. On a spacious campus of the university where I taught, there were vast numbers of raspberry bushes near the agricultural faculty. At the height of the season, the bushes were berry-spangled; there were more juicy berries than there were leaves. It was a sight which foreign wild berry lovers could only dream of. Despite the fact that there were no prohibitions preventing anyone from picking the berries, nobody did. It was understood without question that you should not eat these berries because they are a product of nature and not cultivated, therefore they might not be safe. The ripe berries fell to the ground and rotted, unappreciated by anybody.

Along one city road, bushes of dog-rose extended for almost two kilometers. They were planted for decorative purposes but the berries ripen as they should: red, large and sappy. Dog-rose grows not only along city roads but also in many other places. Is there any need to mention that the Japanese do not eat the hips but only enjoy seeing them? Instead, strangely enough to Westerners, the Japanese eat chrysanthemums, but of course only after special processing by soaking them in a spicy sauce.

Nevertheless, a tendency to improve upon the nearest space is peculiar to the Japanese to a greater extent than in other nations; it is an important element of their attitude toward nature. Having begun this activity in ancient times, they had continued it methodically over the ages and achieved much success with it by the end of the 19th century. Lev Mechnikov, who drew attention to this peculiarity of the Japanese attitude toward outward nature said: "It is most strange that Japanese scenery, with all its fascinating beauty...has nothing wild or primeval in it... There is not a single inch of uncultivated land anywhere" (Mechnikov, 1992).

Today the pace of the improvement of the nearest space is increasing. It is evident when you see the piezoelectric elements that are built into the roadside curbs, even on the sidestreets of small Japanese towns. The bronze-gold lights extend along one side of the road while silvery lights extend along the other side so that drivers and pedestrians can clearly see the border between the road and the footpath and not confuse the left and right sides of the road.

Because nature is so extensively cultivated, its undeveloped part is pushed to the side and becomes more and more strange to a Japanese observer. A dragonfly or bumblebee that strays into a university classroom causes a minor panic among Japanese students. The lecture room is not the proper place for insects and most students will keep their watchful eyes on the invader until it leaves the room and returns to its native environment. In Japanese perception, the perfect society of tomorrow should be absolutely controllable, safe and comfortable. This society should ideally copy unexplored wilderness as well; the copy should be modern, technological and elegant, but it should be no more than a copy.

Globalization has rudely invaded the refined Japanese world. The Japanese worldview and their attitude toward world affairs are changing as they realize that they are part of a messy world. Their intentions of improving their nearest living space collide with the reality of contemporary global processes and international factors. Japan's prosperity now depends more than ever on the decisions made by the international community, including countermeasures against global warming. This problem is of primary importance for Japan as an island country with a mild and humid climate.

A public opinion poll taken in 2005 revealed the priorities and values that are most important to the Japanese people (Table 8.1).

Table 8.1 shows that nearly nine out of 10 respondents put "concern for nature and the environment" at the top of the list while "safety of living space" took third place. Such qualities of life as emotional richness and good fortune were not among the top priorities of the Japanese and material well-being was at the bottom of the list. The item related to adventure and risk was notable as only 26 percent of the respondents said it was important. As we have seen, the Japanese have never been inclined toward risk and this does not seem to have changed.

Taking into consideration the Japanese attitude toward the environment, it is quite fitting that the Kyoto Protocol to the United

Table 8.1:   The most important things to the Japanese.

Priority or value	% indicating that it is important
Concern for nature and the environment	87
Kindness towards people, desire to make them happy	84
Safety of living space	78
New ideas, creativity, opportunity for personal fulfillment	70
Following a strict moral code, desire to avoid other people's disapproval	68
Public recognition of successes and achievements	54
Observance of traditions, family and religious customs	53
Possibility of enjoying one's life and to reward oneself	51
Emotionally rich life with adventure and risk	26
Material values, availability of expensive goods	23

Source: Nihonjin no kachikan henka (Japanese moral values in development). Dentsu soken, 2005, p. 7.

Nations Framework Convention on Climate Change was adopted in the ancient capital of Japan (December, 1997). In the course of the implementation of the Protocol's provisions, Japan even took the liberty of criticizing the United States, its closest ally, for its delay in joining the world community. Since 1998 the Japanese government has monitored public opinion on climate change. In 2005 a full 87 percent of the respondents were concerned with this problem and two years later it was considered to be a serious problem by 92 percent of the respondents.

In their efforts to secure a clean environment, the Japanese have become uncharacteristically un-Japanese; in fact they showed not only their inherent ingenuity but also an unprecedented radicalism. In the spring of 2005, the Japanese Ministry of the Environment recommended that office workers should stop wearing their uniforms (suit and ties). It was noted that, during the hot summer months of each year, work efficiency dropped while electricity bills shot up. The millions of air conditioners that were cooling the buildings were at the same time heating the streets, which of course compounded global warming from the carbon dioxide released by the generation of electricity. A large-scale national campaign called "Cool Biz" was launched from 1 June until 30 September 2005. Millions of white-collar workers were allowed to go without their suit and ties. This would allow the buildings to be kept at about 28 degrees celsius which would reduce energy consumption and the emission of carbon dioxide. Even then Prime Minister Jun'ichiro Koizumi went to work in a short-sleeved shirt and without a tie. He was followed by other government workers, including members of Parliament whose images were eagerly caught by TV cameras. According to a poll taken by the Ministry, one-third of the responding institutions reported their acceptance of the Ministry's recommendation. As a result of the first campaign, 46 tons of carbon dioxide was prevented from being released into the atmosphere. The Ministry continued the campaign in 2006, during which the favorable view of the campaign increased to 43 percent and the carbon dioxide savings grew to 114 tons.

The measures did not result in a decisive victory over wearing uniforms, however. Two years later, fewer than half of offices stopped implementing the measure. Many of the dissenters were simply unwilling to appear before their customers and partners "inappropriately dressed." Nevertheless, the above-mentioned 114 tons is the amount of carbon dioxide released by supplying electricity to approximately 2.5 million houses for one month. The campaign was considered a success by the world community. In 2006 South Korea announced its intention to implement a similar program, and the Great Britain Central Council of Trade Unions appealed to the government to take similar measures.

This is apparently not the last effort by the Japanese in working for climate change. During the 2007 poll, almost half of the respondents expressed a willingness to contribute personally to this effort. Many suggestions included using energy-saving home appliances and refusing the plastic bags offered by supermarkets. However, the most substantial measure, suggested by 57 percent of the respondents, was for the Japanese government to apply Daylight Savings Time, as many foreign countries do. The popularity of this measure has been gradually increasing and the number of opponents steadily falling. In the spring of 2007, this suggestion was made by the powerful Japan Business Federation (*Keidanren*).

At present more than 100 countries change their standard time twice a year. Among the 30 countries who are members of the Organization for Economic Cooperation and Development (OECD) only Japan, South Korea and Iceland do not apply Daylight Savings Time. For the time being, the Japanese government has abstained despite the obvious economic advantage. According to preliminary estimates, the application of Daylight Savings Time would save 970 billion yen whereas resetting computer hardware and the 100,000 traffic lights regulated by these computers will cost about 100 billion yen. The balance of 870 billion yen (about USD 7.25 billion) is a clear profit.

Dawn and dusk come early in Japan. During most of the year, it is dark after 6 p.m. in much of the country. In Japan, it is customary for people to get up early in the morning and work until dark; returning home when it is still bright is not the accustomed practice. This traditional routine is the basis of the conservative attitude of the Japanese toward Daylight Savings Time. Their time perception is of no less importance. Chronologist Yukio Takahashi said that "it's not a technical problem to introduce Daylight Savings Time, but we have no right to make a mistake because the slightest inaccuracy may cause a panic" (*Yomiuri*: 23 April 2005). Changing a clock twice a year would certainly be a big thing for the Japanese, who are very attentive to details and minutiae. Skeptics are apprehensive about Japanese families' ability to adjust all of their clocks and timers; there are five or six such devices in every Japanese household. Experts believe that a change to Daylight Savings Time will result in a sharp increase in the sales of self-adjusting clocks. It seems that concern for the environment within the next few years will change the caution of the Japanese government, and most of the population, toward Daylight Savings Time.

The Japanese government monitors public opinion. For example, the fact that eight out of 10 Japanese are concerned with issues of worsening public security prompted the Cabinet in 2007 to propose increasing the punishment for the possession and use of firearms, for which Japan has always had strict laws. Possession of a firearm was, prior to 2008, punishable by imprisonment for one to 10 years, and the use of a firearm carried a minimum sentence of three years and a maximum of life imprisonment. After 2008, the use of a firearm is punishable by a minimum five years of imprisonment and an additional fine of 30 million yen (US$250,000). This fine is second only to corporate sanction for anti-monopoly law violations.

It is no secret that in many cases of organized crime, the Japanese *yakuza* ("mobsters") consider it an honor to be imprisoned for the sake of the organization to which they belong. Large fines are intended to eliminate the economic expediency of organized crime activities. A high-ranking officer of the National Police Agency says: "We proceed from the assumption that the members of criminal groups will be unable to pay such fines unaided, and that the fines will be burdensome to the whole organization. It should be a restrictive measure for organized crime" (*Yomiuri*: 17 October 2007). Taking into account that the Japanese police have a complete list of the members of the criminal groups on hand, including their addresses and those of their family members, the collection of fines present no difficulty.

Foreigners and Internal Safety

On 24 May 2006, a new law amending parts of the Immigration Control and Refugee Recognition Act was promulgated. The law was aimed at tightening control over foreigners coming to Japan for the purpose of internal security, despite the law's stated purpose of reducing the threat of terrorism. Biometric data recording is currently a compulsory procedure for all foreign nationals entering Japan, even those holding a residence permit and thus being equal to the Japanese in their civil rights (1.57 percent of population). The law caused discontent among Australians, Europeans and Americans, some of whom had resided in Japan for 20 years or more and who considered Japan as their second homeland. They argued that they take an active part in the social and business life of the country, give lectures in

Japanese universities, head businesses that give jobs to Japanese workers, work as volunteers and also pay taxes. The foreign residents were quick to remind the Ministry of Justice that "the only known terrorist act in Japan since the early 1980s, the 1995 sarin gas attack on the Tokyo subway that killed 12 people and injured 6000, was carried out by Japanese cult members," not by foreigners (*The Australian*: 25 October 2007). It is also a fact that in the 1970s and 1980s, members of *Nihon sekigun* (Japanese Red Army, consisting of Japanese citizens) perpetrated terrorist acts abroad. Foreign permanent residents in Japan voiced their opinion that, given these facts, the parliament's decision was not entirely logical.

However, the attitude toward foreigners is a long-standing Japanese eccentricity, a visible manifestation of the reputation of the country. In the 1980s, the Immigration Service at Narita Airport met all foreign guests with an inscription that read *Aliens*. For several years, the foreign visitors complained about this to Japanese immigration officials until then Minister of Justice Yukio Hayashida stopped the practice in 1988.

Nevertheless, this victory did not greatly influence the attraction of Japan to foreigners. Strangely enough, based on the number of foreign visitors, Japan, known for its exoticism, hospitality and tidiness, is ranked a humble 30th in the world and only 7th in Asia. It is hard to say exactly which factor is responsible for this competitive disadvantage — the geographical remoteness from Europe and America or the notoriously closed Japanese society. According to the United Nations World Tourism Organization, the number of foreign visitors to Japan in 2006 was half the number of visitors to Russia or Australia and one-sixth the number of visitors to China. France was the world leader, receiving 11 times the number of visitors to Japan.

From 1952 to 2000, all foreigners entering Japan for stays of longer than one year were fingerprinted. This practice was abandoned in 2000 due to international criticism. However, permanent residents of Korean and Chinese descent who were forcibly displaced from occupied territory in pre-war times have been enduring this procedure for decades. In Japan, they are called *tokubetsu eijusha* (special permanent residents). They were born and bred in Japan, speak

Japanese without an accent, have Japanese names and are completely acclimated to the Japanese social environment. They also do not differ from the Japanese population in appearance. Nevertheless, they are still considered half-aliens. Even today, some employers turn to private detective agencies to determine if the candidate to be hired is of such descent and some parents do the same before their children's marriage. However, a new system introduced by the Japanese government does not affect "special permanent residents"; thus, they have become one step nearer to being ethnically Japanese citizens. As for foreigners married to a Japanese man or woman, they must undergo the usual identification procedures upon each re-entry.

More than seven million foreigners visit Japan each year. This is more than previously but is half the number of Japanese traveling abroad (IBJ, 2007). In January 2004, the United States Citizenship and Immigration Services put into operation a system of biometric controls, called "US-Visit," for all foreigners entering the United States. Some countries condemned this measure and some even took countermeasures in response. For example, Brazil began fingerprinting and photographing only US citizens. Japan followed the United States' lead and introduced a system called "J-Vis" on 20 November 2007. The official reasoning was that the system was a preventative measure against acts of terrorism committed by foreigners. The system was intended to help reduce the crime rate among foreigners and to rule out the possibility of deported persons returning to Japan. Illegal entry into Japan by using forged documents occurs relatively often.

Advocates of the biometric immigration control technology refer to statistics that show higher criminal activity by immigrants than by local residents. In Japan there are 5.4 domestic criminals per 10,000 population but the figures are much higher for foreign criminals. For every 10,000 population, there are 76 ethnic Chinese criminals, 64 Iranians, 33 Philippinos, 31 Koreans, and 16 Brazilians. In 2004, foreign permanent residents (including ethnic Koreans and Chinese) composed about 1.5 percent of the population but 7.7 percent of the convicts imprisoned. Most crimes are committed by ethnic Chinese (34 percent), followed by Koreans (29 percent), Iranians (9 percent) and Brazilians (7 percent) (*Yomiuri*: 5 May 2004). According to data from the Immigration Bureau of Japan, about 200,000 foreigners are in Japan illegally.

Under the J-Vis system, immigration officers fingerprint and photograph non-Japanese travelers as they pass through immigration at air and sea ports. The data is checked against an immigration black-list containing the names of about 800,000 Interpol suspects and 14,000 foreigners who had been deported from Japan. According to the Immigration Bureau, after the implementation of the new system, the probability of illegal entry into Japan plummeted to about 0.001%. Then Minister of Justice Yukio Hatoyama said he was satis-fied with what he had seen during a test of the system at Narita International Airport. On the first day of biometric scanning, finger-print checks identified five people on the immigration black-list, and 21 faults of the new equipment were recorded. The simplicity and reliability of the biometric control system were highly regarded by experts. They pointed out, however, that the new system covers 27 airports and 126 sea ports but cannot be installed in the numer-ous small fishing ports on the coast. It is practically impossible to control these ports, so the threat of illegal entry into Japan remains.

There is also a humanitarian aspect to the problem. The watchdog group Privacy International has protested against the implementation of fingerprinting and face-scanning systems. In a letter signed by more than 70 nongovernmental organizations, they pointed out that the system has done severe damage to the image of Japan as a hos-pitable and beautiful country. Human rights activists in Japan share this approach. "The Japanese government has a long history of not wanting long-term foreign residents, and they really feel they need more control over foreigners," said Sonoko Kawakami of the Japanese chapter of Amnesty International. "The government just wants to gather as much information as possible on people" (*The Seattle Times*: 18 November 2007).

Reproaches like this are rather habitual for Japan. Having joined the U.N. Convention Relating to the Status of Refugees in 1981, Japan undertook obligations worthy of a world leader but is fulfilling them in a peculiar way. The Japanese government spares no expense in accepting refugees (second in the world only to the United States) but does so only reluctantly. Thus, for the first 20 years of the Convention, only 305 refugees took shelter in Japan; a mere 15 per year on average. In 2007, the newspaper *Asahi* was proud to report that the figure had increased to 41 (Asahi, 25 July 2008). But the entrance filter is still extremely tight, even for the very small number of refugees seeking asylum in Japan, as compared with other developed countries. Only one out of every 46 applications is approved by the national government. For comparison, in 2007, around 48,000 political refugees took shelter in the United States, 11,000 were accepted by Canada and 10,000 by Australia.

In the 1990s, *kokusaika* (internationalization) became one of the most popular words in the Japanese language. The media was discussing the internationalization of Japanese society and school teachers time and again told their students about it. The correlation between the unassimilated and unsafe outer world, and the developed, well-conditioned inner Japanese world has a social aspect as well as a natural one. The role and position of Japan in the global community and its relations with it are at the core of the issue. Contrary to past practices, the Japanese government has voluntarily decided to make its country more accessible and open to the outer world. Two main aspects of this process have become clearly visible.

First, the Japanese people are actively encouraged to study foreign languages and cultures. For example, by number of learners, Russian is ranked sixth among foreign languages taught in Japan; still Russian courses are offered at more than 80 Japanese universities. It is taught and studied mostly in a superficial way and is not considered to be a subject of much practical use; the students are mostly driven by curiosity. In addition, numerous community culture centers offer courses in Russian. The same is seen for the major European and Asian languages. There are also an innumerable number of events involving cooking and tasting of dishes from all over the world.

Second, the Japanese government is taking unprecedented efforts to attract non-tourist visitors to Japan, mainly students from universities. At the beginning of the 1980s, about 10,000 foreign students were studying in Japan while twice as many Japanese were studying in the United States alone. In 1983 the Japanese government set an ambitious goal that seemed unachievable at the time: to increase the number of foreign students by a factor of 10 to 100,000. As of 1 May 2006, more than 118,000 graduate and post-graduate students from overseas were studying in Japan, 10,000 of which were studying at the Japanese government's expense. Despite this, Japan is still far from catching up with its European counterparts, France and Germany, both of which accept about 250,000 foreign students. There is no doubt, however, that Japan is on the way to becoming the biggest international education center in Asia. Students from Asian countries are coming to Japan, just as they do to the United States and Great Britain. In 2004 the Japan Student Services Organization (JASSO) was established with the aim of attracting more foreign students to Japan. The organization was given a considerable budget and has ambitious goals. One of them is to increase the number of foreign students to 300,000 by 2020, a feat that was inconceivable not so long ago (JASSO, 2008).

However, the growing flow of foreigners could not but aggravate some old problems and reveal the way of thinking typical of an island country with a closed society. "Japan's concept of 'internationalization' as a controlled ingestion of foreign civilization while keeping foreigners at bay, rests on a perception of racial and cultural

Figure 8.1

Source: Website of the Windmill College of Australia, accessed from [http://www.windmill-college.co.jp].

homogeneity that is both dynamically creative and easily destroyed" (Hall, 1998, as cited in McVeigh, 2002).

Most observers agree that the tightening of immigration controls, including that of long-term foreign residents, could be related to the threat of terrorism, but not primarily so. The Japanese government simply uses the threat as convenient ground for reinforcement of control over those coming from outside, thus strengthening the internal safety of the country. The above-mentioned third priority of Japanese society — the safety of the nearest living space — still determines the government's actions on the international scene.

Chapter 9

Educational Values

Children and Adults

The Japanese approach to child education is quite original. On one hand, it has vast advantages that hardly have any analogues in other cultures. On the other hand, it has grave disadvantages that have proven difficult to eliminate. The advantages, formed over the centuries, have played an important role in the postwar development of Japan. At the same time, the drawbacks became a prime target for criticism when it became clear that specialists educated in the Japanese system had failed to innovatively solve tasks yet to be resolved in the world. Such an ability is of crucial importance to the professionals of a country that has displayed international leadership in many areas.

How can we define a system that lets you catch up with anyone but that does not let you come up first? Piles of books have been written about the Japanese educational system, describing it as a very specific and an extremely exotic phenomenon. Japanese education is a complex set of several main and supplementary principles, rules and methods, the development of which began in the 17th century by founders of Japanese education science Toju Nakae (1608–1648), Ekiken Kaibara (1630–1714) and other scholars. The core principle is that, psychologically, a child differs entirely from an adult, thus a special behavioral pattern should be applied in relating to them. These scholars believed that it was impossible to grow an adult out of a child at once, that each age group should practice definite requirements and that behavioral restrictions should be introduced gradually.

The reports of foreign travelers and journalists that Japanese children do not cry at all and their mothers let them sit and play quietly in puddles are actually quite true. They confirm the fact that modern parents, exactly like those of 100 years ago, dutifully apply a classical educational approach. In 1905 A. Nikolaev wrote: "Starting from early childhood, a child is given a great deal of freedom in the family under the only condition that he should not hurt himself or other people; he is protected but not controlled, he is persuaded but seldom pushed... It is considered unacceptable to threaten a child with abuse or reprimand; every punishment should be imposed as calmly as possible. To give a child a cuff on the nape for some fault means to display your bad manners and vulgar behavior... Commonly accepted ethics oblige a parent to be patient with children" (Nikolaev, 1905). This is the essence of the Japanese approach to the development of a child whose psychological character is considered different from an adult's. From the Japanese point of view, a mother who is trying to control her child by yelling, scolding or threatening looks rather silly.

Adults should behave like adults and children should behave like children; Japan has very strict regulations regarding this postulate. Japanese children normally do not role-play to imitate government officials or the country's top business managers. They do not wear evening dresses and suits and do not perform ball dancing in front of adults. Boys do not have a romantic familiarity with girls and do not act out romantic roles in elementary school. All of these activities are for adults and children should not participate in them.

The scrupulous work aimed at raising respectable members of Japanese society starts in school. According to the principle of gradual maturation, Japanese pupils in their first year of school do not have lessons at the beginning. For several days, they simply come to school with their mothers for a couple of hours, as if for an excursion. They receive explanations on how to arrange things on school desks and how to correctly sit at them, what a school bag is and how it should be used, and other useful information. Special attention is paid to the instruction of etiquette: the correct ways to greet each other, to say goodbye, to listen to the teacher or to ask questions. These first

Figure 9.1

regulations acquaint the pupils with the most important parts of adult life; how to obey the formal rules of behavior. People in many countries believe that the main task of elementary education is to provide primary knowledge while, in Japan, nine out of 10 people think that knowledge of basic moral and ethical values is more important than literacy skills (Takahashi, 2003).

One of the main goals of school education is to develop the habit of working out group rules and to obey them thoroughly thereafter. External limits and norms are always set up for all activities, no matter how creative they are supposed to be, and these limits must not be ignored under any circumstances.

If pupils decide to make a video film about their school, then the film's duration and purpose, the duties of the participants and time schedule will be defined in advance. The plan will be printed and given to each participant.

A pupil who manages to solve math problems in an original and innovative way will be moderately praised by the teacher but, at the same time, he will be criticized for not keeping with established procedure. Accuracy and exactness of actions and compliance with the established rules are praised more than is inventiveness, even if it shows the pupil is highly talented.

If the school baseball team should play a game in another region, then a detailed schedule is worked out in advance to regulate the players' time from morning until night, including the exact time of departure and arrival as well as the trip's duration. According to such a system, the players normally do not have any free time. Actually, this attitude is applied not only to school trips but also to the school regime in general. It is like in the army — an absence of free time is much better than abundance.

The program for a child's growth and maturation is worked out by Japanese society for the child's entire life. Such a slow educational process results in the delayed maturity of Japanese youth compared with their foreign contemporaries. The difference becomes particularly evident when they start student life.

In developed Western countries, a student is considered an adult when he or she begins college. In Japan, the official legal age begins when a person turns 20 years old. He or she is then allowed to vote, to purchase alcohol and to get married without parental permission. Actual readiness for an adult life and full social responsibilities, however, is not expected to be developed until the end of university studies. Until the age of 22 years, when the majority of Japanese young people receive a degree, they are officially regarded as "objects of the educational process." Here we can trace the roots of the evident infantile behavior of Japanese youths.

This behavior can take different forms. For example, many Japanese students cannot reasonably respond to the question of why they have decided to pursue higher education. The most usual answer is that "it is a necessary thing to do" or that "everybody does it." Except for the small portion of students who attend elite universities, Japanese students do not have any idea of what they are going to do or even what they would like to do in the future.

The relationships between Japanese students and their teachers do not resemble the colleague-like relationships observed in other universities. Teacher-student relations in Japan are greatly influenced by a Confucian model of behavior that was adapted for modern life. The most common type of university teacher is an instructor who is more of a licensed organizer and general mentor than a competent professor capable of passing specialized knowledge to his students. He acts like a class-appointed teacher but only at a higher level. Informal interactions between professors and students outside the university are actively encouraged, including at parties. A professor holding a glass of sake and mumbling something to his students is a common sight at such parties. This causes neither surprise nor reprimand. It should be noted here that the Japanese students behave with a great deal of tact and friendliness in such situations.

When studying, Japanese students do not even try to look and behave like adults who are responsible for their actions. They easily admit that they have slept through the lecture, have not prepared for an exam and thank their sensei for his patience with them. Many foreign professors point to this practice with great annoyance. The main duties of students at a university (and in their future life in general) are limited to being honest, obedient and observant. They act according to proverbs such as *shojiki wa issho no takara* (honesty is a lifetime of treasures) and *shojiki ni shite son wa nai* (there is no harm in honesty). In Japan the students are easily forgiven for infantile behavior, ignorance of the simplest things and errors (because the educational process is not yet finished), but they are strictly punished for dishonesty. For example, cheating in exams, which is considered to be usual of students in Russia, is regarded as a shocking incident in Japan. A student caught cheating forfeits all credits and the right to sit for exams for the corresponding semester. He will have to attend all of his classes again, which will prolong his studies in the university and result in extra expense.

Group Pressure

Belonging to a group and recognition of your status by its members are essential conditions of life in Japan. Therefore, one of the main educational goals is to teach children to harmonize their own actions with the group's interests. Unlike in Europe where teachers "tend to develop in a pupil his individual abilities and his own character in order that he grows into an independent and strong person, in Japan, on the contrary, educators aim to prepare a person not for an individual and independent life but to develop in him maximal abilities for joint actions and cooperation" (Nikolaev, 1905).

The first thing the teacher should do after the first graders get acquainted with the school regime is to organize his class into small groups of four to six pupils. Students with mixed abilities, characters and talents are normally united in one group. Naturally, each group has its leaders, its followers and its stragglers. It goes without saying that the teacher is well aware of which students fit which category and the teacher would never reveal to the students to which category he thinks they belong. It is understood by the pupils, however, that during the course of studying, all students will be brought to the same high level of performance. A successful teacher achieves a well-organized effort by the entire group during the accomplishment of the task. Any conflicts within the group must be ruled out completely.

Every Japanese class, like the entire school, consists of a great number of various groups or committees. Pupils are enrolled into the committees according to their preferences, and such committees include those responsible for feeding the animals in the school zoo, for organizing radio programs, for observing sanitary rules, for serving in the school library, for helping with school meals and any number of other task.

Belonging to a particular group is expressed in different ways. In middle school (grades 7–9) and high school (grades 10–12) the students wear uniforms. Pupils in elementary school may wear what they like but some elements of a uniform are already included in their attire. For example, all 1st graders are supplied with bright yellow panama hats or caps easily seen from afar. From 2nd grade, they are given two standard caps of different colors; one for summer and another for winter. The schools send letters to parents informing them when the caps should be changed. During school sports competitions, all of the participants are divided into two teams. The performance of the team or of the individual athletes, depending on the sport, is tallied and a team score is calculated that applies to the entire team; there are no school champions or individual winners in such competitions. The words *winner* and *loser* can be found in every language, but in Japanese these words (*shosha* and *haisha*) are not widely used and are most common in written translations from other languages. Instead, the words *kachigumi* (the winning team) and *makegumi* (the losing team) are commonly used both in conversational and written language.

According to the Japanese educational postulates, a teacher, being an adult person, has a mentality quite different from that of the children and therefore must not be a dictating person. When bringing his class to order, he would not ask for silence in a threatening voice but quietly tell the pupils of his class that they are bothering another classroom. This is an application of the same long-established method of teaching a child to subdue his interests not for the sake of one particular person, even if he is the teacher, but to a group of equal standing, even students of the same age. There are no modern innovations in this method and it remains as it has for 100 years or more. "The class is not managed by the absolute rule of the teacher but most often by a joint agreement of the pupils' will. A particular child is generally restrained by the decision of the whole class and an experienced teacher simply directs the course of the class' decision. Thus, the discipline based on public opinion, as well as by the pressure of the group's interests, is introduced at the early stages of school life. In middle school, the pressure increases and in high school, it becomes most intense, and during all this time the public opinion of the class, not of the individual will of the teacher, remains a constant ruling power" (Nikolaev, 1905).

The standards of Japanese group behavior, especially among children, have not yet been thoroughly studied. These norms define behaviors and actions that seem strange and incomprehensible to foreigners. For example, consider the traditional behavioral pattern of a leader of a Japanese group. Any children's group has a leader who is usually physically stronger than the others and has less fear of danger; in other words, he is bolder. However, the Japanese leader should also be able to organize his group members and to protect them when necessary. Sometimes his concern can resemble fatherly care and take a form of service to his group members. For example, if a "protected" inferior is robbed of something valuable (theft is quite common in Japanese schools), then the leader should be the first to start searching for it and to organize the others in the group. While other group members might stay inactive, the leader should take action. A failed search or unsatisfactory actions might cost the leader his reputation. His behavior in such situations has nothing to do with his personal relationship with the protected child and in other situations, he can demonstrate his superiority in any form, including the use of force.

Educational Standards and Uniformity

Japanese children study for six years in elementary school and during this time, they receive very few marks. The marks that they do receive come at the end of each academic year but this is a formality to advance the pupils to the next grade. The main criterion for moving smoothly to the next level is not the acquired knowledge but a pupil's actual age. The unbreakable rule of the Japanese educational system states that all children should go to elementary school at the age of six years and graduate from it at the age of 12 years. Gifted children do not skip grades and those who lag behind are not retained in their current grade. In Japanese elementary schools, it is not permitted to form special "gifted" or "remedial" classes and the early introduction of specialization in education programs is regarded as a negative practice. Classes with intensive learning of mathematics or the English language can be found only in private elementary schools, which are very rare in Japan.

Japanese education is designed in such a way as to provide the minimum amount of required knowledge that is understandable to the average pupil. It is designed not to provide society with high profile talents but rather to provide everybody with modern basic knowledge. Thus, gifted pupils with high potential and aspirations receive little attention, and the main goal is to prevent average pupils from lagging behind. We can trace this to the traditions of the samurai warrior code. In the 16th century Kenshin Uesugi (1530–1578) taught his vassals the following: the main thing is not to always win but never to lose. The well-known warlord Soun Hojo (1432–1519) instructed his warriors that they should not rely solely upon their own talents and abilities: "Do everything together with others and you will escape troubles" (Sato, 1999).

What about those students who want and can achieve extraordinary results? There are a number of private tutor schools (*juku*) specially designed for such pupils. There, pupils can study as they like and for additional money attain their personal goals. Such schools are attended by those students who want to receive a higher education, which in Japan is an absolute majority of students. Standard school programs are not designed to prepare pupils for a university, which is why an average pupil upon returning home from school should have a quick meal and then go to another school where classes start at 5 p.m. and finish at about 8 or 9 p.m.

In the past, Japanese pupils went to school six days a week, but in 1993 a five-day school week was introduced. At that time *juku* were open all week, with six days assigned for evening studies and Sundays were set aside for tests. Today Sundays are free of studies in all schools. In ordinary schools, summer vacations start on 20 July and on the same day students of the 6th, 9th and 12th grades begin intensive full-day studies in *juku*. They prepare for exams after which, if they pass, they advance to the next level. Additional studies cost parents about US$300–600 per month, depending on the school's status and the number of subjects. In *juku* schools, only one age-old and well-proven method is usually applied: everything should be learned by heart. In case of any difficulties, *juku* tutors will work with students more directly, giving everybody as much time and attention as necessary.

Another very useful habit being taught in ordinary schools is learning how to manage time. Schools have an exact time schedule and always open their doors at the same time, usually at half-past seven in the morning. Classes begin at nine in most schools but it is necessary for the pupils to arrive at the school by eight. Coming after a quarter past eight is officially considered late and the teacher on duty will note this fact in a special registration notebook that is later handed to the pupil's teacher. Repeated tardiness is punished by pinpointing public attention on the student: the name of the tardy student is written on the blackboard, which is a dishonor.

Widespread unification is a distinctive feature of the Japanese obligatory nine-year education, which enrolls nearly 100 percent of Japanese youth. It is almost wholly controlled by the state with the help of local authorities. Ordinary public schools receive about 97 percent of the students, with the remaining enrolled in private schools. It can be assumed without any doubt that, at any given time, pupils of the same age throughout Japan are studying the same material and taught by the same methods. School buildings, classrooms, gyms and other school facilities — everything is built according to a uniform plan and is equipped in a unified way. A pupil who moves from the capital city to a rural area will hardly be able to spot any difference in his school setting.

Judging by school curricula, Japanese elementary schools are the most uniform among the developed countries. Speaking about uniformity we can note here that the antipode of the Japanese school are French elementary schools, where annually about 10 percent of all pupils are retained in their grade and only half of all students are promoted to higher levels without being retained at least once. For comparison, in the Soviet Union schools of the late 1980s, about 2% of all pupils were normally retained.

Japanese middle schools, which experience the most problems with the pupils' behavior, have a practice of rotating the pupils in each class once per year. At the end of the school year, students are asked to write the names of classmates with whom they want to stay with and the names of those with whom they prefer to part from. School authorities try to consider these requests as much as possible during rotations.

Japanese schools only run single sessions. After classes, pupils normally clean the school building as a daily routine, five times a week. Students of different ages never study in the same place. Elementary, middle and high schools have independent organizational and juridical

Figure 9.2:   Elementary school.

structures, different addresses and different teachers. The overall number of students in one school is therefore usually not large and this makes school management much easier.

Japanese society has a strict hierarchical structure and pupils from the first grade are taught to respect its laws. The Confucian system of superiority has penetrated the relationship between students and is further reinforced by special events. Many schools introduce "superior curators" from the 5th grade to future first graders when the latter are still in kindergarten. When first graders arrive in school, their personal "superior curators" are from the 6th grade. The relationships between them are based on the long-established Confucian postulate, "respect from the junior in exchange for protection from the superior."

From an early age, children are taught to observe the accepted rules of communication. Boys of the same age can call one another as they like — by name, family name or even by nickname — when they communicate. But in the presence of the teacher, they have to address each other only by their family names and add the ordinary honorific suffix *-kun*, which is used primarily toward males. Any senior pupil who is at least one year older should be addressed only by his family name with the addition of a polite honorific suffix *-san*. Nobody breaks the rule, including the most commanding and gutsy of class-room leaders. "Etiquette is a full-fledged compilation of knowledge that a child should learn from the early ages and is equally acknowl-edged by both rich and poor people. From childhood on, much attention is granted to etiquette norms and rules, and in schools...the Japanese have special subjects devoted to studying etiquette. All of the gestures and motions used during every meeting, farewell and conversation completely exclude roughness and clumsiness. Etiquette is strictly observed by all people" (Nikolaev, 1905).

The Japanese have a great love for doing things in unison, and one of the best ways to achieve this goal is through synchronized action. The National Center Test for University Admissions, held yearly since 1979, is a good example of this. The standardized test is admin-istered nationally by the National Center for University Entrance Exams, which is under the control of the Japanese Ministry of Education. Those who understand the Japanese way of thinking immediately grasp that there are few things comparable to the Center Test in terms of synchronous unification. The actions of everyone taking part in this event are regulated to the second. This is not an exaggeration. One hour prior to the beginning of the test, all faculty members are instructed to check their watches. A digital chronome-ter with a voice recording announces: "The exact time is eight hours thirty minutes ten seconds, eight hours thirty minutes twenty seconds," and so on. Japan has only one time zone, therefore, thousands of high school students, who have also synchronized their watches to the same chronometer, enter university classes at the same time. At the same second, they begin the test and at the same second, they finish. Hundreds of faculty members read aloud, to the second, the same phrases that have been handed down from the Ministry. Not a single word is omitted or added, because these guidelines have been carefully thought out and checked in previous tests. Having read a phrase, a senior member of the faculty puts a mark beside each phrase. After a proper pause, he reads the next phrase. The second faculty member is a timekeeper, and he or she checks the time required for every action completed. A third member of the group watches the class to answer questions, if any. The actions of the test takers are regulated even more strictly. Guidelines determine every detail, including the types of graphite pencils permitted to be used when answering exam questions and the quantity of tissues for those who have caught a cold. The tissues should be taken out of the package and the package itself should be put away. The instructions are seemingly endless.

The synchronization of the National Center Test for University Admissions might surprise a foreigner, but not Japanese students. Unification is a cornerstone of Japanese education that can be seen elsewhere, starting from obligatory school uniforms and finishing with a standard set of foods for the school lunch (*bento*), all of which have been arranged in a certain order in small boxes. The least regulated element of a school uniform is the color of socks. The requirements only state that socks should be of light color. The color of underwear is not regulated, but schoolmates who are taught to be identical will immediately spot a fellow who has an undershirt that is not white. Once spotted as different, the child becomes a target for mockery and if he does not "coordinate" his behavior at once, he risks becoming the victim of *ijime* (bullying). There is nothing worse for a Japanese pupil. Its victims often commit suicide from being unable to withstand its harsh psychological pressure. *Ijime* most often happens in the middle schools while in the high schools, it is rare. The targets of bullying are usually pupils who cannot adapt themselves to the group's standards and requirements for various reasons. For example, such a child might have lived abroad for several years and therefore failed to learn the crucial norms of behavior.

The fear of standing out by not complying with standard norms becomes a powerful physiological motivation and a regulator of behavior. In Japanese schools, there is a special program intended to monitor the pupils' health and the main physical parameters of all students are regularly taken. The results are then recorded in two types of files; one for physical data (height, weight, etc.) and one for medical information. Data on height and weight are calculated according to a special formula and the results are then divided into five categories: excessively obese, obese, normal, thin, and excessively thin. Most pupils watch these results very carefully and with the first sign of weight gain, they go on a diet. The stimulus is not propelled by their parents, but by a threat of *ijime* from their peers.

It is evident that group psychology takes a central place in the *ijime* problems of Japanese schools. Over the past 10 years, about 20,000 cases of group bullying were registered annually and a minimum of one suicide per year was connected with it. In 2006, Japan hit an unhappy record: 125,000 *ijime* cases and six suicides, five of them in the middle schools and one in the high schools. However, a six-fold increase in registered cases should not necessarily be referred to as a worsening of the situation, given the intensification of the fight against violence in schools, it is simply being reported more often. The Japanese Ministry of Education has recently increased the list of actions that are classified as harassment and humiliation, including those involving the Internet, email and mobile telephones.

This long-standing problem of *ijime* has become extremely acute in Japanese schools and the fight against it might involve non-standard and sometimes very innovative measures. A schoolgirl in the 8th grade at Mizunami School (Gifu Prefecture) committed suicide on 23 October 2006, her birthday. Her birthday cake remained untouched that day. The tragedy shocked the girl's parents and the entire school. Teachers and school management decided to keep the girl's name in the records and at the end of school year, they symbolically advanced her to the next grade. Her desk and personal drawer for clothes and footwear were not given to other pupils and the class decided to take her photograph along on all school excursions. The 23rd day of each month in the school became a day of compassion. On this day, pupils fill in special questionnaires that draw their attention to schoolmates who might be facing *ijime* problems. All of these steps are taken to prevent similar tragedies in the future.

Sensei Means "One Born Before"

The teacher is at the top of the school hierarchy. Respect toward him is directly connected with his age, and it is clearly seen in the translation of the well-known word *sensei*, which literally means "the one born before." He plays a more significant and extensive role than do teachers in European or American schools, whose major task is to provide subject knowledge. A Japanese teacher is first, an instructor and mentor and only second, a teacher of a certain subject.

According to Japanese perception, a school teacher bears more responsibility for his pupils than do their parents. During the school year, the family plays only an auxiliary role in the child's upbringing, and the mother's responsibility is to contribute to school events and to prepare her child for them. Her subordinate role is defined by two factors. First, the mother is an individual while the school represents a group. Second, she is a woman, while the teachers are almost always men. Ann Conduitt, an Australian woman whose son attended a Japanese school, gives a typical example of the role separation here.

On the day of the school baseball match, the mothers were asked to bring breakfast boxes (*bento*) to the stadium. Being a foreigner, Ann did not know what to cook and she was greatly surprised when she saw elaborate and sophisticated boxes of food being brought by the Japanese mothers. Besides being amazed by the food itself, she was slightly puzzled by all the thermos bottles with hot tea and boiled water, miniature tablecloths and napkins, decorative sticks and other table-setting paraphernalia. In Japan, the daily regime is strictly observed so dinner at 12 o'clock is as sure as the sunrise. It was not surprising then that by half-past 12, all of the mothers were quite hungry but they were all waiting patiently for the end of the match, although the food was already set on the tables ready to be eaten. Anna then asked whether they could have a snack while waiting but the Japanese women told her that, first, all of the instructors and teachers should be served their dinners. After the match, the women were serving the men who were eating at the improvised tables. Only after all of the men had left could the mothers eat the remaining food

(Conduitt and Conduitt, 1996). By knowing the rules well, the mothers cooked enough food for everyone. But a strict order must be observed.

Joint committees of teachers and parents are created in schools where the families are always represented by the mothers. Participation is voluntary and schools organize different events to interest mothers, like courses in aerobics under the guidance of a physical education teacher. In their turn, members of a committee can look after children on Saturdays when there are no lessons but the children may want to play at the school. The Japanese believe that unsupervised outdoor play is unwise. That is why schools willingly provide sports fields and other facilities for children during weekends under the surveillance of members of a parents' committee. The classical pedagogical approach requires that adults should continuously and purposefully control the educational process.

In Japan, parents cannot choose a school for their children and if there are no special circumstances, they should send them to the nearest school. As has been mentioned, all schools are unified and each school functions as an organizational center in its neighborhood, collecting all operational information methodically.

If an adult Japanese man see something unusual and relevant to children in the streets, he will first report this to the school. If a school excursion is planned for Sunday, then at 6 o'clock in the morning, a white flag appears on the top of the school building, signaling a meeting; a red flag means that the trip is cancelled due to weather conditions. The schools usually send parents notifications about dangerous crossings or intensified, and thus more dangerous, traffic at certain roads or other pertinent information. Before summer vacations, schools also send little booklets warning parents about the dangers of swimming in summer, excessive sunbathing and other hazards. During vacations, the schools continue to control their pupils by coordinating their meetings, for example, by notifying them that they should not gather for collective games before 10 o'clock in the morning. Pupils also receive a long list of summer tasks that should be fulfilled before the beginning of the next academic year (to keep a herbarium, make summaries of weather observations, read books for a literature course, etc.).

The Japanese elementary and middle schools work 240 days a year, more than in the United States, Great Britain or France. Given the fact that most pupils stay in school daily for after-class activities, the school's role in a child's life is immense.

Schools bear the main responsibility for the pupils' safety, so they have broad authority over the students. The school management selects the walking routes and the means of transportation to get to school safely. Many city schools do not allow their pupils to cycle to school, which are a very common means of transportation in Japan. The main reason is that during rush hours, the narrow streets and intense traffic present a significant danger to cycling students. Bicycles are allowed in rural areas but even here, the schools require that the pupils wear protective helmets when cycling. Generally speaking, Japanese schoolchildren have more than enough rules, regulations and bans. Girls must not wear cosmetics or accessories, and even the types of hairpins allowed are specified. Parents are instructed not to let children bring noticeably original, stylish or expensive things to school to avoid theft and excessive ostentation. Until the end of the 9th grade, pupils are not allowed to visit convenience stores on their way to school or back home without an adult present. All pupils wear standard uniform that are well-known in the district so that any violations are easily traceable. Salesmen in shops (usually part-time working students) are notified of the rules and follow them.

Schools receive, through various channels, any information regarding breeches committed by their pupils. Here, the Japanese again apply the method of group education. During a lunch break, it is announced via the school radio that students of a particular class have been spotted in nearby convenience shops, but the family names of the violators are not publicly announced. Punishment for violations can take the form of the entire class losing the right to go to the gym during a lunch break. If pupils break this ban, a stricter punishment will be imposed. Decisions concerning punishment of the pupils are made not by teachers but by a school council, and the execution of such decisions is controlled by the students themselves.

Chapter 10

Reluctant Workaholics

Encouraging Social Activity

Japan lives and works at a very fast pace which, in its big cities, is almost beyond human capacity. R. Levine, an American psychologist, once estimated that the Japanese have the fourth fastest tempo of life in the world. According to his research, the Japanese are outpaced only by the Swiss, the Irish and the Germans. The author provides data on 31 countries in total, with Mexico, Indonesia and Brazil having the slowest living tempo. Levine measured the living tempo by using three parameters: walking pace, mail delivery time and the precision of a public clock that presumably helps people time their actions. The Swiss took first place mainly due to the precision of their national clock, the Irish turned out to be the fastest walkers and the Germans have the fastest mail (Levine, 2002).

The Japanese, being of generally short stature, have difficulties competing with Europeans in pace, and there is nothing that they can do about this. Thus they placed seventh in walking pace in Levine's analysis. Their public clock took sixth place among the most precise ones, and these two factors prevented the Japanese from being placed better than fourth in Levine's overall standing (Levine, 2002). But why would they need a public clock when half of their wristwatches automatically adjust the time by use of a radio signal, and the remaining half cannot be considered the worst in the world? The mail delivery time was only slightly longer than it was in Germany. Without calling the American psychologist's methods into question, I would like to note that, in my subjective opinion, the Japanese in total perform more active bodily movements than most other nations.

Figure 10.1

The tempo of life in Japan and active participation in the life of society did not appear suddenly. When adapting Buddhism to suit their needs, the Japanese discarded anything that did not go along with their initial expectations, including deep meditation and withdrawal from real life. Shotoku Taishi (574–622), who took a great interest in the idea of Buddhist altruism and who is considered to have been the first Japanese legislator, would often say that a real Buddhist should make himself useful to people. He removed the phrase about the necessity of deep meditation from the Lotus Sutra and substituted a different one: "Do not approach a person who always sits in religious meditation," meaning that this person is of no use to the people around him (Nakamura, 1960).

Buddhism was initially professed by a narrow circle of priests. As a religion that propagates spiritual perfection and withdrawal into reflections on life's fleeting nature, it did not spread widely among the people. On the other hand, Confucianism, which determined social standards of behavior, was readily accepted and became the cornerstone of the Japanese state structure. A few centuries later, Buddhism captured the hearts of Japanese followers in a significantly modified form, not as a philosophic doctrine but as an ethical one. Later philosophers, such as Soko Yamaga (1622–1685), Jinsai Ito (1627–1705) and Ekiken Kaibara (1630–1714), unreservedly recognized the authority of the material world and rejected the philosophy of passive meditation. This philosophy was also criticized by Sorai Ogyu (1666–1728), who wrote that even gambling looked more preferable than withdrawing from real life and being absorbed in philosophic speculations (Nakamura, 1960).

In India, with its year-round warm climate and fertile soils, religious and philosophic doctrines did not often focus on labor but instead on the principles of wealth distribution. For example, charity and almsgiving were considered socially significant. But beggars in Japan have never been in favor; it was considered humiliating and disgraceful to panhandle and to live at the expense of other people. Although they lived in poverty, the lower classes earned an honest livelihood for a bowl of rice. This attitude earned them respect from both society and the government. A foreign observer once wrote: "I have noticed a significant disparity in the attitudes of the government officials; they harass outcasts, poor men, truants and frauds and at the same time sympathize with the honest toilers who drink, fight and disturb the city dwellers" (Humbert, 1870).

The ethics of production relations that create goods and services took a central place in the works of Japanese philosophers and religious thinkers. Production and economic management traditionally received significant attention. The works of Dogen (1200–1253) and other well-known Buddhist preachers spoke extensively about apprehending the essence of the doctrine through active labor. They taught peasants: "Farming is nothing but the doings of the Buddha" and admonished even the merchants who work only for the sake of profit: "Renounce desires and pursue profit single-heartedly. But you should never enjoy profits. You should, instead, work for the good of all the others" (Nakamura, 1967a).

In 1890, Emperor Meiji signed the Rescript on Education (*Kyoiku chokugo*). Until 1945, this document formed the ideology and morality of the citizens and had a great influence on public moral principles. The minister's archive contains 22 draft versions of the Rescript; the Cabinet discussed this question 24 times before ratifying it (Katayama, 1974). The appeal of the Emperor "to strive for knowledge and professions" was never disputed; it successfully went through all the debates and survived in its final version.

In the Meiji Period (1868–1912), the government, being true to its paternalistic traditions, encouraged the development industry and trade. In major cities, they opened so-called commercial museums that displayed samples of goods manufactured in Japan and abroad. Almost always, foreign goods exceeded local ones in quality and were visually categorized into three groups: goods competing with Japanese goods in the domestic market, goods competing with Japanese goods in foreign markets and goods not made in Japan but could be manufactured by local industries (Nikolaev, 1905).

Encouraging hard labor is closely related to the idea of economy and frugality as the most important virtues. In medieval didactic manuscripts, the scribes were urged to spare ink and brushes, and the craftsmen and peasants were instructed to keep their tools. Even the military was supposed to be rational and economical. The Warrior's Path taught: "The samurais in service should always be economical" (Daidoji, 2000). In addition "Hojo Soun's 21 Articles: the code of conduct of Odawara Hojo" contained one specific demand: "Don't wastefully pour out the water used for washing, even though it may be abundant" (Sato, 1999).

The merchants were especially ardent in their desire to be economical. Soshitsu Shimai (1539–1615), the head of a major trading house, left written instructions to conserve food. He wrote that they could save a lot of rice if the household added barley into their diet. He recommended that the traditional Japanese soup *miso* be thoroughly filtered and the residual bean mass be mixed with the scraped vegetable peels (which were usually thrown out) and served to the apprentices and servants. To prevent any resentment, the head of the family and his wife should sometimes eat the same dish (Ishikawa and Naoe, 1978). Knowing that these recommendations were made by quite a wealthy merchant helps us to better understand Japanese attitudes toward economy and frugality.

The results of these age-old attitudes are still obvious in modern times: the Japanese have the largest savings accounts in the world. In 2007, total deposits came to the astronomical sum of US$14 trillion. The average Japanese family has 16.3 million yen in savings (about US$136,000). The deposits of ordinary citizens in the Japan Post Bank make its assets the largest in the world. The balance between consumption and saving leans towards the latter, which dilutes the attractiveness of the domestic market and boosts the export of Japanese manufactured goods. This balance also attracts major international investment companies, such as Vanguard and City Group that tap personal savings.

The drive to conserve material resources can be observed throughout Japan. The number of coaches in commuter trains of the same line changes several times per day, depending on changes in traffic flow; there are two to three times more coaches during the peak rush hours. During the "economical" daytime hours, even the doors do not open automatically but only on demand when the rider presses a special button. In this way, the Japanese save power that is otherwise wasted on opening and closing of doors and on maintaining the temperature inside the coaches.

Diligence versus Talent

Throughout their long history, the Japanese have cultivated many very uncommon views and ideas. One of them is the attitude toward the role of a person's inherent talents in shaping his destiny. Western tradition assigns primary importance to talent and diligence to achieving success in life. In Japan, diligence takes priority. For a long time, the Japanese were convinced that "people are born possessing an equal degree of talent; that they can develop it and achieve success if they make an effort" (Miyano, 2000). Or stated slightly differently: "Originally people possess equal talents; the various results are determined by their various displays of effort" (Kanayama, 1988). Simply speaking, it is persistence, strength of will and diligence that makes the difference. The entire system of classical education and child rearing was based on the principle of equal talent *(noryoku byodo)*.

However, Sorai Ogyu (1666–1728), a Japanese philosopher, said that people possessed various talents from birth and this should be taken into consideration in their education (Takeuchi, 2000). As the social barriers and restrictions of the Tokugawa Period (1603–1867) were being strengthened, this attitude was lost in social practice. In the 18th century, Norinaga Motoori (1730–1801), the founder of orthodoxy in Japanese culture, wrote that it was not the method that was important in academic research but the scientist's diligence. "After all, long and intensive effort is much more important for a scientist than the way in which he works" (Nakamura, 1967). Therefore, in Japan selflessness and diligence are the key elements in achieving success in life.

During the Pacific Campaign of World War II, the plans and decisions of the Japanese military continually surprised the Americans. When the American military analyzed the enemy's mission planning they observed that the Japanese had overestimated their own morale and had insufficient logistics. The intelligence data confirmed that the Japanese commanders placed more trust in the combat spirit and morale of their soldiers than in the development of weapons or of sophisticated tactics. In pre-war Japan, the expression *seishin itto* (the power of the spirit knows no boundaries) was popular. The most extreme example was the dispatching of suicide pilots to attack American targets at the end of the war. Japanese tank drivers and artillerymen were de facto suicide soldiers as the service regulations did not allow them to leave their weapons and equipment during combat. If the equipment was damaged, the soldiers were required to stay with it and "to share its destiny" which often meant to die on the battlefield. Japanese tank armor was last improved in 1938, but the Soviet and American shells were already more advanced and easily penetrated their targets. Japanese soldiers who fought in the war enviously said that, in disabled American tanks, they used to find plates with the words: "Soldier! This tank is enforced with armor of X thickness. Your life is securely protected" (Shiba, 2000).

The idea that labor and persistence can solve any problem is also widespread in Japan today, in the time of efficiency and rationality. Poll results indicate that the Japanese think that "talent" is almost

Table 10.1: The number of people agreeing or disagreeing with the indicated statements.

Statement	Agree (number of respondents)	Disagree (number of respondents)
All people are born possessing equal talent.	62	37
The majority of the people can develop their talent through diligence.	88	12
A person's working manner shows his talent.	79	30
Diligence guarantees success.	66	24

Source: Miyano (2000).

equal to "diligence." This attitude is expressed not only by public opinion poll respondents but also by the polls' organizers. Table 10.1 presents the results of one of these polls.

The table shows that almost two-thirds of the respondents are convinced that all people are equally talented from birth and that nearly nine out of 10 respondents think that diligence can help develop their talent. Can you visualize Albert Einstein developing his intellectual skills by daily diligence? In the Western tradition, outstanding intellectual abilities can give birth to ideas like the theory of relativity and diligence alone is not sufficient. On the other hand, if we take into account that the theory of relativity is not developed too often and thus cannot serve as a common criteria, then the Japanese might be right in a way.

In either case, there is no doubt in the Japanese mind that diligence and a strong work ethic are directly connected to a sense of happiness and satisfaction. According to recent opinion polls, more than 70 percent of Japanese take greater satisfaction in the recognition of their efforts than they do in the actual outcomes of their efforts (*Yomiuri*: 29 September 2008). In other words, polls show that diligence and hard work are still the most cherished and sacred of Japanese values, more so than are personal abilities and the efficacy of their efforts.

A few years ago, one major regional bank of Japan asked me to organize a basic Russian language course for some of its employees.

The Russian language and culture were much more popular in Japan then and the bank's managers decided to train their employees for future business activities in Russia. We began discussing the schedule and when I was told that the one year course was supposed to include one three-hour class per month, I thought I had misheard them, but actually I had not. The appointed employees would assemble once a month on Saturdays to study basic Russian conversation and grammar. With my strict Russian educational background, I was doubtful that it would be possible to learn even a simpler language, let alone Russian, in a mere few hours a month. But I was assured: "Don't worry, our employees are very talented, they can work as much as needed." That is how I was introduced to the Japanese perception of talent. Now my doubts seem excusable: I did not know at that time that Japanese bank employees work up to 3,000 hours a year. Although I could tell that the employees were studying very hard, I was unsure about the results until the very end of the course. I was surprised when I graded the final exam: my students knew much more than I could have expected them to given their schedule. Later it became obvious that the bank's management had put more faith in the diligence and efficiency of their employees than it had on my teaching skills.

As the Japanese do not see much difference between talent and diligence, it is not surprising that, even today, many of them think that employees should be paid equal salary for equal labor, regardless of their skills and proficiency (Miyano, 2000). Therefore it becomes more obvious why the Japanese use a system of lifetime employment and remuneration of labor based on length of service. In short, employers who do not believe in the great power of diligence would not hire an employee of average or low skills for life. Therefore, equalizing trends are embodied in the labor remuneration system. In the United States, top industry managers make 30 times as much as their lowest paid employees; in Japan this disparity is only 10 times.

Everyday life should make the Japanese realize that people do not possess equal skills and talents, nevertheless they maintain that a significant difference in talent is not frequent and that slight differences can be equalized by outstanding diligence. Maybe that is why, before starting an important task, they wish each other "diligence" (*gambare*), unlike Americans who wish each other luck and Russians who wish each other success. The Japanese answer to this would be "thank you," as if they had received a compliment.

Diligence: The Authentic and the Assumed

The fast pace of life in Japan requires efficient and fast action from everybody. A relaxed and lazy employee who takes his time at work immediately becomes a black sheep and receives everybody's scrutiny. Offices in municipal buildings, banks and companies are not divided into separate personal offices, and the boss sits in the common room with his back to the window and his face to his subordinates. Special guest rooms are used to conduct confidential discussions and negotiations with clients. If a boss has his personal office he never closes his door during office hours so that he is able to see and to be seen by everybody. Diligence is augmented by visibility and mutual control. During office hours, Japanese employees never conduct private conversations on the office telephones. I have not seen any instructions prohibiting this; it just seems that everyone knows not to discuss personal matters during work hours.

The rules of office layout and workplace design gave birth to several new words and concepts. In the 1980s, the word *madogiwazoku* came into frequent use to describe employees who did not perform to expectations, or did not quite wear themselves out at work. Those employees were separated from the others in a special way: they were assigned workplaces closer to windows where they had to sit with their faces or sides to the window, thus the moniker *madogiwazoku* (those who are sitting by the window) was born. Those employees sat either perpendicularly or at a 180-degree angle to their coworkers to emphasize their degraded status. The lifetime employment system in use at the time prevented them from being fired, so the *madogiwazoku* were not given any work to perform and sometimes were allocated separate offices with never-ringing telephones. They were supposed to arrive at the office on time and stay there without doing any work. If they left their workplace or dozed off they were subject to further disciplinary action, warnings and eventual dismissal with a "black mark" in their labor records. Later, methods for disciplining negligent employees were toughened and in the economically distressed 1990s, those employees were simply laid off without any black marks.

Long before Ray Kroc developed the McDonald brothers' idea for rapidly prepared food into the McDonald's phenomenon of today, the Japanese understood the connection between biological necessity and a person's business qualities. The proverb *hayameshi mo gei no uchi* (to eat quickly is also a craftsmanship) praises high performance labor. It means that a competent and energetic person even eats quickly to conserve time for more useful activities. Therefore it seems quite natural that it was the Japanese who were the first to make instant soups. They adored the idea. When they learned about McDonald's, the Japanese, true to tradition, borrowed the idea and improved upon it. Thus on 25 August 1958, the world became acquainted with a dish called *instanto ramen* produced by Nissei Shokuhin.

The Japanese think that the greatest sin is to work slowly, to conserve efforts and not to try hard. The surface impression that coworkers have about a colleague should not be neglected. Like any other country, Japan has always had incompetent, lazy and incapable workers, but such workers also know a golden Japanese rule: assumed diligence (*tatemae kimben*) is just as important as genuine diligence. Just as with food and personal dress, appearance is as important as the substance. That is why the standard answer to the polite question "How are you doing?" is a polite *isogashii desu ne* (I am very busy), sometimes accompanied by the popular Japanese proverb *bimbo hima nashi* (a poor man has no time to rest). Official modesty requires that a person understate his virtues and possessions.

A serious and responsible attitude toward work is the quality that defines an ideal Japanese employee. It is this very serious and responsible attitude that does not allow the Japanese to joke at business meetings, at negotiations or in the office in general. It is not a Japanese virtue to combine wit and good business qualities. The implication is that a person who jokes is thinking about something other than work, and this is not good. The employees follow the principle of "the work does not look for the man, but the man looks for the work." In other words, an ideal employee should be constantly busy simply because it is good to be busy. This is another source of assumed diligence.

In 1991, blue collar workers from Russia began working in small Japanese companies. Different approaches to management immediately caused misunderstandings. Russian employees were surprised to see the Japanese walking quickly or even running around the shops, regardless of their work load. The Japanese were likewise amazed to see the Russians (or other foreigners, for that matter) buying soft drinks from vending machines and consuming them at their leisure. In most cases everybody was summoned into the office and informed, through the interpreter, that they had one 15-minute break before and after lunch for cigarettes, soft drinks and to use the restroom, and that they were supposed to work quickly during the remaining time. For the sake of propriety, I will not cite the responses of my fellow citizens.

This is how G. Reynolds, who once worked for Sumitomo Electronics, describes the Japanese atmosphere at the workplace: "The Japanese think that, regardless of the actual workload, a person should look very busy. The best way of showing this is to be in a hurry. For example, Japanese workers would not walk but almost run the three-meter distance to the copying machine, hit the keys feverishly when typing a business letter, jump up from the chair when called by the boss and momentarily freeze before him, saying *hai* [yes, I am listening to you]. Both genuine and assumed diligence is considered equally virtuous, therefore a habit of working quickly and with elements of slight panic is supposed to show the others the employee's busy schedule and his compliance with the ideal of an employee" (Levine, 2002). It is interesting that an employee's response to the boss' call is exactly the same as the instruction left in the early 16th century by Soun Hojo (1432–1519) to his descendants: "When the master calls your name, quickly say 'yes, master.' Even if you are sitting far away from the master, promptly approach him and kneel. Listen to his words with respect" (Sato, 1999).

These personal observations are supported by statistical data. The time spent in the office by an employee is the most obvious indicator of his serious and responsible attitude toward his duties. According to the International Labor Organization, in late 1980s and early 1990s, when business growth rates were high, the Japanese spent more time in their offices than the employees in other countries, but their efficiency was markedly lower than in Western Europe and the United States. In 1990, the French worked on average 1646 hours per year and the Japanese worked 2044 hours, about 20 percent more. The employees of Japanese banks, where the salary is much higher than average, worked nearly 3000 hours per year, or 10 hours per day for a six-day week or 12 hours per day for a five-day week. This resembles the Western factories of the 19th century. The International Labor Organization report for the year 1993 says: "Japanese employees spend much time in their offices to demonstrate their devotion to the company, but their working efficiency per hour is only 46 percent that of the French and 39 percent that of the Germans" (World Labor Report, 1993). It is only natural that when diligence is appreciated as much as talent, it is almost impossible to keep from demonstrating such a valuable quality.

Working late has become a national tradition that did not yield even to the changes introduced by the Americans during the postwar occupation. In 1948, the Americans introduced Daylight Savings Time in Japan. The idea was to intensify daytime labor, minimize man-hour losses and increase nighttime relaxation. The daylight hours became longer but the employees remained at their work places until dark; the American innovation actually increased the number of working hours. In 1952, after the Americans had withdrawn, the Japanese cancelled the yearly shift to Daylight Savings Time and have yet to return to it. As discussed earlier, the issue is regularly reviewed and limited experiments have been conducted. The main reason not to introduce this system is the concern that longer daylight hours will encourage people to overwork and to reduce their amount of sleep instead of providing them with more time for relaxation at night.

Japanese employees cannot think of leaving their offices before dark. A midnight walk around the governmental district *Kasumigaseki* in Tokyo can easily demonstrate this fact, as many windows in the office buildings are still brightly lit. The same picture can be observed in Marunouchi, the central business district of the capital. That is why the cab drivers congregate there around midnight, after the last trains have left the stations. They are more aware than anybody else of the time when the business elite leave their offices. An official from the central ministry writes: "Sometimes I managed to leave my office at 7 p.m. This quite seldom happened usually only when the everyday current issues were suddenly resolved. But in other cases, the working day would by default finish shortly before the last train's departure… This was mostly for economical reasons: if an employee missed the last train, his boss has to issue him a cab coupon, the number of which is budgeted and strictly limited. Both by train and by cab, one usually gets home by 1 a.m. Thus an employee spends 16 hours per day with his coworkers" (Miyamoto, 1994).

Working undoubtedly occupies the major portion of overtime hours, but not always. The employees of a Japanese company are treated as a family and a family is supposed not only to work together but also to spend time together outside of the office. That is why when a Japanese mother tells her kid that "tonight father has much work and he is coming home late" she means that her husband will be with his coworkers, whatever they may decide to do. One member of these "families," who did not completely accept their ideology, writes: "It's still difficult for me to understand something. I can understand when employees stay late at work when they have many tasks to complete. But it's much more difficult to understand when they start a party during overtime hours. The borderline between home and job becomes elastic; there is no rush or pressure any more. Everybody has lunch together; at night they drink and have a tasteless *bento*. If they slept together, they would make a perfect group of same-sex love. I have noticed that the parties in the office organized for any or for no reason unite the employees like nothing else. They start perceiving themselves as an organized and united team" (Miyamoto, 1994).

Another factor that reduces the efficiency of the labor force is business etiquette, no matter how strange this might sound. In

Japanese companies, the regular rotation of an employee's duties and projects is a common rule. After each appointment, every employee, together with his predecessor, is supposed to spend a few months visiting the most important clients and introducing himself personally. In this way, all of the parties concerned can witness the transfer of authority. The clients are happy with the new person paying such obvious attention to them; they feel an increased trust and fidelity toward the company. At the same time, however, the workload of the employee goes up and his efficiency goes down.

Numerous etiquette norms are counterproductive in the work place. When an employee is visited by an older colleague, or by a co-worker to whom he feels obliged, the employee has to postpone his current tasks and to attend to the visitor — to have some green tea, exchange office news or just to have a little talk about nothing. Labor efficiency is important but it cannot compete with business etiquette, which is not much different from the principles of the military high command during World War II; the human factor predominates over everything else. While Americans take the shortest path to the goal, using the most efficient resources and methods, the Japanese have to follow a sophisticated route that is dictated by numerous unwritten rules and traditions. That is why the Japanese often have to exert redundant efforts to achieve their goals, and this is a problem in the current conditions of the business world.

In recent years, Japanese companies have begun to search for the means to increase their labor efficiency by focusing on previously overlooked areas. Some companies turn off the air conditioners at night, thus making their employees leave the offices. The Tokyo company Ryohin Keikaku, which runs a distribution network in Japan and abroad, issued a policy forbidding overtime hours. Five months later, the company reported increased labor efficiency and salaries despite the shortened working hours.

Throughout history, the Japanese have not taken regular vacations. In ancient times, people had a day off once every 10 days in addition to religious and local holidays. Leave for family reasons (death of a relative, a wedding) were given for two or three days but were not regular. Modernization did not change traditional attitudes.

A 1970 public opinion poll showed that working without leave or absence took the fourth position in the list of the main Japanese virtues (*Nihonjin no kachikan*, 1970).

Western countries have criticized the Japanese government for their vacation policy. On the surface, the situation has begun to change. According to the Ministry of Health, Labor and Welfare, since 2000, the average paid vacation in Japan has been 18 days per year. This is less than in the United States and much less than in Europe where people have an annual vacation of four to six weeks. Although allowed more time, the Japanese do not use all of their vacation, usually only about half, or eight to nine days a year and some do not even take this much. For example, in 2006, only 47 percent of Japanese wage earners took any vacation at all.

After graduating from a Japanese university, Masao Miyamoto went to the United States to study and stayed on to work. On returning to Japan in the late 1980s, he was appointed as the deputy manager of a subdivision in the Ministry of Defense. In due time Miyamoto applied for a two-week vacation, in full accordance with labor legislation. He had not known that the unwritten rules were more important than the written ones. A few days later, he was summoned by his immediate superior who said: "I have been informed that you have asked for a two-week vacation. Are you crazy? Do you have any idea what being a government employee means in Japan? It is not customary to take more than three days off for a person holding your position." The superior was not the only one shocked by his employee's application; the entire office was buzzing. Any employee who wanted to be promoted had to be very modest with the duration of his vacation. The old-timers of the subdivision could not remember anyone taking a vacation that lasted more than seven days. Some of them sincerely resented their new coworker's shameful behavior, but others secretly hoped that he would be able to break the tradition and create a precedent that would make their lives easier. Finally Miyamoto was given official leave on the condition that he invent a reasonable excuse for it. The desire to have some rest was not reasonable enough, and the fictitious reason is also one of the forms of *tatemae* (outward stance). Thus everything was resolved in a traditional way as a compromise.

It is worth noting that the subdivision did not have a very heavy work-load at that time and everybody knew it. But the principle of *tatemae kimben* (assumed diligence) did not allow them to speak about this (Miyamoto, 1994).

In many Western countries, any worker is automatically granted five days of paid vacation for seasonal illnesses (flu, cold etc.). Those who did not use these days get a certain allowance at the end of the year. Japanese personnel departments try hard to prevent sick leave. They suggest that employees who have come back to work after sick leave consider the time off as their vacation since the latter is not usually taken anyway. These veiled statistics made *The Economist* conclude that Japanese workers fall ill less often than do Westerners. Such inaccuracy benefit the public image of Japanese industries; their employees appear healthy, are full of energy and capable of working efficiently.

Japanese doctors face especially challenging issues when they themselves fall ill. The Japanese mind can hardly assimilate the idea of a "doctor-patient" and "the shoemaker's wife is the worst shod." The conformity principle does not allow these ideas to come into their minds. An ill doctor will stay at work as long as he can although his "heroics" will not bring much benefit to anybody. It takes consider-able time and effort to make an ill doctor leave his workplace. This is how the inseparable unity of two major principles, *tatemae* (outward stance) and *messhi hoko* (sacrifice of self in service to the public), triumph in Japan.

On the other hand, many companies grant their female employees a monthly two-day paid vacation for their periodic indispositions. According to the managers, a cold or a hangover could either be pre-vented or overcome but natural physiology should not be disregarded.

Paying the Price for Success

So, the Japanese live fast and work long and hard. There are, of course, limits to human endurance and the time will come when these limits are reached. Japan's unprecedented growth in the 40 years following World War II ended in enormous damage to the physical and spiritual heath of the nation. The crisis broke in the late 1980s when Japan was at the peak of its economic powers. The most significant indicator of the situation was Japan's high rate of death, in fact the highest in the world from chronic fatigue. The phenomenon of working to death was even given its own special name: *karoshi*. This word was later borrowed by some of the European languages and became known internationally. In 1988, the first telephone line for those experiencing problems with overwork was opened in Osaka. Within the first day, the service received 309 calls from city residents. Now there is hardly any prefecture in Japan that does not have such a service.

A young and promising man under 30 worked in a Japanese chain of restaurants. He was promoted rapidly and soon became the director of a restaurant in the eastern part of the country. He worked up to 20 hours per day, took reports and other paperwork home and worked until after midnight. Soon after his promotion, he began suffering headaches, nausea and chronic irritability. In 2006, he lost control of himself and physically abused a subordinate, for which he was demoted and later fired. It might have saved his life; he later told his doctors that he was on the verge of suicide. He was then diagnosed with a serious mental disorder caused by chronic overwork (*Yomiuri*: 22 May 2007).

Many are not lucky enough to be fired. According to non-governmental organizations, in recent years, over 10,000 people in Japan have died as a result of overwork and overwork-related health problems. Companies heatedly dispute any connection between the deaths of their employees and overwork, and they are quite successful. The problem is quite complicated; even the latest research techniques cannot prove a direct relationship between these two phenomena. The data of the NGOs contrasts with that reported in the Japanese media, which states that, from January 1988 to December 1990, chronic overwork killed 89 people, or about 30 per year.

In the spring of 1995, the Tokyo district court heard the case of the suicide of a 25-year old employee of a major advertising company. The court established the fact that the victim overworked by about 147 hours in a month — almost six hours overtime every day, including Saturdays. Four months after starting work, he would often return home at 1–2 a.m. by August and at 4–5 a.m. by November. By March the following year, he stopped going home entirely and spent the nights either in his office or at the nearest hotel. Ten days prior to his suicide, he told his co-worker: "There is something wrong with me. I can't understand what I am doing. I must be incompetent in my work." The company managers produced the evidence of their care for the employee's health and their attempts to help him. They recommended that he see a doctor, issued him cab coupons, paid for his hotel and took other measures. They only failed to lessen his work.

The Japanese have never been indifferent to the Western media's perspective of them. In the early 1990s, the world started talking of Japan as a country of chronic workaholics who have nothing in life but work. In response to this criticism, the Japanese government took some unprecedented steps, dispatching public relations practitioners to explain the significance of the family vacation to the citizens. The results were rapidly seen: in 1996, the Americans topped the list of workaholics. Today Americans work 1800 hours per year while the Japanese work only 1780 and the Germans 1440. But can we really trust official statistics that do not reflect overtime hours? In Japan, overtime is usually rated as "voluntary unpaid labor for the benefit of the company." According to public opinion polls, the number of Japanese who work more than 50 hours per week is twice that of England, eight times that of Belgium and 20 times that of Holland. One out of every three Japanese between 30 and 40 years old works over 60 hours per week (*The Economist*: 19 December 2007).

As a rule, Japanese employees do not leave work before their boss signals that overtime has ended. Only a few would dare to leave the office in view of their boss and coworkers still beavering away. However, foreigners can do so because they have no fear of any unwritten Japanese rules. Sociologists say that the lack of a definite demarcation between company time and personal time has led to corporate malpractice and subsequent overwork. This practice also reflects the *messhi hoko* principle (sacrificing personal needs for the sake of the community) that has been adhered to by the Japanese through the ages. Masao Miyamoto writes that "even though an employee has no important tasks to complete, he is pressed to stay at work with his coworkers" (Miyamoto, 1994). According to the OECD, the affiliates of foreign companies in Japan achieve a much higher rate of performance than do the Japanese companies. In manufacturing, performance is higher by 60 percent and the service sector by 80 percent (*The Economist*: 18 August 2007). The gap is impressive, even considering the fact that only the most successful Western companies enter the Japanese market.

Public opinion polls show that a feeling of moral responsibility toward the company causes the highest workplace tension. Most Japanese employees dread making a mistake that can result in moral or material damage to the company. They are also afraid of failing to complete everyday tasks or of making a mistake when dealing with clients.

An exaggerated responsibility and the fear of making a mistake at work reflect the unique perception that the Japanese have of individual competition and competitiveness in general. According to Yasuo Takeuchi, a Western businessman gets involved in business competition to show his superiority over his rivals, while a Japanese businessman does it to prove both to himself and to the people around him that he is the equal of his rivals. In other words, foreigners try hard to win but the Japanese try hard not to lose. Therefore, in a problematic situation, the Japanese tend to retreat into themselves and to shoulder the blame for everything (Takeuchi, 2000). That explains why 10 days before his suicide, the advertising executive worried not so much about his health but about his reputation in the company. This feature also explains why the vast majority of Japanese companies avoid risks by all means possible and prefer reliable long-term projects.

In 2006, the Ministry of Health, Labor and Welfare confirmed that it was aware of about 355 cases of overwork-related situations that had resulted in 137 fatalities, which is 3.5 times higher than six years previously. These statistics cover only the most obvious and undeniable cases. To investigate these cases, the Ministry compiled a detailed list of signs that make it possible to recognize the work-related illness or death of an employee. As a result, the Japanese courts have been receiving a constantly increasing number of lawsuits.

In 1988, only 4 percent of overwork-related death lawsuits were sustained, but in 2005 this number has increased tenfold to 40 percent. If the families of affected workers win the lawsuit, they get an annual government allowance of US$20,000 and the company responsible for the employee's death might have to pay up to one million dollars in compensation.

There are many less serious cases in Japan and the number is constantly growing. According to the Ministry, 44,100 patients were diagnosed with "depressive syndrome and mental disorders" in 1999. This figure more than doubled to 92,400 patients in 2006. In June 2007, the NHK television company publicized the results of a study of mental disorders among Japanese men aged between 30 and 40. One of the conclusions was as follows: "The number of mental disorder cases among the most able-bodied men is steadily growing. Of the companies surveyed, 60 percent reported an increase in mental disorder cases among their employees in recent years, with employees between the ages of 30 and 40 years suffering the most. In many cases, these are related to overwork. It's a fact that truly illustrates the need to implement changes in labor management" (Koseisho, 2008). Big business could not help but react to the worsening situation and in 2008, more than 90 percent of all Japanese companies with more than 1,000 employees had mental services policies in place.

The Japanese are amazed when they read in the Western media that the Japanese love to work. "What does love of work have to do with it? We are working because we have to, not because we love to." Public opinion polls confirm this attitude. Only seven out of 10 Japanese think that "working hard will enhance their lives in the future." This is low in comparison with other countries, with Japan placing 12th out of 23. Labor enthusiasm is also not typical of the Japanese: less than half of the respondents said that they possessed this quality, which put the Japanese in 19th position in the list of 23. Labor enthusiasm is more typical of countries like Peru and Venezuela, whereas economically developed countries mostly appreciate performance, efficiency and labor discipline (*Sekai*, 1999). So, the Japanese reputation for being hard workers has come about not because they like to work, but because they have to.

Chapter 11

The Unpretentious Joy of Being a Group Member

Japanese Balance Between Work and Play

Longer office hours, shorter vacations and a high sense of responsibility for the company make employment the main purpose of life for the modern Japanese. It there any relief to this infinite cycle? The situation is not really as bleak as it may seem and pockets of recreation do exist.

There are 15 official holidays in the Japanese calendar. They comprise the so-called Golden Week, several holidays that occur in late April and early May. In mid-August, the Japanese have a second important holiday, *obon* (commemoration of the ancestors), which is not a festive holiday on the calendar but nevertheless consists of several consecutive days off, including public holidays and leave. For example, in 2007, the average number of *obon* days off was 8.2 days. The situation is the same on New Year's day, for which there is only one official day off but, unofficially, there are more. Those who work in transportation, trade and services have the least amount of time off (three days), while others have between seven and 10 days. So, in Japan, people annually have three one-week holidays plus 10 separate occasional holidays. They currently enjoy a five-day working week. The days off partially compensate for the short paid leave.

Seven out of 10 Japanese are happy with the number of holidays and days off in a year (Takahashi, 2003). Both in Europe and in Russia, people are used to having long vacations once a year. Some people say that it is good for one's health, but others say otherwise. The dissenters point to the stress of returning to the usual work routine after a long vacation; they are backed by doctors who say that it is better to have frequent short vacations. The optimal frequency and duration seems to be a matter of maximizing one's options. For example, the Russians have no choice but to take extended vacations; there are few areas with favorable climate near the population centers and the distances to such areas are too great to make it practical to get there and back in a reasonable amount of time. Meanwhile, the Japanese have a wide variety of recreation areas within a two-hour car ride. Therefore, they have many convenient options for rest and recreation.

In recent years, the Japanese have begun to enjoy longer vacations but they remain the leading work horses. Do intensive workloads have any impact on the health of the nation? Global statistics show that in Western countries, heart and blood vessel diseases are the number one killer followed by cancer. The gap between these two health problems is substantial. Cardiovascular diseases kill three times as many people as cancer, and cerebral vascular problems kill twice as many people as cancer. The situation is quite different in Japan. Cardiovascular and cerebral vascular problems taken together kill fewer people than does cancer (238 and 254 per 100,000 population respectively). As mentioned above, between January 1988 and December 1990, overwork killed 89 people, and the majority of them (62) died as a result of massive heart attacks and strokes. So, in Japan as well, extensive workloads lead to the same results. But why is the incident of heart attacks and strokes in Japan lower than elsewhere and why do the Japanese live longer than people of other nationalities? What helps them?

In addition to the qualities of Japanese cuisine and moderate consumption of weak alcohol, psychologists speak of a culturological factor. They say that a Japanese person who overworks for the benefit of the team or group first and for himself last receives a powerful psychological return in the form of appreciation, respect and support from his coworkers. According to this point of view, in the individualistic West, people cannot count on anything similar, even after achieving personal success and wealth. The favorable influence of this factor, together with advanced health care, is presumably crucial for the outstanding longevity and cardiovascular health of the Japanese.

Edvin Reischauer (1910–1990) also emphasized this aspect of the Japanese office atmosphere. He wrote: "One may have an impression that employment for the Japanese is something more than just performing their contractual obligations. It is also a realization of that deep and powerful feeling that is a part of the general Japanese mentality... In Japan, an employee is not treated as an insignificant and easily replaceable part of the huge industrial machinery, this attitude being typical of Western management" (Hamaguchi and Kumon, 1989).

Sazo Idemitsu (1885–1981) is known in Japan as a hero of the postwar "economic miracle." He is the only Japanese to have established an oil company amid the cut-throat competition of the Western oil giants. His explanation of the Japanese's lifetime devotion to a single company is: "Our predecessors have never used written contracts; they'd just pat you on the shoulder and say, 'Take care of it' and you'd say 'OK' and then you would do it. You'd risk your life to do what you were supposed to do. So the Japanese people, even though they may be offered better pay somewhere else, would not necessarily leave their company. To us, the spiritual relationship with our superiors is a big part of it..." (March, 1996).

In the Western view, any company is considered a commodity that can bring either profit or loss. The common ways of modern capitalism involve buying a failing company, firing a portion of its employees, hiring new ones, modernizing and increasing its efficiency and then selling it at a good profit. The Japanese think differently. "In Japan companies are regarded not as money-making machines but as self-perpetuating institutions that are expected to pursue 'service to society' first and profit second. Many firms date back centuries, and changes of ownership are rare. Atsushi Saito, the president of the Tokyo Stock Exchange, says it is hard for the Japanese to accept that a firm can be traded like a commodity" (*The Economist*, 22 December 2007).

The system of lifetime employment and individual devotion to a single company originate from the samurai code. Western employment is based on market requirements, encouraging employees to look for the most profitable application of their professional expertise.

Figure 11.1:   A family-like company.

If the contract fails to satisfy them any longer, or if they have a better job offer elsewhere, they change jobs without aspersion. "I am doing what is best for me and my family" is the standard refrain of modern Western society. On the contrary, the Japanese have long lived by the principle "a true samurai can have only one master." The military estate could never think of rushing toward profit and changing their suzerain. The medieval moral codes threatened the renegades, not with divine retribution, but with the rejection of their master (Sato, 2004). The worst shame for a samurai was to have his services rejected by his suzerain. Modern Japanese management has preserved this principle in the form of lifetime devotion to a single company that guarantees a lifetime of support to its employees, much as a feudal duke would have several centuries ago.

Not only do the Japanese leave their offices late but they commonly have a drink with their coworkers afterward to talk about work and life in general. After they retire from their careers, they often engage in various activities. However, some are so accustomed to socializing with their coworkers that, following retirement, they become clients of a newly popular service: paid conversation. Some retirees go to a professional "counselor" simply to chat. It is not that they need any counseling or help; they just need somebody with whom to talk. It is quite difficult to understand their motivation. Either the retirees are not able to converse with family and friends or their fellow coworkers are irreplaceable. But the fact is Japanese retirees need what they can get only from after-hours socializing. Their financial needs are not sufficient enough to explain why 70 percent of 60 to 64-year old Japanese men would like to continue working fulltime. No other developed country can boast that many active retirees. In the United States, such people make up 58 percent of all people in this age group, while in Great Britain, the percentage is 56 percent and in France, 19 percent (Data as of 2005, *Yomiuri*: 9 May 2008).

Doctors have shown that prolonged psychological discomfort and related stress cause many somatic illnesses in otherwise mentally and physically healthy individuals. It is also known that patients recover from severe brain and heart injuries much more quickly in an atmosphere of love and care from the people around them.

R. Williams of Duke University puts the 5-year survival rate at 50 percent for cardio-vascular patients who live alone, and at 82 percent for those who recover in a family environment. According to polls, 66 percent of the Japanese treat their companies like they would their own families (Levine, 2002). Could this be the factor that supersedes any medical device in helping the Japanese to survive overwork?

The inner stability of the labor market should not be overlooked. Despite employment changes that have occurred during the past decades, the majority of Japanese companies continue to practice lifetime employment as reciprocity for employee loyalty. A Japanese team or group does not normally expel its members; an erring member either reforms or leaves voluntarily. The Japanese are very sensitive to critical remarks and opinions, so even negligent employees tend to begin working with the team for the benefit of the company. Of course, sometimes employees are fired but much less often than in other developed countries.

The stable atmosphere of Japanese companies is also supported by the often-criticized system of salary and promotion that is based exclusively on age and length of service. Modern managers may be right in saying that this system is becoming outdated and inefficient. Nobody, however, is likely to deny its role in creating a stable working atmosphere in the office. A preset and publicized schedule of promotions and wage increases helps to minimize the psychological stress of intrigues and denunciations which many Western corporations are notorious for. This approach works even when promotions and bonuses for long-term service fail to satisfy the employees, which also happens in Japan as it does everywhere. Given the workload distribution among employees of equal age and expertise, this process of like remuneration and promotion is open and quite fair in the

Figure 11.2:   The business ritual of exchanging visiting cards.

majority of cases. The major drawback of the Japanese system is the wage leveling and slow promotion of younger employees who, among other things, receive lower salaries.

This system has been in effect for over 150 years and the Japanese have only recently begun modernizing the process, gradually introducing contracts, inside competition, performance assessments and other Western management techniques. The recession of 1997 made personal performance assessments especially important for Japanese companies, but the following year witnessed a dramatic increase in the suicide rate (over 30,000 a year) and the prevalence of mental problems. Since then, efforts to reduce these rates have been failing.

People in general follow four main criteria when selecting a job: salary, stability of the company, atmosphere and professional fulfillment. Comparative polls conducted in different countries made it possible to reveal the peculiarities and preferences of the Japanese. Japan ranked 53rd of 55 countries in terms of placing a high importance on salary. In other words, in almost every other country in the world, money plays a greater role in job-hunting than it does in Japan. The Japanese placed their highest priority on the psychological atmosphere of the company, and was 1st among the nations that ranked this criterion highly. The stability of the company and professional fulfillment ranked 2nd and 3rd, placing Japan in the 27th and 16th position, respectively (Takahashi, 2003).

A similar poll has been taken over the course of 30 years in Japan in which the respondents were asked to rank the priority of each of 10 criteria in their job-hunting process. The psychological atmosphere has always taken the 1st position. Moreover, between 1973 and 2003, the number of those who gave top priority to this criterion rose by 30 percent. The differences in working hours between different companies are so insignificant that less than 4 percent of job seekers take them into consideration, putting this criterion in the 8th position; the significance of this criterion has dropped by 20 percent over the 30 years this poll has been conducted (*Gendai nihonjin*, 2004).

Unlike many other developed countries, Japan does not appreciate individual competition, placing 21st among 23 countries polled. Only the Spanish and the Chileans showed less appreciation for individual competition (*Sekai*, 1999). These poll results do not indicate a readiness for between-group (as opposed to between-individual) competition, where the Japanese have few rivals to challenge them.

Working within a group and for a group, although unattractive and inefficient from a Western point of view, has one indisputable advantage: it frees people from having to make various large and small decisions. Working for a Japanese company requires loyalty and diligence but not initiative or enterprise, thus making the burden of responsibility considerably lighter. Recent studies show that only a small minority of the global population (4 to 8 percent) are able to make complicated (and correct) decisions while remaining mentally balanced. The people who possess these qualities comprise the most active part of mankind and define the rates of social progress. The overwhelming majority, however, prefer to follow somebody else's decisions and work under their authority.

Due to their unique historic, ethnic and cultural traditions, the Japanese had acquired their work ethic long before the Industrial Revolution. When the then current economic patterns required these qualities, the Japanese immediately made the best use of them, first during modernization in the late 19th century and then again after World War II. In both cases, Japan showed unprecedented rates of economic development and social reforms. Ninety years before Japan won the Russo-Japanese War, Lieutenant Commander Vasily Golovnin predicted: "If the Japanese sailors acted in the European way, their fleet would soon be as good as the best in Europe." The Japanese postwar economic miracle fulfilled another of his predictions: "I am not sure that anything is impossible for this industrious, diligent and patient nation" (Golovnin, 2004).

The Most Common Vocation in Japan

The specific Japanese character of hiring and using the labor force has resulted in an interesting and almost unique phenomenon. The Japanese seldom ask each other, "What do you do?" Even if they do, they do not ask about a specific profession (an accountant, an engineer, a construction worker) but about their employment in the most general sense (government employee, private company employee, etc.). For instance, the word "salesclerk" (one who is employed to sell goods in a store) cannot be adequately translated into Japanese; "shop employee" (*ten'in*), which has a broader meaning in Japanese, is the nearest equivalent.

The names of specific professions are not common for one important reason: a company does not hire an expert but a wide-ranging team. Of course, more specialized employees are hired to work in the field of technology, but these are in the minority among Japanese wage earners. In answer to the question about their employment, the majority of Japanese would say "*shain*," which literally means "a company employee"; a member of the team, somebody who is hired to follow orders and work where he is assigned. The majority of able-bodied Japanese work for private companies, so *shain* is the most common form of employment. "Specialization and professionalism, the trademarks of American culture, are the antitheses of the multi-skilling so dominant in Japan. American specialists consider that they are doing their job when they promote professionalism... But specialists are almost anathema in Japan's industrial/business society. It is the generalist..., the multi-skilled manager, who is dominant" (March, 1996).

When hiring a new employee, a Japanese company provides many guarantees. If the applicant's education is insufficient or does not comply with the company's specialization, the employee is educated on the job. The basic training takes one to two years and then the employee masters the vocational skills throughout the remainder of his career. The employee is guaranteed a lifetime job and advanced vocational training. Over the years, he receives a larger salary, which reaches its maximum in the years immediately before retirement. Twice a year, in June and December, he receives a bonus of roughly two months' salary. In the northeastern areas of Japan, many companies provide their employees with a once yearly stipend to compensate for their heating bills in the winter. When a person retires, he can receive a bonus of 40 months' salary in addition to his government pension.

In return for these benefits, Japanese companies expect loyalty and diligence from their employees. This involves constant overtime work, short vacations and no sick leave. The tradition of *tenkin* (job transfer, change of job location) must be added to the list of conditions. According to this tradition, the employees are transferred to different company departments, which can be within Japan or abroad. In addition to the internal rotation, they practice an external rotation when employees are temporarily transferred to different companies according to the preset schedules. These transfers are unilaterally decided by the employer and do not require the employee's consent. The employees are simply informed of their new assignments. In the majority of cases, the employee moves to the new destination in a different city or prefecture by himself, without his family. This type of transfer is so common that it has a name every Japanese child knows: *tanshin funin*. Along with *tenkin*, it is among the most commonly used words in the Japanese language, used as frequently as the words for "home," "family" and "school."

In Japan, both the business and the school year begin in April, and at this time, the rounds of relocation and reassignment begin. Thousands of private industrial, governmental, prefectural and other institutions go through a standard ritual of introducing new employees. The personal name, family name, position and responsibilities of the new person are announced and the reassigned person gives a short presentation about himself to the applause of his coworkers, and the ritual is over. Then follows a corporate dinner to help the employees get to know each other a little better, then the employee is ready for new accomplishments at the new workplace.

Lifetime employment and the priority the group takes over that of the individual define the human resources policy of Japanese companies and help to better explain the Japanese system of education. The main peculiarity of Japanese higher education is that teaching specific skills is not its main target. Today, over half of high school graduates enter institutes of higher education, and this proportion is expected to increase. Japanese higher education has become a phenomenon unseen anywhere else. Even in Great Britain which is famous for its quality education, only 30 percent of high school graduates enter universities, about half the proportion of students in Japan. The main purpose of Japanese universities is to provide students with broad basic knowledge, to develop the skills of adult life and to teach the students how to study and to learn. Only a few elite universities require serious effort from the students. Intensive training at these elite universities is viewed as the cost of getting a prestigious diploma and a privileged job. In general, the average Japanese student spends only 25 hours per week studying and 15 hours per week working at a part-time job (Teichler, 1997). In private universities, which comprise the majority of Japanese higher education institutions, even home-work assignments are uncommon. Highly specialized courses are considered secondary, especially for students majoring in humanities.

A Japanese educational expert, Nishio Kanji, once wrote on this topic: "Companies don't expect that universities would teach specific subjects. According to them, general training is completely sufficient. Specific professional training starts after the employee is hired. A university is viewed as a place where a person is taught a broad-minded approach and moral values. In other words the companies give priority to human qualities over professional training" (Kanji, 1982). Why would anybody try hard to get professional skills not demanded by a consumer (in this case, an employer)? Having explored the Japanese system of higher education in 1980s, American experts gave it an uncompromising evaluation. Said Professor Ezra Vogel: "Faculty devotion to teaching and to students is limited, student preparations are far less than prior to the entrance examination, analytic rigor in the classroom is lacking, and attendance is poor" (Vogel, 1979). According to Edwin Reischauer: "The squandering of four years at the college level on poor teaching and very little study seems an incredible waste of time for a nation so passionately devoted to efficiency" (Reischauer, 1977).

The most important function of Japanese higher education is to certify the students. A system of the most challenging admission exams known as *shiken jigoku* (examination hell) is designed to select the most industrious and ambitious students out of the thousands of graduates. These qualities are necessary to survive the tough training environment of the so-called cram schools (*juku, yobiko*) for admission to the prestigious universities. These same qualities are required for the training in high, middle elementary and even kindergartens which are affiliated with the famous universities. These qualities are sought after by employers as Japanese companies appreciate loyalty and readiness to work in a team while disregarding one's own interests more than they value professional skills and training.

To get a permanent job in Japan, one has to pass qualification exams and go through an interview. Elite companies and government institutions first conduct a document contest, which eliminates all but 10 percent of the applicants who are allowed to take the admission exam. Those who pass are invited for individual interviews. What qualities are in greatest demand in the Japanese job market?

A survey of 200 Japanese companies conducted by Kajihara (1997) showed that companies of different profiles have different requirements. For example, manufacturers value honesty and sociability above all. Financial companies place more importance on enterprise and responsibility while trade and service firms appreciate flexibility and adjustment. Only the engineering and industrial enterprises value independence and creativity. The survey also showed that unlike Japanese companies, major transnational corporations prefer employees with "good professional training." At the same time, all Japanese companies emphasized qualities such as initiative, dedication and readiness to face challenges; the qualities considered to be "typical Japanese features." This is not surprising. Lifetime employment and remuneration based on length of service are more financially beneficial for the older generation. The younger generation gets guaranteed employment and promotion but their remuneration is not commensurate with their contributions. Insufficient professional training both promotes and perpetuates this trend. Surveys show that Japanese university graduates highly rate their own general training level and related qualities such as responsibility, cooperation and optimism. At the same time, they are not confident of their abilities to show initiative and enterprise, to be mentally flexible or to be able to clearly state their ideas (Nguyen *et al.*, 2005). This self-appraisal shows insufficient specific training in universities but completely complies with employers' expectations. Japanese experts on this subject confirm this: "The companies' expectations coincide with the graduates' aspirations to become generalists, not specialists." Kanji's (1982) research paper, "Training of the industrial elite" says: "Companies seek not those who have special skills or training but those who have a great inner potential. They select these people to be 'raw human material' and to make them real experts in the office."

The economic recession of the 1990s affected all aspects of life in Japan. The increased internationalization and dissemination of information and improved technological efficiency in the world have made the Japanese dismissive of everything that does not work well enough. In looking for new solutions, Japanese national universities have been transformed into independent administrative corporations, the system of funding has been dramatically changed and other steps have been taken to help the education system meet the needs of the business community. The Japanese companies have restructured as well. They have introduced remuneration based on performance, temporary employment (contracts) and other market economy strategies. The year 2004 witnessed an unprecedented event: the owner of a small company was changed according to market practice without the consent of its employees and minor stockholders. In other words, the company was simply bought out. In December 2007, the same approach was applied when a middle-sized company registered in the Tokyo Stock Exchange was sold. The deals that are so common in the West are gradually becoming a part of Japanese business life.

Those Left Behind

Like everywhere else in the world, Japanese elders grumble and complain about the younger generation. They say that the youth do not want to work, as their fathers did, for the same company with wholehearted devotion and loyalty. Taking their cue from the West, young people want to have more time for recreation. In addition to the unemployed, which have always existed everywhere, new categories of young people have emerged in Japan: *furita, nito, parasaito* and others. These words have their roots in other languages. *Furita* is a portmanteau of *furi arubaito*, which refers to an adult who, by choice, only holds a part-time job, excluding homemakers and students. *Nito* comes from the English acronym NEET, which stands for

Not in Education, Employment or Training. *Parasaito* obviously refers to parasites, those single people who live with their parents despite being able to strike out on their own. Can it be that the Japanese have changed so much and have become lazy?

These borrowed words imply that a large group of young Japanese people, between 15 and 34 years old, of both genders fail to find or do not want to find a permanent full-time job. They work as part-time employees at gas stations, cash counters, ticket offices and so on. According to some estimates, there are 2.2 million such people in Japan, of which the *furita* comprise a little over 10 percent. It is not the case, however, that they all deserve a stern reprimand from their fathers. According to the Ministry of Health, Labor and Welfare, only 8 percent of these people are completely satisfied with their status and between 70 and 80 percent would like to find more traditional employment.

But Japanese companies work in an assembly-line fashion and prefer to select their new employees from university graduates. It is easier to train graduates, as well as foster company discipline and loyalty among them. Those who fail to become part of a team before they turn 30 are doomed to temporary, low-paid, unstable jobs for their entire lives. For Japanese companies, these individuals are "second-class workers," "spoiled employees," the last to be hired and the first to be fired. Even during the economic growth of 2003 to 2007, these people had problems finding permanent jobs.

The English were the first to invent the category of *nito* workers; the Japanese simply borrowed the idea to describe a section of the population in their midst. Unlike the unemployed, these people do not do anything to change their status, although half of them say otherwise. In recent years, the number of Japanese *nito* has been about 640,000, but in 2006 it dropped to about 620,000 (DSKK, 2006).

The adult kids who stay with their parents after finishing high school are called *parasaito* or *parasaito shinguru*. The definition sounds a little bit harsh, as unlike *nito*, these people do earn their own living; the criticism stems from their late separation from their parents. One must bear in mind that there are standards for everything in Japan. This is a rather complicated phenomenon and therefore will not be discussed in depth here. It is quite evident that it involves many societal issues, including late marriages, high real estate prices, optimization of personal income and so on. This problem is not purely Japanese and is common in South Korea, Italy and other countries.

The modern Japanese economy is increasingly becoming more and more efficient and rational, which places stricter requirements on its people. It is no wonder that some people fail to comply with these requirements; they do not want to participate in the rat race and are satisfied with the little that they have. Such people can always be found in any society at any point in history.

Among those outside of active office life are experienced, highly qualified employees who are approaching retirement age. These individuals often prove unprofitable for the Japanese system of lifetime employment. By the age of 60, they are drawing a maximum salary but their performance has begun to decline. To get rid of aging employees, companies offer higher retiring benefits to those who quit voluntarily before their retirement age. For example, Japan Airlines has announced that, from 2008, it will be annually reducing the salary budget by 50 billion yen (US$417 million). Therefore, different categories of flight personnel are now eligible for pensions at the age of 50 or 54. In most Japanese companies and institutions, employees are forced to retire between the ages of 60 and 65, regardless of their experience, expertise or health. In Japanese, the expression *kata o tataku* (to pat on the shoulder) is used to remind somebody that it is time to retire. Many Japanese people retire not because they want to but because they have to. Some people are allowed to work longer under certain circumstances, such as if they are raising underage children or caring for an ill relative.

Due to the remarkable longevity of the Japanese, there are many pensioners who are able to keep on working but they are circumscribed by the law. Since 2005, the number of pensioners has gone up rapidly because of the postwar baby boom. In the near future, this situation will aggravate the growing demographic imbalance in Japan.

Currently, the emerging Chinese economy is coming to the rescue. The expertise and skills of leading specialists from Sony,

Fujitsu, Mitsubishi and other world-famous companies are in great demand in China. Chinese manufacturers are planning to compete with global brands but they do not yet possess the quality to do so.

In the fall of 2006, a seminar on the employment of Japanese pensioners was held in Tokyo. It was organized, not by the Japanese government, but by the authorities of the Chinese city Dalian. One-tenth of the 200 Japanese participants signed one-year contracts with the Chinese companies on the spot. Although the salary offered by the Chinese rarely exceeds one-third that of Japanese companies, many of the business veterans readily took up the contracts.

Some Japanese companies have expressed their concerns over the potential drain of technical information to China. Of the 625 companies polled, one-fifth confirmed that such a drain has already occurred. Upon dismissal from a Japanese company, employees usually sign a non-disclosure statement. However, one cannot hope that they will honor it; Japanese experts are hired for the sake of this information. Some analysts are confident that there is nothing to worry about and that the modern rate of technological progress is so rapid that transmission of the outdated information to rivals cannot cause any harm.

Chapter 12

Humans Judging Humans

Power of God, Power of Man

In Christian countries, divine powers are seen to readily intercede in human life, their main task being to help those who are confused. The Supreme Being will guard you against temptation, help you in your hour of need and forgive your sins. Throughout its centuries-old history, Christianity has developed a long list of human sins to be resisted, together with the mechanism for their forgiveness: confession, repentance and prayer. It is important that remission of sin can be granted without any unnecessary publicity (seal of confession) and without directly addressing the person who had been harmed. The most important thing is to be purged of sins in the eyes of God. In the Christian religion, the Supreme Being acts as a wise and impartial intermediary.

This tradition has become so rooted in the Western mind that even today, the age of efficiency and rationalism, people call on the Father, the Virgin Mary and Jesus Christ in critical moments. Such expressions as "swear by God," "in the name of God" and "for God's sake" are used daily and even by inveterate atheists. To prove their sincerity, Russian Orthodox believers kiss a crucifix while Protestants swear on the Bible. When absolute honesty or trust is required, Christians call to God for help. They also believe that marriages can be sanctified through recognition by a higher ecclesiastical authority — the church.

The Japanese have no such tradition. The judgment of other people has always been the main criterion for guiding human deeds, with public disgrace being the worst punishment ever. The samurai commandments refer to a man called Morooka Hikoemon who, when asked to vow fidelity to the gods, replied: "A samurai's word is his bond. I have given the word, so what do buddhas and gods have to do with it?" (Yamamoto, 2000) His answer was considered correct and was preserved.

Marriages in Japan have always been secular affairs. The parents of both sides would come to an agreement, the future bride and bridegroom would meet a few times and then a formal ceremony in the presence of several witnesses would take place. Mortal beings would pronounce other mortal beings husband and wife. Divorce was also a simple procedure: a husband could pronounce his marriage invalid, send a simple notification to the town council and the deal was done. The Japanese did not involve any divine powers in significant human affairs and preferred to proceed on their own discretion.

Religious bigotry has never been popular in Japan and the Japanese have never had a custom of burning anybody at the stake for their religious beliefs. There was a terrible struggle between the Buddhist sects but it was held in a humane manner. For example, Nichiren, one of the most isolated Buddhist sects, forbade its apologists to give or to receive donations from its ideological opponents. It is true that, in the late 16th and early 17th centuries, Christians in Japan were persecuted and both Japanese and foreign Christians were mercilessly tortured and burned at the stakes. However, this medieval brutality was a result of a perceived threat to the local authorities and national security rather than a threat to the Japanese religions. It is not so important now whether or not that threat was real, but what is important is that the Japanese did not seem to be against Christianity per se; they were scared of the possible occupation of the country by Europeans. So it was not the believers who were executed but the fifth column — the traitors. This clearly shows that the repression was triggered by purely human interests. The situation in Europe, exemplified in the extreme by the Inquisition, was, as we know, different.

The eternal dilemma of "what is good and what is bad" was also addressed by the Japanese but in a different and simpler way. Good actions were defined by widespread approval while bad actions were met with condemnation. When a person made a mistake, he knew for sure that he should confess in public, which was of paramount importance, and ask to be forgiven, most importantly by the person harmed. Both of these conditions had to be met before one could atone for a wrong.

One February morning in 1856, six peasants went hunting for wild boars in the Harima Province (southwest of the modern Hyogo Prefecture). During the hunt, one of the shooters, named Kyohei, accidentally wounded a fellow villager. The wounded man was given care immediately but the wound was fatal. The accident was not that uncommon at that time, and the government rules said that a thorough investigation is to be conducted in such accidents to find out if the murder was intentional. If the murder was not intentional, then it is to be considered a mistake and the killer is to be sentenced to penal servitude. If, however, before dying, the wounded person was able to forgive the guilty person and to ask for mercy for the later, then mercy should be granted. Although it is unknown if the wounded man was able to voice forgiveness in the Harima Province case, it is known that the guilty peasant was not punished. He and his relatives visited the family of the deceased, and the case was settled peacefully without judicial recourse. The only extant document on that case is a statement filed by Kyohei in which he admits his guilt and asks for forgiveness (Hirota, 1994). We can therefore understand that either the victim himself or his family forgave an involuntary killer and the case was not passed into court.

In medieval Japan, a lone person did not amount to much; everything was decided by the family and community. This is why a group's powers and authority were to be relied upon in an emergency, even those involving crime and punishment. Penitential letters were written according to standard patterns and although the writer's individuality was not always obvious, the key phrases about admitting guilt and asking for forgiveness were formulated clearly and unambiguously.

One interesting fact is that the guilty person was never the only one to sign this letter and his confessions and petition would be supported by many others, first of all his relatives. These signatures would be followed either by that of the head or those of all of the members of the five-household group *goningumi* (alliance of families that was responsible not only to help each other and settle village disputes but also to keep an eye on each other), the village headman, a middleman-guarantor (any influential member of the commune), Buddhist priests and other members of the local community.

The aggrieved party was addressed in the plural, as the crime, even if committed against an individual, was committed against the entire community. This community could be a local trade guild, residents of the neighboring village, the dwellers of the inn, or others. To reflect this, the letter was supposed to start with special forms of address, such as "your whole family" (*shinruichu*). The divine powers were not asked to interfere in secular problems and this is why multiple people were involved. This followed a simple and worldly logic: group repentance weighs more than that of a single person.

Thus, a written confession has long been viewed not as a sincere emotional impulse but as a conflict-settling and highly formalized legal tool. In 1720, the Japanese government passed a law forbidding the Supreme Court from accepting written confessions from the parties involved in the trial, the reason being to disregard personal confessions and apologies, and to judge by rights. By this law, written

Figure 12.1:   Giving an apology and compensation.

confessions, should they be submitted to the court, were to be ignored. Such documents had been taken into account and had influenced the court's decisions in the past. It was immediately clear that the party that wrote the confession was guilty. For many years, the Japanese "asked to be forgiven not by the Lord but by the secular authorities. And they more often apologized to their fellow villagers and neighbors than to the authorities" (Hirota, 1994).

Today's state of affairs is not much different. On 16 July 2007, a strong earthquake shook the Niigata Prefecture with the epicenter at Kashiwazaki which houses the world's biggest power plant. When one of its units caught fire, the operators tried to extinguish it but were unable to due to a failure of the fire control system. The facilities were abandoned, the reactors were shut down automatically and nobody was injured. Four days later, the top managers of the facility, headed by director Akio Takahashi, gave a press conference where they explained the causes of the fire control system failure, admitted their responsibility for the accident and offered official apologies that included ritual bowing to the employees. Pictures of the bowing director and his deputies were printed in all of the national newspapers.

In his book, *Non-apologizing Americans and Apologizing Japanese*, Tetsuya Takagi writes that in everyday life "the Japanese apologize easily in any situation. They often say 'I beg your pardon' and 'Sorry' automatically, without thinking. These words are very important for maintaining human relations; they release tension" (Takagi, 1996). On the other hand, the author expresses his surprise over the Americans' ability to avoid apologizing, even when their wrongdoing is obvious and undeniable. The Americans would admit their mistakes and correct them but will nevertheless try to avoid making formal apologies. The author gives many examples to illustrate this point.

The explanation for this probably lies within the context of Christian morality. In the formal ethics of many nations, a public confession and an appeal for mercy cut too close to personal humiliation. It is not for nothing that the winner in a conflict often makes his opponent confess and ask for mercy in public in an attempt to humiliate him. Is it not easier to admit one's fault to God and atone for one's sins by prayer than to ask somebody for forgiveness in public?

In general, the Russians are similar to, or even worse than the Americans in their reluctance to apologize and to ask for forgiveness. They would rather silently correct their mistakes than to admit them publicly. The Russians have long been celebrating Forgiveness Sunday at the end of Pancake Week, when people are supposed to ask each other for forgiveness and hear the ritual answer "God will forgive you." Probably, it is an axiom of the Christian mentality: "I have no right to forgive you. Almighty God can see and know everything; he will forgive you." Or, put slightly differently: "As for me, I will forgive you, but it's more important that God forgives you." Therefore in Christian morality, God's forgiveness carries more weight than does that of a human being. On Forgiveness Sunday the ceremonial liturgy includes reading the portion of the Sermon on the Mount that refers to forgiving our neighbors before obtaining remission of sins by the Father. Thus, only after forgiving our neighbors can we expect to be forgiven by God.

Considering how strictly the Japanese regarded even unintentional wrongdoings, how did they treat those who committed serious crimes? Severe punishment, group responsibility and mutual control, when "the whole nation is watching itself with thousands of eyes" (Ziebold, 1999), have for ages been stabilizing society and keeping its citizenry honest and law-abiding. In the 18th century a foreign observer wrote: "The Japanese laws are bloodthirsty; they almost never contemplate guilt of different degrees... Justice is given to everybody regardless of their rank and wealth... An offender cannot find asylum in the whole of the empire and there is no other country where theft would be such a rare occasion. In Japan, you can sleep with your doors open without any fear of being robbed. But this security comes at a high price" (Ziebold, 1999).

It is true that in the Tokugawa Period (1603–1867) the rulers succeeded in their battles against dishonesty and theft. The results are obvious in Japanese society today. Foreigners report with surprise when their lost valuables are returned, when wallets come back with the money intact and when other contemporary miracles occur. This invariably evokes respect for a nation that is mostly unaware of the commandment "thou shall not steal" but nevertheless follows it.

In the course of a year and a half, I have read two stories in Japanese newspapers about money found and then turned over to the police.

On 8 March 2006, the workers of the waste incineration plant in Saitama Prefecture found a bag with 500,000 yen (about US$4,000) in the garbage. The money was passed to the police and an advertisement was published in a local newspaper. Eleven days later, the owner of the money was found; his wife had thrown the bag out without knowing about its contents (*Iwate Nippo:* 13 April 2006).

In September 2007, in the town of Han'yu, an amount 20 times larger was found in similar circumstances. The money was also passed to the police and now its officers are visiting houses in the "suspicious" area to find the owner of the money. In any other country, this situation would become the theme of a joke, but, in Japan, these cases are treated very seriously. If the police fail to find the owner of the money within 27 weeks, then it will be given to the person who found it.

However, fast growing public wealth and current urban individualism seem to be altering even the law-abiding Japanese. In late 2008, a total of 69 public libraries reported thefts of 284,000 books during the pervious year, or about 12 items per library per day. Perhaps not all thieves were professional because some of the stolen books were anonymously returned to the library or were thrown out not far away.

Good Neighbors and Distant Relatives

In fact, human justice as a criterion of virtue is typical of any communal consciousness, not just of the Japanese. Criteria, however, change with time and the rate of these changes varies greatly in different countries. When 80 percent of the Japanese population was concentrated in village communes that exercised group control, everything went relatively well. When disobedient, eccentric and criminal elements commited various improper deeds that could neither remain unpunished nor be taken into court, the Japanese applied a form of public boycott of the offender. Everybody broke all contact and economic relations with the person or family that had violated any written or unwritten laws. This group punishment was called *mura hachibu* (the village eight).

The term *mura hachibu* comes from the fact that, in those days, the villagers united their efforts to help members of the community on 10 specific occasions such as weddings, illnesses, deaths, and others. If somebody was to be punished, the commune would prohibit anybody's involvement in eight of them, hence the term. The commune would help the outcasts only in case of fire or funerals and only to prevent potential danger to the village from a burning building or a decomposing body. In a way, they showed common sense and "healthy group egoism."

An "eight" was a serious punishment at a time when rice-growing required mutual help; the outcasts were almost completely excluded from communal life and could not survive very long. Since the punishment was a civil one, it was not always applied fairly or consistently. In some cases, powerful people used it for mercenary ends. But as a tool of establishing group discipline, the measure was quite effective. Today this punishment is illegal but it is not forgotten in distant mountain and fishing villages.

With time, this communal tradition became wide-spread in Japanese society as the foundation for group behavior regulation. In modern Japanese schools, outcasts are harassed in the same manner and suffer complete isolation and the overt contempt of the entire group. According to some Japanese linguists, even the young people's slang word *haburu* (to unfasten, to separate from the group) is related to the old expression of *mura hachibu*. The connection between generations of modern schoolchildren and peasants from the past shows the collective nature of group behavior regulation in Japanese society.

Members of Christian civilizations are accustomed to drawing a clear and uncompromising line between good and bad. Here, Jesus Christ embodies good deeds and the Antichrist embodies evil deeds. In Japan, religious doctrines do not have as deep an influence on the moral and ethical beliefs of the people and the Japanese cooperative-centered morality does not allow black and white attitudes. Seiichiro Ono (1891–1986), a well-known criminal lawyer in Japan, wrote: "A principle of harmony doesn't go along with opposition; harmony disappears as soon as life is divided into good and evil" (Kawashima, 1967). A similar opinion was expressed by Ruth Benedict (1887–1948): "The Japanese have always been extremely explicit in denying that virtue consists of fighting evil" (Benedict, 1994). Japanese culture has elaborated its own categories of opposing ideas to maintain harmonious relations with the surrounding world.

One of these categories is formed by the opposing concepts of an inner circle (insiders, *uchi*) and an outer circle (outsiders, *soto*). They can be applied to all things in this world, including those most essential for human existence: home and its insiders (or family).

Traditional Japanese houses, both rural and urban, were always divided into inner and outer spaces. The portion visible from the outside, the street-facing portion, was called *zashiki* and had a standard appearance and decoration. The inner part of the house, which was forbidden to visitors, was called *nando daidokoro* and was designed according to the owner's taste, usually in a more luxurious and exquisite manner if he could afford it.

All of the people around a person were divided into an inner circle and an outer circle, which of course is not a uniquely Japanese concept. Such a practice might be typical of any group with a tribal past but the Japanese attach a greater importance to it and observe it more consistently than do most others. In Japan, there is an invisible but insurmountable barrier between the inner and the outer circle, between insiders and outsiders.

This barrier is a combination of two attributes: a community of space (living or working) and a community of membership (a profession or a group). To be considered a "complete insider," one must share both a spatial proximity and a similar group membership. Those who share neither are "complete outsiders." Those who possess only one of these attributes belong to an in-between group. Thus, the peasants who live in the same village and grow rice represent complete insiders to one another, while the craftsmen and the merchants from the same town form two different inner circles that overlap based on location.

In the Japanese perception, the community of space is more important than is the community of membership. People who work in the same space (a company) and the people living in the same space (a family) form the two major Japanese groups of insiders. When two Japanese visitors who do not know each other meet in the same building, they usually greet each other but if the same two men meet on the street, nothing happens. This observation is reflected in a popular Japanese proverb: "A close neighbor is better than a distant relative" (*toi shinseki yori chikaku no tanin*). The community of space can be more important than even ties of real kinship. The idea ingrained in this proverb is of profound ideological and practical significance to the Japanese people. It is not just a proverb but is at once a principle, a worldview and a guide for action.

In April 1804, an incident happened in one of the villages in the existing Hyogo Prefecture. A group of teenagers got together and started gambling. The *Bakufu* (Tokugawa government) edict prohibited gambling and encouraged witnesses to inform the authorities about any such incidences. The neighboring family ignored the activity. When the community leaders learned of it, the family was accused of withholding information. The family wrote a letter of confession admitting their guilt, asking for mercy and promising never to repeat their inaction. Moreover, they asked the community to plead for them and to assist in dismissing the case. The letter extant in the archives was signed by 12 family members and four guarantors from the village. The community accepted the apologies and helped to dismiss the case with no punishment being enacted. If the information had become known outside of the community, however, its leaders would have been punished for concealment.

There was a drunken brawl in 1837 in Musashi Province (near the border between Kanagawa and Saitama Prefectures and the Tokyo capital district). One of the participants was wounded and later died. The perpetrator was forgiven after obtaining the support of his family and community. The widow balked at granting him forgiveness but eventually agreed to a compromise after receiving a tribute. After a while, the capital court was informed about the incident and re-opened the case. The offender was punished and the widow was found guilty of concealing the crime. The widow was sentenced to exile and her property was seized. All 10 of the people involved in the incident were also punished for not informing the police; among them were a village headman, the local priest who performed the burial service and a few others (Hirota, 1994).

It was therefore honorable but not quite prudent to protect those within the inner circle. These incidents from Tokugawa legal history are a demonstration of how the Japanese set priorities between their obligations toward insiders and toward outsiders. The situation is similar today. As in previous times, these priorities help in some cases and harm in others, but always dominate in human relations.

Japanese culture did not originally have a concept equivalent to the English word "privacy." The Japanese borrowed this concept from the West along with many other things. This word is now heard everywhere but its content is much different from its American prototype.

Mr. and Mrs. Devits describe a Japanese woman who lived in the United States with her husband and child. The woman could neither fit into the parent-teacher association nor did she feel comfortable with her American girlfriends because American women do not recognize the same boundaries between their inner and outer circles. Americans easily talk about the school performance of their own and other couples' children as well as about their teachers' professional skills, their husbands' businesses and many other things that are simply not discussed by Japanese women. For the Japanese, family members are within their inner circle and their affairs are not discussed with those who do not belong to the inner circle. This is as forbidden as openly discussing the affairs of the company to which one belongs with a stranger in a bar. The American friends of the Japanese woman described her as very polite and well-mannered but distant, reserved and even arrogant (Devits, 1996).

A Japanese psychotherapist who practiced in the United States has shared the opposite observations, where private information was not shared with the inner circle. He was greatly surprised when his Japanese clients asked him to ensure the privacy of the session by not billing their medical insurance. The clients paid the full fee to prevent their company from seeing their medical bills: "If the company finds out about my visit to a psychotherapist, my career is over." When reminded about a law that guarantees privacy, the clients responded that a Japanese company is a family-type organization and information known to one person becomes known to everybody else (Miyamoto, 2000).

There are no beggars on Japanese streets but there are many religious sects that build their cash reserves by using masked forms of begging. On one occasion, I encountered members of a sect collecting money for starving African children. Armed with pictures of poor kids, they were asking decently dressed Japanese to donate money to the noble cause. A legitimate Japanese aid organization would not put people on the streets, and this is why there was no doubt that these people were frauds. The Japanese are well aware of these tricks, and, even while donating money, they understand that the members of the sect are simply doing what they are told to do. Due to their upbringing and the *tatemae* effect some people (especially women) have trouble saying no to a person when asked for a favor, especially when this person has a noble story to tell. Japanese etiquette prohibits an outright denial of the favor and the money collectors have counted on this. One of the Japanese when approached for money replied very briefly: "Excuse me, I am not related to your organization." This short reply was quite enough. If I were him, I would probably have asked for an ID, a license to collect donations or something of this kind. The Japanese approach was more understandable and thus more effective: "I don't belong to your organization, and know nothing about it, so you have no right to ask me for any donations."

This approach works flawlessly in other situations, whether for a good or bad cause. For example, one cannot possibly imagine a Japanese policeman letting a criminal go in exchange for a bribe or revising his charges in an attempt to preserve the honor of an inner circle (as obviously the policeman and the criminal are in different circles). This is explained not only by the high moral principles of the policeman but also by the impossibility of any individual bargaining with people of different social groups. I shall emphasize the word "individual" because, with a different approach, the results can also be different. For example, a leader of the local community can congratulate the head of the local police department and personally express his sincere gratitude to him and to the whole police department for their vigilant maintenance of order. Then a gift (an envelope) will be presented on behalf of the community as a gesture of gratitude.

In these situations the results vary widely and some of them can be legally controversial (see the earlier discussion on gift giving in Chapter 4). Many experts say that Japanese corruption is based on this approach, a point of view that is not in contradiction with official data. In 2008, Japan ranked 18th (of 180 countries) on the list of least-corrupt countries. The ranking is not very low internationally but Japan lags far behind the least corrupted on the global index — Denmark, Sweden and New Zealand (*Yomiuri*: 25 September 2008). In any case, the alienation between the ordinary members of different groups impedes low-level corruption, which is the most difficult to deal with.

The opposite can be demonstrated by the following example. On 30 August 1974, a technical failure caused an explosion at a Mitsubishi facility. A foreign reporter was shocked to witness a weird situation at the scene: some people were frantically trying to help while others were just silently observing. Later, the reporter found out that those who were helping were the coworkers or friends of the victims. Those who were not related to Mitsubishi remained detached onlookers and made no attempts to help (Mori, 2005). A few Japanese newspapers later raised the question of immoral group psychology.

It seems more important not to stigmatize but to understand the reasons for this behavior. The observers were not heartless egoists, as it might initially seem. Their behavior can be related to the same invisible barrier that separates and isolates any significant group from others in Japan. Everybody in this country knows that a group is closed and sovereign, that its territory is off-limits, especially if the group is a first-class company with an elite self-identification. This extraordinary incident simply revealed the ordinary and habitual attitudes of the average Japanese.

Everything accepted and approved by the inner circle is moral and appropriate for the Japanese and everything outside this circle is vague and indistinct. The Mitsubishi accident showed that Japanese morality is specific to the circumstances and is localized; it is inside-oriented and lacks the universal significance so typical of religious moral values. To put it in simpler words, a Christian fulfils the commandment, "Thou shall not kill" because their religious beliefs forbid killing people in principle. The Japanese, however, follow this commandment because the group behavior rules say so. These rules determine their set of human values and mostly agree with them. If the rules do not agree with their moral values, then the rules lose their priority. This is why those not belonging to Mitsubishi's inner circle did not participate in the rescue attempts.

According to Chie Nakane, who has been studying this issue for many years, Japanese society is characterized "by a distinct division into 'inner' and 'outer' circles. There is an obvious contrast between opposing forms of human relationships when a person from the outer circle is not recognized as a personality. A Japanese group can treat anybody outside the group very coldly. Any behavior is allowed towards a person who is not considered one of them and who is therefore inferior. This cold attitude can be observed in other peoples, especially among the residents of isolated islands or mountain villages. They treat anybody outside their little world with a dull hostility" (Nakane, 2000).

Religious beliefs can reach unprecedented depths, as demonstrated by the history of both Christianity and Islam. A Japanese society deprived of these religious attitudes accumulates and directs all human emotions toward relations with other people. Thus, the numerous manifestations of Japanese spiritual strength, both in the past and at present, as well as the tragedies of those who suffered as a result of these attitudes do not seem surprising.

From Inner Circle to Outer Circle

Social progress intensified the economic relations of the Tokugawa Period and often encouraged members of village communities to leave their homes. The process lasted for two centuries and became especially active in the 19th century. By that time, the country had been divided into 273 feudal fiefs, each of which lived according to their own laws. All of them were equally subordinate to the central government but were so different in their way of life that their residents often spoke, both literally and figuratively, different languages. Special guidebooks and reference books were printed for travelers where the latter could find the correct names and spellings of different towns, villages and the sights for which they were famous. During the 270 years of Tokugawa rule, at least 394 guidebooks of this kind were published.

Everyday life could be torture for peasants or craftsmen when they left their communities for the first time. Not only did they have to obtain a permit to travel (usually people were only allowed to go to temples or to hot springs), but they had to travel on foot. Victual houses (restaurants) and inns charged them twice as much as they charged travelers on government or public business. The food names and prices were different but asking anybody for explanations might be considered awkward and would identify the traveler as a country bumpkin. The customs and language were also different in each place the traveler visited. It is not for nothing that the Japanese have a proverb *kawaii ko ni wa tabi wo saseyo* (if you love your child let it travel alone), which implies that the outer world will teach a child to grow up more quickly.

In the second half of the Tokugawa Period, the number of travelers increased dramatically. Surviving manuscripts show that three million people annually obtained permits for pilgrimage to famous temples (Inoue, 1977). During this period, community moral beliefs first began to deteriorate. A new proverb came into use: *tabi no haji wa kakisute* (one should not be ashamed of anything while traveling), meaning that you can blunder in strange lands where nobody knows you and leave your shame there. The only concern was not to let the inner circle learn of it. The Japanese are the first to admit that this proverb reflects the peculiarities of their attitude. Until the mid-19th century this proverb had only one meaning, but with time it became broader and was modified to: "There is no shame in the lands where nobody knows you" (Mori, 2005). The list of deeds that were allowed in the outer circle but remained unacceptable in the inner circle began to expand.

Figure 12.2:   In a strange land.

The rapid modernization and technical progress of the late 19th century accelerated this process, and people began travelling more and spending more time amid their outer circles. In 1905, Chamberlain wrote: "One can't explain why the Japanese, being so demanding about tidiness in their everyday life, became so slovenly when it comes to certain European ways of life. While getting into even a first-class carriage, you have to climb over piles of orange peels, spilt tea, cigar butts and empty beer cans. Half-dressed (or half-naked) passengers sprawl about on their seats" (Frederic, 2007). Seen in the context of inner and outer circles, Chamberlain's observation is not so inexplicable. Because the railway represents a "European way of life" it was a place where "nobody knows you" thus "there is no shame" and everything is allowed.

Today, 150 years later, feudal isolation has vanished completely and Japan has become unified in all aspects — political, cultural and linguistic. One would think that the division into inner and outer circles has sunk into oblivion as well — but it is not the case. The Japanese are invariably friendly, attentive and considerate in a group, whether the group is a company or a calligraphy fan club. When two members of a group want to let each other enter a door first, the situation can resemble a comedic movie or children's cartoon. But when many Japanese strangers get together, their behavior changes rapidly and their ancestors' customs become quite obvious. Where can crowds of strangers be seen most often? At transportation facilities and supermarkets.

Imagine the following situation: you are in a commuter train in a four-seat compartment. The seat next to you and one seat opposite are vacant. The seat diagonally across from you is taken by a neatly dressed Japanese gentleman. He takes off his shoes and puts his feet on the seat next to you, reaches for a newspaper and starts reading. His socks are impeccably clean so the problem is not in the hygiene; it is his manner. The gentleman continues reading a newspaper without paying any attention to you. Then more passengers get onto the train and the carriage gradually becomes more crowded. Here the two scenarios are possible: the man removes his feet from the seat, puts on his shoes and continues reading or nothing changes. I have witnessed both scenarios, and I cannot say which one is the more usual. The gentleman's behavior is traditional and could not have developed in modern times.

Imagine a supermarket full of customers on a weekend with a long line at each cashier station. A man (or a woman) makes his purchases, slowly takes out his wallet, counts his money and then ponders over something for a while... The other customers in the line begin to get angry but nobody says a word. The cashier does not dare to tell the customer to hurry up. At this moment, only two people in the entire world exist for the customer: the cashier and himself. The cashier is a service staff and thus can be ignored. When I witness these situations I would always wonder: does the customer fail to realize that the people behind him are silently hating him or does he understand but simply does not care? The Japanese to whom I have asked this question reply that, most probably, such a man does not notice anything around him. "They are used to just turning their heads off," said one of the respondents. Some people do it due to chronic fatigue and others due to the Japanese custom of ignoring people outside of their inner circle. When young people behave in this manner, the Japanese tend to interpret this as poor upbringing, reasoning that if a young person is not told that this behavior is inappropriate, he will not realize it by himself.

Might they be right? I do not know; we would need to conduct a survey to find out. But I have witnessed many times how Japanese schoolchildren, particularly girls, usually quiet and obedient in the presence of their teachers, will turn into an uncontrollable yelling crowd in, for example, a public bus. At some bus stops, this crowd is capable of not only causing severe headaches among Japanese elder women but also of infuriating the usually unflappable, stone-faced bus drivers. I have never seen a Japanese public service employee admonish a customer in any situation. The only exception is when some bus drivers try to call the schoolchildren to order by using a metallic note in their voices. And I still don't know what exasperates other passengers more: the impudence of the youngsters or the lack of professional self-control of the bus drivers.

In 2001, the East Japan Railway Company received 3,275 complaints, about nine per day, from passengers regarding the behavior of their co-passengers. This number is 2.4 times the number received in 2000. The airlines received 416 written complaints in 2001, which was a five-fold increase from 1996. An overwhelming majority of the complaints concerned violations of cell phone and laptop etiquette (Mori, 2005). There were other complaints as well, as Chie Nakane noted: "A Japanese person doesn't hesitate to rush in order to take a seat first [in public transport] when traveling among strangers, but the same person will never do it in the presence of those who know him. No matter how tired he might be, he would keep offering a seat to the other person, especially to one superior in rank" (Nakane, 2000).

Are the Japanese losing their famous politeness? Or is the rapid pace of life turning them into irritated neurotics? The answer is somewhere in the middle. There is no doubt that the proverb *tabi no haji wa kakisute* remains relevant today; Japanese behavior in the inner circle is completely different from their behavior in the outer circle. When among strangers, the Japanese commonly manifest shamelessness, indifference and other negative features. Partly (but only partly), this behavior can be due to the tremendous nervous and emotional costs of maintaining a comfortable atmosphere within their inner circle. Indeed, it is not so simple to control yourself fully and to maintain a polite and friendly Japanese-like atmosphere on the job day after day and week after week. Of course, one can relax a little after office hours and have a drink with coworkers, but only a little, as they are part of the inner circle and group behavior rules are still in effect. The cost of the group's emotional comfort may seem overrated but one cannot escape it. Although the principal of *mura hachibu* (the severing of the group's ties to an individual, see above) is not well known today, it is in fact still valid.

Having entered the outer world, the Japanese become relaxed and nonchalant; that is why they do not see that their behavior bothers others and they do not observe any rules. Maybe this is the reason why so many Japanese men in suits and ties sit alone in bars and drink highly-diluted whisky while staring blankly at the TV-screens. In response to this demand, some bars have begun hiring staff to provide solitary customers with a person to talk without having to follow any particular rules. This job is offered not only to young and attractive women but also to older and wiser ones.

According to public opinion polls, the relations among inner circle members are also changing. In the last 30 years, the number of Japanese who would like to establish very friendly relationships with their close neighbors has decreased by 1.5 times while the number of those who would be satisfied with "hello/good-bye-type" of relationships has increased by 1.7 times. This same trend is obvious among relatives, where the percentage of those who advocate close family ties has decreased 1.6 times and the percentage of those who would be satisfied with exclusively formal relationships has increased by 2.5 times. The majority of the respondents prefer an intermediate variant: light relationships that are not strictly formal (*Gendai nihonjin*, 2004).

The strict requirements of the outward aspects of behavior have always been a significant feature of interpersonal relationships in Japan. When travelling in Russia, the Japanese are surprised at seeing women put on their makeup or tidy their hair in public places. They are especially shocked when they witness this behavior in the office.

Etiquette rules do not allow Japanese women to look in the mirror, put on lipstick or comb their hair in public. Putting on makeup is considered an intimate affair and should be done before leaving home. Until recently, loving couples did not even dare to touch each other in public places, let alone hug or kiss. Morals and manners have become less stringent in major Japanese cities, but are not yet as free as they are in the West.

Conventional Japanese etiquette forbids people to eat, drink or smoke while walking. You cannot even chew gum when others can see you, let alone spit or blow your nose. Such behavior is considered poor manners (*gyogi ga warui*). Although it is not customary to give up your seat to the elderly in public transport, you will also hardly see anybody chewing, drinking or eating while walking along a street in Japan. Considering these strict public rules, it becomes quite obvious that the Japanese are very sensitive to any displays of inattentiveness by others. This is another reason for the huge numbers of complaints filed at the public transport companies. But complaints are not the worst of it; nowadays more and more Japanese are punishing their offenders on the spot.

Figure 12.3:   Eating while walking.

In his article, "Rudeness makes people mad" A. Tanase, a *Yomiuri Shimbun* columnist, cites extracts from police reports. A police officer, 57, grabbed a girl who was standing next to him by her hair and explained that she could not speak loudly on her cell phone in a crowded commuter train. A school teacher, 28, hit a woman who was sitting opposite him on the head after she accidentally struck him with her heel and forgot to apologize. A woman driver, 38, fired a shot from her air pistol at a car that had cut her off at an intersection. All of these people were detained and had to explain their actions to the police.

In many countries, these skirmishes are an everyday occurrence and people usually disregard them; people are human and anything can happen. But just a short time ago, the Japanese read about these incidents only in foreign newspapers. According to the police, in 2006, over 20,000 people, 3.4 times higher than 10 years previously, were detained for hooliganism or displays of violence. Tanase wrote: "There is a dramatic increase in the number of young Japanese who fail to see the difference between their behavior at home and in public and who do not notice anybody around themselves, even in a crowd. They fail to take a detached view of themselves; when they are reprimanded, they perceive it as a personal insult and lose control" (*Yomiuri*: 1 June 2007).

The situation has been aggravated by the computer technology boom of the 20th century. Cell phones cross the time and space barriers that had securely separated the inner and the outer circles for centuries. The members of the inner circle can call you when you are among strangers, and it is quite clear who is more important.

In order to know how to behave in certain situations, one needs a *kata* (algorithm or pattern, see Chapter 3). The Japanese cannot survive without such sets of rules, but new technologies are advancing so rapidly that the rules have failed to keep pace. It is obvious that it will take some time for new rules to be set as a matter of routine, although the work has already started.

Plates displaying the list of "appropriate cell phone manners" are gradually taking up the remaining free space in commuter trains, waiting lounges and student canteens. The Japanese, true to themselves,

Figure 12.4

believe that moral principles are to be taught consistently and systematically. I cannot help but mention that the Japanese have already made some progress. The most receptive minds have learned patterns that can be barely seen anywhere except in Japan. Unlike nonchalant supermarket customers, some Japanese drivers have bumper stickers that say: "Sorry for driving slowly." Both new and simply inexperienced drivers follow this pattern of showing their concern for other people.

Chapter 13

Enacting Law and Justice

Confession — The Trump Card of Investigation

In recent years, rather astonishing information has received much public coverage in Japan, revealing events that contradict the country's traditional image of a rational and well-mannered Eastern nation. In April 2003, 13 residents of Shibushi, a small town in Kagoshima Prefecture, came under investigation on suspicion of violating election laws. More precisely, they were charged with buying votes in the assembly elections. During interrogations, six people confessed, one died from the unbearable stress and one tried to commit suicide by drowning but was rescued by a fisherman. The remaining five refused to confess. The investigation continued for more than three years, but in January 2007, the Kagoshima District Court acquitted them all, announcing that the confessions were evidently coerced by the police. The incident was extraordinary in Japan but it later received much more international publicity when the police's questioning methods were revealed.

One of the accused men in this case, a 61-year-old named S. Kawabata, who had no previous experience of being questioned by police, was forced to go through marathon interrogations lasting for up to 15 hours per day. After failing to receive Kawabata's voluntary confession by using requests, reproaches and orders, the investigator decided to apply a classical method dating from the Tokugawa Era. He wrote messages with the names of Kawabata's family members on pieces of paper and forced the man to trample them. For any Japanese man with a deep-rooted esteem for family and ancestors, such a method can be considered mental torture. Yielding to violent pressure, Kawabata confessed to things that he had never done and, after the interrogation, was hospitalized for two weeks. Another man in this case, a 58-year-old named Toshihiro Futokoro, tried to commit suicide after three days of continuous questioning. It should be mentioned here that he was interrogated on a voluntary basis and police let him return home after each questioning. A woman, charged in connection with this case, was forced by the investigator to undergo a shameful procedure as well: he made her shout her confession through an open window to attract public attention. Several people were arrested and served jail time from three to 13 months.

The increased numbers of such cases fuel a desire to investigate more fully the balance between contemporary concepts of human rights and traditional crime-fighting methods in the Japanese justice system. The style and techniques of the Japanese police are closely interconnected with people's awareness of the laws and their attitude toward law enforcement. Russia has a long-established tradition concerning justice and the question, "Shall we judge according to law or according to conscience?" has always been one of great importance. Many people in Japan face the same dilemma.

The Japanese can hardly be described as a nation that is well informed about their country's laws. Japanese nationals gradually started to change their attitude toward laws, the police and legal procedures only in the 1990s when Japan experienced a large-scale socio-economic crisis for the first time since World War II. However, the juridical consciousness of the late 1980s can serve as a clear example of the Japanese population's ignorance of national legislation. According to a survey conducted by lawyers of Kyoto University, almost 70 percent of the Japanese had never opened the Civil Code to read about their rights and obligations, and 87 percent of the people surveyed had never experienced situations that even required a thorough knowledge of the laws. Only 8 percent of the respondents had ever sought legal consultation. The survey also revealed that the obedient Japanese population had a very vague and old-fashioned comprehension of law and justice. For example, six of every 10 people interviewed stated assuredly that Japanese laws equally defend the interests of all groups of citizens. However, only three out of 10 surveyed expressed readiness to follow a law that seemed unfair to them while the rest said that they would disobey such a law (Shibata, 1986).

At the beginning of the 21st century, only one of every three Japanese nationals is aware that freedom of speech is guaranteed by the Constitution and only one out of five citizens knows that the Constitution grants the right for free gatherings. Of the people polled, 42 percent believe that paying taxes is their right rather than their duty, 15 percent think that Japanese law permits left-side traffic while 7 percent believe that the law gives them the right to follow the instructions of superiors. According to Japanese sociological estimates, the population's level of awareness of the legal system has declined as compared with 1973 (*Gendai nihonjin*, 2004). At the same time, 70 percent of the Japanese population think that the government is mainly responsible for maintaining qualitative life standards and 67 percent of respondents believe that public security is more important than a person's rights and freedoms (Sekai, 1999).

Japanese juridical understanding greatly differs from that of Western nations not only regarding general knowledge of the laws. Article 38 of the Japanese Constitution says that no person should be compelled to testify against himself, thus, during an investigation, an accused man can keep silent. However, the Constitution was adopted only 60 years ago while the moral obligation to cooperate with law enforcement organizations has been planted into the Japanese mind for centuries. The Japanese Procedure Code gives broad powers to the investigative bodies, from the use of moral pressure to stopping of the prosecution. In the early stages of an investigation, police actions are regulated very generally and transcripts of interrogation sessions are not written down. This is not coincidental.

According to Japanese law, a suspect can be held in custody without any charges and isolated from the outside world for up to 72 hours. Meeting with an advocate can be limited to a nominal 2–3 minutes. A judge can prolong the detainment period for up to 10 days, and then for another 10 days if he wishes. Overall, a person can be held in custody for up to 23 days without charge. During this time, the police apply all efforts to make the suspect confess.

At this stage, the detained person can considerably improve his relationship with the police if he behaves correctly. Those who confess and repent sincerely may count on a noticeably lighter sentence. Police can appeal to the court to lessen the punishment, or even recommend that the suspect be absolved, and as a rule the court takes this into consideration. The investigators determine the degree and sincerity of the suspect's confession, as well as his readiness for cooperation and the prospects for improvement in the suspect's future behavior. During the rehabilitation period, the police might provide some support and even pay some of the suspect's expenses, such as transport costs. Perhaps this is one of the reasons the Japanese population regards their law enforcement bodies with such confidence, and overall the Japanese have a much higher opinion of the police than do people in many other countries. Until 1999, three-fourths of the Japanese population had complete confidence in the police (the third highest index in the world) and the same proportion showed confidence in the entire law enforcement system (which was the highest in the world) (*Nihonjin no kachikan*, 2005).

However, this policy has a so-called carrot and stick approach. Those who knowingly obstruct justice or try to avoid it are usually strictly prosecuted in Japan. The impediment of justice is considered a fault, sometimes even worse than the offense itself. For example, a driver who has fled the scene of an accident will be severely punished with a fine and his driver's license can also be suspended for 10 years. Meanwhile, the maximum period of license suspension for an intoxicated driver involved in an accident is only five years.

All of the law enforcement bodies in Japan — courts, prosecutor's offices, advocate offices, police — act like an integrated and well-coordinated state mechanism. They cooperate with each other without having any competition for winning a case, in contrast with the United States where personal ambitions usually prevail. In Japan, all law enforcers are colleagues united by one objective. Japanese advocates work together with prosecutors in a state structure supervised by the Supreme Court. An advocate can be dismissed only for professional incompetence or for misconduct, and both cases are quite rare. Being state employees, advocates receive salaries depending on their qualification, employment period and amount of monetary settlement.

The association of professional lawyers in Japan is not extensive and it is rather difficult to join. For example, there are only about 22,000 advocates in Japan (compared to one million in the United States). Law departments of the universities train future lawyers but graduates must receive a state license, which requires the advocate to pass a bar exam. The exam is centralized, held only once a year, has an official pass rate of three percent and can only be taken three times. Such statistics have made the Japanese judicial system renowned throughout the world. By comparison, the California bar exam is held twice a year and the number of successful candidates varies from 30 to 50 percent. In Japan there are only 22 licensed lawyers per 100,000 population; much lower than in other developed countries. For example, this index is nine times higher in Germany, 10 times higher in Great Britain and 17 times higher in the United States. By imposing strict admission requirements, Japan tries to avoid the possibility of an excessive number of lawyers overloading the legal system. Nevertheless, in 2004, the government allowed graduate studies in jurisprudence for the first time, so the number of practicing lawyers should grow in the near future. Since 2005, the pass rate for the bar exam has been gradually increasing (Jones, 2006).

The mission of Japan's police is more instructive than it is punitive, and the first step expected from an offender is his sincere confession of guilt. According to the Japanese concept which is Confucian by nature, a wrongdoer can improve his conduct only if he feels earnestly sorry for his misbehavior. Rehabilitation of lawbreakers is therefore the final goal of all Japanese law enforcement bodies. Regardless of how serious the crime may be the police must exact a confession and make the criminal feel remorse. The most important formal sign of repentance is when the offender apologises sincerely to the victim or the victim's family. Without this, the investigation is considered unfinished.

The Japanese courts do not consider confessions to be absolute evidence of guilt and they require more solid verification. However, the case against the accused cannot be passed to the court if he or she has not made a confession. Such an attitude explains Japan's justice statistics, absolutely atypical for a democratic country: 95 percent of people sued in court admit their guilt and 99.97 percent of all cases are closed with convictions (*The Economist*: 10 February 2007). The time factor is not an obstacle as the police have as much time as they need to obtain a confession from an accused person. Justice is in no hurry in Japan.

Court proceedings against Shoko Asahara, leader of the *Aum Shinrikyo* (Supreme Truth) cult took eight years. It is common that the final execution of a convict occurs 20 to 25 years after the court's decision. In another case, 27-year-old Tsutomu Miyazaki, suspected of committing four murders, was arrested in March 1989 and confessed soon after. In 1997, the court delivered the death sentence but the case was not closed as there were doubts whether the man was mentally competent to be held responsible for his crimes. It took another eight years to investigate the matter. The last trial was held in January 2006 when the convicted man turned 45 years old. He has spent half of his life in prison on death row.

Kenzo Akiyama, a former judge now serving as a lawyer, said: "In Japan the confession of the suspect is traditionally viewed as the 'queen of evidence,' especially when it concerns significant cases. Even if the accused person has not committed a crime, the law enforcers will attempt to make him plead guilty" (*New York Times*: 11 May 2007). Koichi Aoyagi observed: "Japanese suspects almost always make confessions and report all of their deeds, including those not yet discovered. They apologize to their victims for having caused harm and to their parents for the family dishonor" (Foote, 1991). John Haley, an expert in Japanese criminal law, wrote that in Japan the vast majority of those accused of criminal offences confess, display repentance, negotiate for pardon from their victims and submit to the mercy of the authorities. In return, they are treated with extraordinary leniency (Haley, 1989).

The Japanese moral perceptions that value the rehabilitation of the offenders and their return to society are reflected in national folklore. In Japanese fairy tales, all of the villains usually repent at crucial moments and receive forgiveness. For example, the Japanese *Yamamba* (mountain witch), who is similar to the Russian folk heroine *Baba Yaga*, behaves according to the following scenario. Like the Russian folk witch, *Yamamba* is always keen to catch a lonely stranger walking in the mountains and to use him for a snack, although the Japanese witch never attempts to roast her victim in the oven. Apparently, Japanese villains are less aggressive than Russian ones.

In the Japanese version of Little Red Riding Hood (*Akazukin*), a wolf that has eaten a grandmother and her little granddaughter, upon meeting an angry hunter kneels down, confesses his guilt and asks for mercy. Taking into account the wolf's sincere remorse, the hunter does not cut the wolf's belly open to release the two victims like he does in the original tale by Charles Perrault. Instead the wolf vomits out the grandmother and her granddaughter who are still alive, thus making for a happy ending. The Japanese Little Red Riding Hood also feels a little guilty for having gone alone into a forest and for causing trouble for her grandmother. She repents of her wrongdoing, promises never to let such things happen again and thus becomes an exemplary little girl (Ames, 1981 as cited in Winston, 2003).

Another mythical creature, *Kappa* (the river imp), which lives in rivers and ponds, also behaves differently compared with similar Russian folk heroes. Being rather mischievous, *Kappa* pulls its victims into the water and sucks the life out of them. But when he is finally caught and taken to the village to stand trial, he earnestly apologizes and publicly promises to never be naughty again. To display his good intentions, he rewards the fishermen with a good catch. Thus, *Kappa* not only stays alive but is reprimanded and then released.

Anyone familiar with Japanese culture will clearly see here a connection with the national idea of reaching a compromise in any situation and minimizing the damage resulting from a conflict. To reach the maximum possible accord between a victim and an offender and to minimize the punishment for the latter, with a prospect of his quick rehabilitation, is the ideal scenario for Japanese criminal proceedings. This model reigns in all Japanese juridical and law enforcement bodies, ensuring their corporate unity and efficient co-ordination of action. The concept has its roots in the Japanese general category of *wa* (accord, harmony). Article 248 of the Japanese

Figure 13.1:   Asking for forgiveness.

Criminal Code directly states that criminal charges should be insti-
tuted only after weighing all of the considerations, such as the
offender's age, character, environment and the circumstances of the
crime, and also the potential for rehabilitation. The accused person's
confession, remorse and cooperation with police are considered favorable circumstances. Generally speaking, the Japanese believe that the
fewer criminal cases that go to court, the more professional their
police work. In the 1990s, more than 70 percent of all cases registered by police were later solved by mutual agreements and without
court proceedings. Even during court hearings, before reading the
verdict, the judge asks for the final time if the parties wish to stop the
proceedings and resolve the issue through negotiations.

The unshakable faith of the Japanese in cooperating with law
enforcement bodies sometimes takes rather interesting forms. Examples
can be found even in high-level official circles that intermingle with

business in the exchange of mutual services that often extends to questionable moral limits. A recent case is the scandal involving former Vice Defense Minister Takemasa Moriya who came under scrutiny in connection with lavish gifts he had accepted from a company in return for lobbying for its interests. He was often seen in restaurants and golf courses with a president of a trading company that was bidding for defense contracts — dealings that are prohibited by the Charter of the Defense Ministry. In the autumn of 2007, when the retired official admitted the facts, the Japanese government suggested that he voluntary compensate for damages to the state by returning part of his salary and his severance pay, which was estimated at US$600,000. Interestingly, no formal procedures have ever existed in Japanese law for such monetary refunds and bribery was not proven at that time. However, in Japan, the absence of an established legal procedure is not an obstacle to carrying out justice. Here is an example of the dilemma "justice according to the law or to conscience?".

Looking Back at Tradition

The Japanese practice of coercing an accused man's confession originated in ancient China. During the Qing Dynasty, a confession was obligatory for reaching a verdict and torture was allowed in order to obtain confessions. However, in China, the confession was considered as the moral suppression of the suspect and his total submission to the juridical authority of the state. Therefore the confession was not used for the benefit of an accused man and only rarely, if ever, affected the penalty. Present Chinese laws do not give a suspect even a formal right to refuse answering questions during the investigation. Torture is officially prohibited but there is some skepticism about whether or not this prohibition is enforced.

As an expert on the Japanese legal system, Kenneth Winston believes that in this respect the Chinese and Japanese were in great contrast to the ancient European regimes, where torture was applied when there was some proof but not enough. There is also an evident difference between China and Japan concerning to whom the duty to confess is owed. The Japanese believe that it is owed to other citizens while in China the responsibility is to the state (Winston, 2003). The role of the Japanese police is to mediate between citizens on behalf of the state and usually the police are not criticized for being too zealous in their work. After the scandal in Shibushi, a probe was launched to investigate the situation and although the allegations were credible, the police officers were not punished. The head of the Police Department routinely apologized to the citizens by saying that his officers "took the recent events deeply into their hearts."

The Japanese tradition stands in contrast with the US justice system, where expressions of remorse are largely unexpected and may even aggravate the offender's situation. When the latter agrees to a plea bargain, he usually admits some guilt in exchange for a lighter penalty. His expression of remorse can be greeted skeptically by US prosecutors who are likely to consider it a negotiating ploy rather than a strong intention to rehabilitate. If the defendant pleads innocent and fights to the end counting on acquittal, then there is no need to appeal for mercy. Unlike Japanese courts, those in the United States do not give much consideration to expressions of remorse and convict offenders on the basis of evidence and facts presented by prosecutors and advocates. It should be mentioned here that the US legal system is far from being perfect and faulty rulings occur often. Perhaps not coincidentally, many prisoners in the United States insist on their innocence, and recently discovered evidence (usually based on DNA found at the crime scene) show an alarming rate of false convictions, even in death penalty cases (Winston, 2003).

From the 8th until the 12th centuries, ancient Japanese society lived according to *Taihoryo* laws enacted by the government. The laws were compiled in seven volumes of administrative regulations and six volumes of criminal norms. However, Japanese historians assert that there exist records of earlier regulations of social issues in ancient Japan. According to the oldest chronicle *Kojiki* (*Records of Ancient Matters*), the 13th Emperor Seimu (mid-second century) used to write laws about land utilization and the systematization of his vassals' family names (Nakamura, 1967).

After the military class came to power in the 12th century, the laws were changed in favor of those based on family moral guidelines (*kakun*) bearing a local character. The tradition was further developed during the Tokugawa Era; justice was executed by appanage lords. The lords stood for power and justice while their entrusted representatives controlled the implementation of the policies of the central government. In the central court, a government-appointed person acted both as a prosecutor and as a judge. Middle-ranked samurai maintaining public order (*yoriki*) were assisted by low-grade samurai called *doshin* who typically performed police patrol duties. Lower police assistants chosen from among commoners (*okappiki*) were employed to assist them. Such appointees ensured the execution of justice and order and were regarded as superior to the commoners.

On the whole, punishments were always severe and the system was neither unified nor formal. Foreigners visiting Japan observed: "Japanese laws are pitiless and there are hardly ever different levels of guilt" (Ziebold, 1999). "The despotism of the ruling class was the only law in the country; a commoner's life cost nothing and every owner of vassals...could punish or forgive them at his own will and

Figure 13.2:   Police patrol in the Tokugawa era.

wish. Torture and the cruelest death penalties like crucifixion and burning alive, boiling in hot water or in hempseed oil...were usual; and cutting off the head was barely considered a hard punishment" (Mechnikov, 1992).

Group regulation of behavior was widely practiced in Japanese villages. Five neighboring households and the family of the offender were punished for the misdeed of one person. Neighbors and relatives were condemned for their failure to prevent the offender from committing a crime and had to apologize in front of the community for their negligence. Community psychology was hard on those who happened to have any contact with the offender.

A foreign traveler of that time once wrote: "The entire community is divided into sets of five households whose residents are responsible for each other; every villager should report about others to the *kashira* [head of the five-household group]. The *kashira* further reports to his supervisor while the latter passes all information to the town's council. It is not just that one-half of the nation watches the

Figure 13.3:   Interrogation of witnesses during an investigation.

Figure 13.4: Special police forces of the Tokugawa era. Capture of the armed offender.

other, but the entire nation watches itself with thousands of eyes. Family heads must constantly monitor that part of the street that is adjacent to their yard; the slightest incidents, fights or quarrels between strangers are considered to be the result of their neglect. Those who forget to make the smallest of reports may be penalized by a fine, corporal punishment, imprisonment or house arrest. The last of the mentioned penalties is much stricter than in other countries; the entire family of the punished person is banned from contacting anyone; the doors and windows of the house are locked to prevent escape" (Ziebold, 1999).

A similar attitude toward the family of the convicted person can be observed in modern Japanese society as well. Shoko Asahara, leader of the *Aum Shinrikyo* (Sect of Supreme Truth) was arrested in 1996, soon after his youngest son was born. All of Asahara's children experienced the echoes of this old tradition: they were scoffed at in school, banned from university, employment and even refused rental accommodation. Because of pitiless bullying, the youngest son was forced to change from a municipal school to a private one. Asahara's daughter suffered from chronic depression and was refused admission to a Japanese University on the grounds that she "may damage the environment of the educational institution, though she is not accountable for [her father's actions]." Koichi Kikuta, a former criminology professor at Meiji University and who is currently working as an advocate, affirms: "In Japanese society, the family of the convicted man usually shares his dishonor and guilt with him. The above-mentioned case reveals that the Japanese people do not have a clear understanding of the rights of the convict and his relatives" (Kakuchi, 2006).

Current Japanese traffic regulations confer the responsibility for intoxicated driving not only on the motorist himself but also on the passengers and those who saw the motorist drinking alcohol. It is written in the law that the police may impose a rather strict punishment (suspension of the driver's license for up to three years and a fine of 500,000 yen) on anyone who has given his car to a drunk driver or who has offered the driver alcohol when knowing that the

Figure 13.5:   Execution of a commoner.

person will soon be driving. Formally, these norms are difficult to apply in real situations since it is practically impossible to prove that a third person was aware of the driver's intentions. There is, after all, always the possibility of calling a taxi with two drivers. Besides, a passenger cannot know if the motorist has consumed alcohol before driving and it is difficult to prove otherwise. It is clear that the regulation has an educational and preventive point and relies solely on an earnest admission of guilt. It reflects the psychology of group responsibility that is especially common in Japanese rural communities. The same psychological motivation makes the managers of Japanese companies resign and publicly apologize when their employees are at fault. It does not matter at all that the managers may have no relation to the incidents.

However difficult and almost impossible a mission may be, this is not a problem for the Japanese police. At the end of 2008, the country's police headquarters released reports stating that more than 1250 people were detained on charges of assisting drunken motorists. However, modern times and morals negatively influence even law-abiding Japanese nationals who used to admit their guilt at the first convenient opportunity. According to reports, only 72 people were arrested on the above-mentioned charges; less than 6 percent (*Yomiuri:* 10 October 2008). Presumably, these are people who voluntarily confessed their misbehavior. In the autumn of 2008, the Japanese media reported a rare case that occurred a few years earlier in the city of Kagoshima. The case concerned an intoxicated driver and his passenger who were both found liable in an accident. The two men had been drinking alcohol and drove a car that hit and killed a pedestrian. The driver of the car turned himself in four hours after the incident and was sentenced to three years in prison while the passenger was ordered to pay the victim's mother compensation of more than 53 million yen (more than US$420,000).

The Japanese legal system underwent significant changes after 1868. In 1880, a new Criminal Code, a replica of the French model, was adopted. It was the first time that citizens were pronounced equal before the law and the penalty system was unified. Group responsibility and group punishment were banned but a new penalty was introduced for insulting the Emperor's honor. At that time, the first advocates appeared in courts but as well as the accused, the advocates did not have many rights. The judge and prosecutor had rights to interrogate witnesses while an advocate could only ask questions via the judge and with his permission. The prosecutor represented the state and always sat on the same upper level with the judge. The accused and his advocate, as in the Tokugawa Period, had to sit at a lower level so the disposition in the court showed clearly who had the power. The judge used to take to court only those cases that were thoroughly investigated and completed. The investigation process was also led and controlled by the judge. As in previous times, the confession of the accused man remained the first and foremost of all evidence. The investigators usually collected enough facts for conviction so that the defendant's guilt became evident to everyone, including the defense. An advocate could hardly influence anything in court. If the accused man confessed, repented and did everything that he was supposed to, then he was given a lighter penalty. If not (which rarely happened), then an advocate was of no help.

In 1907, the Criminal Code was revised and the German code was used as the model. The revision greatly expanded the powers of judges when considering additional subjective facts and circumstances accompanying the charges. From 1923 to 1943, a panel of jurors was used in Japanese courts. Although a jury was not used in all trials, the number of convictions then was not very high.

In 1947, the Code was changed again. The punishments for such crimes as insulting the Emperor's honor, war crimes and adultery were removed from the Code. The rest of the Criminal Code stayed unchanged although protection of the defendant's rights was intensified upon demands from the United States. Advocates were given seats on the same level with prosecutors, and both sat below the level of the judges. The judges made rulings on their own after listening to both sides. Formally, the defendants received the right to remain silent during the trial and not to testify against themselves.

After World War II, the accusatory character of the Japanese legal system became even more evident. When panels of jurors were abolished, trials turned into internal affairs of professional lawyers who have their own ethics and relationships. Such relationships demand precise and coordinated actions, the absence of internal contradictions and protection from public disclosure if any conflicts might suddenly emerge. If the Japanese court rules an acquittal or orders a re-investigation, this means that the investigators have not been proficient enough in their probe. Such a judgment by the court is viewed as a public declaration of disagreement with the investigators in their evaluation of the circumstances of the case, which is unacceptable in Japan. This is why convictions in the Japanese courts are almost guaranteed.

In 2002, a taxi driver in the Toyama Prefecture was arrested on charges of rape and attempted rape. Despite the fact that he had an alibi, the police squeezed a confession out of him after three days of continuous interrogations. He was sentenced to three years in prison. This relatively light sentence can evidently be explained by the man's eagerness to confess. He had already served most of his term when another man was arrested and confessed to these same two crimes. The taxi driver was immediately released amidst a public scandal and, on 26 January 2007, then Justice Minister Jin'en Nagase officially apologized for the wrongful conviction. The taxi driver later told reporters that he "had lost all confidence in the Japanese judicial system."

In March 2007, Japan's Supreme Court acquitted another suspect facing charges of murdering three women in the 1980s. His confession obtained by police on the 17th day of daily 10-hour questioning was the only evidence of guilt that the police had managed to collect.

Well-known Japanese filmmaker Masayuki Suo, winner of two Japan Academy Awards, released a movie in 2006 entitled *I Just Didn't Do It* (*Sore demo boku wa yattenai*) based on a true story. A 28-year old man was arrested on charges of molesting a schoolgirl on a crowded train. The man refused to buckle under the pressure to sign a false confession and had to spend 14 months in prison. Critical of Japan's justice system, Masayuki Suo intended to attract public attention to the unjust methods that police use to forcibly obtain confessions.

On 28 May 2004, the Japanese Parliament adopted a decision to introduce a mixed jury system in serious criminal trials. The jurors only started working in May 2009. Six jurors and three professional judges now work together during a trial; for minor cases, four jurors and one judge are engaged. The Japanese justice system is not yet prepared to delegate to ordinary citizens with no legal training the full authority to rule on guilt or innocence. Besides, Japan has a longstanding tradition of never introducing rapid and fundamental changes.

In 2007 the courts, prosecutors, and the bar association collaboratively held mock jury trials in various areas of Japan in order to reveal potential hurdles of the upcoming reform. During those educational sessions, the jurors experienced the most difficulties with cases that are quite rare in Japanese legal practice: when defendants stated that their confessions were coerced.

Punitive Sanctions

Once a conviction is announced by the court, punitive sanctions are imposed upon the lawbreaker. The penalty phase of Japanese legal proceedings has its own traditions and is considered the most important stage of rehabilitation. In 2007, there were 81,000 convicts in Japanese prisons (compared with 2,200,000 in the United States). Almost half of Japanese prisoners, 37,500 people, served their sentences in solitary confinement. The Japanese prisons maintain stringent discipline and most who have committed violent crimes are kept in solitary confinement. However, those who are abused by other inmates can also be transferred to solitary confinement for their own protection. The number of violent criminals in Japanese prisons has grown in recent years, increasing by 1.6 times between 2001 and 2007. As a result, Japanese prisons are experiencing a growing need for solitary rooms, and the country's Justice Ministry plans to bring the number of solitary cells to 70 percent of total prison capacity.

The role of prison officials is not limited to maintaining proper order in prison; they also serve as the inmates' educators and often apply non-standard tactics. In 2007–2008, four private jails were opened in Japan to house offenders with sentences of less than eight years. The inmates are rehabilitated according to a special and recently developed program. In private prisons the inmates solve math problems, crosswords and other puzzles, conduct mental exercises that develop imagination and wit, and practice writing hieroglyphic scripts. By assuming that crimes are committed by intellectually and emotionally backward people, the program aims to assist the convicts in eliminating ignorance. A 20,000-volume library is soon to be opened in the Tochigi Prefecture prison. A special rehabilitation program is foreseen for those inmates suffering from physical or mental disorders. All of these steps address faults revealed during a recent inspection of Japanese prisons.

Japanese society has always given much attention to the reeducation of criminals, especially after the Meiji Restoration and the creation of the unified national state. A. Nikolaev wrote that "there were 32 public organizations in Japan in 1900 that took care of offenders who had served their terms." He also cited the observations of a contemporary: "Prisons let go only those who will receive the care and attention of relatives and friends. I was told a story of a 23-year old medical student who was sentenced to 60 days in prison for book theft but barely escaped staying there for the rest of his life... This is why it should be said here that public organizations played a significant role in liberating many prisoners" (Nikolaev, 1905). The Japanese felt that it was better to keep someone incarcerated than to let them go with no support system.

The prisons were also designed, first of all, for the reeducation of the inmates: "Humane approaches are steadily implemented with much effort in new prisons, which the government builds according to the European model, starting around 1900. Every inmate is given much attention. 'A convict is not regarded as a scoundrel who should be excluded from society — one contemporary writes — as society does not discriminate either morally or financially between a convicted man and other people. The goal is not to punish in revenge but to discipline the criminal and make him reenter society...' The prison regime is hard and militarily structured but it does not oppress the inmates and the absence of runaway cases proves its fairness. The Japanese prisons actually are guarded by a limited number of staff" (Nikolaev, 1905). David Shreider gives another example. In the

Figure 13.6:   Prison guards of the Tokugawa era.

Ishikawa prison, situated on a small island, 1,500 inmates were watched by only one guard. Prison discipline at the end of the 19th century was also extraordinary. Foreigners who happened to visit the prison in Tokyo were surprised to learn that not a single prisoner had been confined to his quarters for misbehavior during that year (Shreider, 1999).

Currently about 30,000 inmates are released annually from Japanese prisons. Only eight percent of those who manage to find work later commit other crimes, but the number is five times larger for those who fail to find work. Hence Japanese society pays close attention to the adaptation of former criminals. Those who do not have a personal guarantor among relatives or friends require the most consideration. Without such guarantees, a former inmate can hardly win other people's confidence. There are many rehabilitation agencies in Japan that perform the functions of guarantors and assistants to former inmates. Although privately owned, the agencies are licensed by the state. The main work is performed by volunteers and currently Japan has 101 such agencies serving up to 2,300 people.

Unlike the European Union, Japan practices the death sentence like many other Asian countries — South Korea, Indonesia, Thailand, Taiwan and the Philippines. In fact, the only members of the G8 group of countries with the death penalty are Japan and the United States. According to data provided in 2005, about 81 percent of the Japanese support this practice. Like many other procedures, capital punishment in Japan is unified and all executions are by hanging. Sentences of death in Japan are rare and executions are even rarer. From 1946 to 2003, only 766 people were on death row and only 608 of them were executed; roughly 10 per year. As of December 2007, Japan had 104 people on death row. Japanese officials never hurry when it concerns the death penalty and the dates of execution are never set beforehand.

Recently, Japanese media reported on a 69-year-old prisoner named Iwao Hakamada who was found guilty of stabbing four people to death, arrested in 1966 and sentenced to death in 1968. To this day, he has been on death row while his friends, relatives and advocates continue to insist that the man is not guilty because his confession is almost the only proof of his guilt.

In Japan, executions are personally ordered by the Minister of Justice. Death sentences wait for approval for tens of years while ministers change every one to two years. Being professional politicians, they try by any means to avoid the unpleasant duty of ordering an execution due to political or moral considerations. For example, Seiken Sugiura, Japan's Justice Minister from October 2005 to September 2006, did not authorize a single execution while his successor, Jin'en Nagase, in a rather short period of time approved 10. In 2007, Justice Minister Kunio Hatoyama asked the government to relieve him and his successors of this painful duty and to make the procedure more formal and independent from the personal views and beliefs of the Justice Minister.

Until recently, Japan was quite secretive about its executions and everything connected with them. No information was provided to the family of the convicted nor to the press, and the prisoner himself was not informed until one hour prior to his execution. Until 1998, even the statistics relevant to the topic were securely guarded. Recent reforms of the country's justice system promise changes, however. On 7 December 2007, the Justice Minister, for the first time in postwar history, made public the names of three convicted men who were executed upon his order a few days earlier. Each of the three men had been found guilty of several murders.

Chapter 14

Preventing Crime and Educating People

Mentors in Uniform

Over the last 15 years, Japan has experienced a continuous rise in its prison population. Despite this, the country still remains the safest among industrialized nations. Among the 137 countries for which crime statistics are available, Japan places 107th in number of prisoners. As of 2005, the United States had the highest prison population rate in the world, some 737 per 100,000 population, followed by Russia (611). Compared to these two countries, Japan resembles a paradise with only 62 prisoners per 100,000 population. Great Britain's is 2.5 times higher than Japan, while Australia's is twice as high and Canada's 1.5 times as high. Japan's index is close to those of Djibouti and Burkina Faso (Walmsley, 2007).

In Japan, all of the state authorities must have an impeccable reputation or it should at least be presented as flawless to the public eye. Officials working for state bodies serve as models of accuracy and diligence and police officers are no exception. Appointed as public mentors, they apply all of their efforts to act as guardians, advisers and supporters of the people in everyday situations. The Japanese police do not maintain order over the population but are instead integrated into an orderly system by keeping in close contact with the citizens. Police officers at ministations are respectfully addressed as *mawari-san* (the term originates from the verb *mawaru* "to walk around, to patrol") and are regarded as helpful friends in difficult situations. Police officers keep detailed records on each household and everyone in it, and know many of the residents in their patrol areas by name.

Officers can make home visits in the area and, sitting with a cup of tea, inquire about everyday life as well as experiences related to crime. They may give tips on crime prevention or help resolve a troublesome situation. In Japan, this method of collecting information, rather than the use of elaborate analytical schemes and deductions, has always been considered the best means of crime prevention and detection. Finding himself in an unknown area, a Japanese man would rather approach a policeman than a stranger to ask the way. The Japanese policemen, after all, share with the population a common group mentality and attitude toward the law.

The Japanese police have introduced various technical innovations to update their relationship with the public. In January 2001, the police department of the Tottori Prefecture unexpectedly posted detailed instruction on baby care on its Internet site. This was done after a newborn baby had been kidnapped from a maternity hospital by unidentified strangers whose motives were not known. Therefore the police posted instructions on how to take care of newborns on the chance that the kidnappers would see them and minimize any possible damage to the baby's health.

In 2004, the Tokyo Police Department started to email crime reports to its registered users. Within three years, all of the police departments in Japan followed suit. In all, these reports reach about 45,000 people. School teachers are among the most scrupulous subscribers since a great part of the emailed information concerns the prevention of crimes against children. By the end of 2007, more than 4,000 of such reports have been sent by the police.

Emerging technology is transforming crime prevention in Japan into, as Ziebold stated, a nation that "watches itself with thousands of eyes." In the spring of 2008, an official crime line was launched by the police for receiving information from the public. Should a Tokyo resident witness anything suspicious, he or she can discreetly send a text message to a police officer on duty. The police started the continuous crime line after receiving more than 722 alarm calls from residents in September 2007 alone. The campaign has been incorporated into the general plan to combat crime. In 2002, 2.85 million offences were registered with the Japanese police, a shocking number for a country that had never seen such high crime indexes before. In the following four years, the police managed to cut the crime rate by 28 percent to 2.05 million cases, which was considered very good. Professor M. Maeda, one of the project's initiators, commented that "public safety has improved equally in all regions of the country, and the main reason is that the government and local authorities have taken energetic steps after 2002" (*Yomiuri*: 6 December 2007).

The police reinforce contacts with local residents in more areas than just crime prevention, often acting as lost and found bureaus. According to the *Article on Lost Items*, a person who finds a lost item must submit it to a local police station. Since 2001, the Japanese police have annually returned to forgetful citizens more than 10 million lost and found items, with a record 10.2 million objects in 2006. In 2008, the police introduced a new and helpful service by which residents can search for their lost property via an Internet database. All they need to do is to enter a description of a lost bag, purse, telephone or other item as well as the approximate date and place of the loss. The search system will report the item's status (found or not found) and will guide the user to the police station where the item is kept.

Japanese police also try to prevent minor offences in a special way, acting, especially toward younger offenders, as educators instead of as arrogant representatives of the Law. According to the observations of Kennett Winston, this practice "may seem more attractive from a moral point of view since it is oriented toward remorse and social rehabilitation rather than punishment. It is more humane and thus more effective in the fight to reduce crime" (Winston, 2003).

A teenager who is suspected of a bicycle theft will be lectured in the police station about his responsibilities to his parents, his school and his neighbors. The police officers will also inform the teenager about the trouble he has caused to the owner of the stolen bicycle. The police will then contact the teenager's family. After the offender has fully realized his guilt, he will be asked to write an official letter of apology and leave it in the police station. It is considered particularly laudable if the teenager's apology is not only to the victim but also to the police officers who have been inconvenienced by his misbehavior.

Figure 14.1:   The public's desired image of a policeman.

Source: Website of Yamaguchi prefectural police.

This letter will be put in a special file to be kept permanently. There are thousands of such apologies for minor misdeeds in police stations across Japan. They are actually the only documentary evidence of the petty crimes committed and neither the offenders nor their relatives know that such documents do not have any legal status and thus cannot be used in court. They do, however, realize full well that the police have a file on their crime and that this knowledge is the best way to prevent a repeated offence.

Such a strong aspiration to reach a compromise is common for all sides involved in the case and at all levels where the case is considered. Central and local authorities are often engaged in resolving issues that might actually be very far from their jurisdiction.

An elderly woman who lived with her daughter in the small town of Soka (Saitama Prefecture) was often visited by salesmen. Within two years, the woman had signed 15 contracts amounting to some 10 million yen (US$83,000). On a regular visit, the woman's son discovered six huge boxes of "ecologically clean products" in her house. The woman was concerned about her health and regularly ordered these products and other related goods. Her son decided to complain to the city authorities that the salesmen had taken advantage of his mother. The salesmen were invited to the city hall and were requested to return to the woman the 3 million yen that she had paid for their goods. The salesmen refused, citing legal grounds and the voluntary nature of the purchases. Negotiations between the city authorities and the trading company continued for three months until a compromise was reached and half of the claimed amount (about 1.5 million yen) was returned to the woman. Remarkably, part of the money was paid by the city authorities (*Yomiuri*: 23 July 2005). This incident is striking because the authorities acted as mediators in a civil dispute between a customer and a trade company and both sides found such intervention quite normal. It seems that the residents of Soka also accepted the administration's right to participate in such disputes since the compensation to the woman was paid from the taxpayers' purse. In any Western country, the intervention of the city authorities would have been illegal because civil conflicts should be resolved in court.

Overcrowded Japanese cities desperately lack free space and face a serious problem of abandoned bicycles in parking lots. The police continually monitor the situation in downtown areas and near the railway stations. After countless notes are placed on abandoned bicycles, tens and hundreds of them are confiscated but the police always leave a telephone number and an address for information. The police conduct instructive work with those who later claim their bicycles, and inform the owners of the addresses where the seized bicycles are kept. Fines or other penalties are not imposed. The police believe that a person who has had his bicycle confiscated will try to avoid a similar situation in the future and be more attentive to warnings.

There is also a "no fines" policy toward people traveling without a ticket in public transportation or against those committing minor traffic violations. A careless driver might receive two punitive points for some insignificant breech but if he drives faultlessly during the following 90 days, the points are automatically deducted. The system of punitive measures is primarily designed to make people recognize their misconduct while the action of imposing a penalty is secondary. Ethical values still play a significant role in the everyday life of the Japanese.

While the moral nature of the police's educational methods is clear, some of the innovative techniques used by the Japanese police might be surprising. For example, police officers in the city of Morioka (Iwate Prefecture) have introduced a new method of working with troublesome youngsters. For over a year and a half, female workers at the police station wrote about 130 so-called love letters (*ai no reta*) to juvenile offenders who were causing problems within the station's jurisdiction. About 100 teenagers are reported to have received the letters and there was a threefold reduction in repeat juvenile delinquency in the area. In fact, the index became lower than the average for the entire country.

However, the attitude of the police and society toward offenders will change if the violations are no mere accident. Japanese moral obligations to aid the police make the Japanese population itself the police's best agent.

In June 2005, the police in the small town of Shisui machi (Chiba Prefecture) received a report from residents about a violator who had been leaving garbage in inappropriate places for two months. Within one month, the police managed to catch the wrongdoer red-handed at 4 a.m. The 38-year old unemployed man admitted that he had been leaving garbage one hundred meters away from his apartment near the railway station simply because it was convenient for him. Several national newspapers reported the incident and celebrated the triumph of justice. The man's actions stem from Japan's complicated scheme of sorting trash into a number of different categories (combustible waste, non-combustible waste, aluminum etc.) prior to disposal. Although his actions might seem to be merely annoying to many Westerners, the ire of the Japanese citizens is raised by the impudence of someone who is not well mannered enough to follow the rules that they follow so scrupulously. In some cases, neighborhoods have posted patrols at garbage collection sites to ensure proper sorting.

The idea of waste recycling is deeply rooted in the Japanese mind, and Japan is the undisputed world leader in this field. It might be interesting to relate some facts from the Tokugawa Period (1603–1867). In the beginning of the 18th century, the Japanese capital, located on the site of modern-day Tokyo which was then called Edo, already had more than one million residents. Dense and as busy as an ant hill, the city produced many things, not the least of which was excrement. According to Japanese historians, the amount was truly enormous, on the order of 510,000 metric tons annually. Because animal husbandry was never a large industry in Japan, human feces from the capital were in great demand among farmers in the densely populated surrounding areas. In the large cities of that era, youngsters used to run after horses and oxen to collect the droppings and sell them to rural folk for fertilizer and fuel. This is one of the big reasons why, compared to European cities, the Japanese could boast the utmost in sanitary cleanliness. It is ironic that, in the Tokugawa Era, a human being did not enjoy much respect but his excrement did. Many landlords supplemented their incomes by selling the contents of the lavatories to sewage collectors. Hundreds of sewage cleaners (*koetori*) used to transport buckets daily to the city's suburbs. These painstaking efforts of carrying buckets of sewage on shoulder yokes gave the Japanese capital an extraordinary image as well as a fetid odor. The residents tried all means to avoid meeting with *koetori* in narrow streets and even had a proverb for this situation: *koetori wa nukimi no yoni kowagarase* (fear the sewage cleaner as you would a sharp sword). This is why pedantic Japanese historians are correct when they say that although TV programs may give many realistic details about the life of Edo, they always fail to deliver the aroma of the age.

Sewage collection was not spared the rigor of Japanese classification. After all, the Japanese penchant for sorting everything according to categories and ranks reached its peak in the Tokugawa Era. Sewage was categorized into several types according to its quality and sold under different trade names and at different prices. There were

Figure 14.2:   A sewage cleaner of the Tokugawa age.

five groups of sewage and the best quality sewage was produced in the toilets of the central government and the Edo residences of appanage lords (*daimyo*). The poorest and the cheapest sewage came from prison and detention pits (Furukawa, 2008).

Modern Japan fights for ecological purity in its own characteristic way: by applying elaborate technology and on a cosmic scale. In 2009, the Environmental Ministry began using images from the earth observation satellites to track illegal dumping of industrial waste. In Japan, companies must be granted permission from the authorities for the temporary use of land as a waste disposal site. Many businesses try (surreptitiously and illegally) to expand their sites. Local authorities cannot closely monitor remote areas so the government of the Iwate Prefecture proposed satellite observation. The idea was accepted enthusiastically. The images are received from the *Daichi* earth observation satellite which can take photographs at resolutions high enough to distinguish objects as small as 2.5 meters in diameter. The cost of a one-time image capture is US$2,000 and the Japanese were happy to state that it is one-tenth to one-eighth the cost of using a US commercial satellite for the same purpose. Companies that have been caught illegally dumping industrial waste are given administrative guidance on how to rectify the situation. A "no-fines" policy is implemented here as well.

The Police as Role Model

Historically, the Japanese police performed a special public mission that has evolved into a ritual. Every newcomer to the force will receive ideological training about his acceptance into this unusual organization. Every New Year for the Japanese police begins with a traditional demonstration of martial arts that is staged for local residents in the gym in which the policemen train. This ritual show is called *budo hajimeshiki* (New Year's demonstration of martial arts) with "honesty, purity, solidarity" as its motto. Uttering battle cries, the policemen display their perfect hand combat techniques which are based on judo and kendo fencing. Their physical strength, accuracy and agility as well as solemn facial expressions would convince the spectators that not a single criminal would be able to escape from such a brave constabulary.

The police officers are well aware of their educational duties toward the public and this knowledge sets the standard of their conduct. The main requirement of professional ethics for a man in uniform is to be a role model. This is why policemen deliberately and demonstratively obey all the rules designed for the citizens. Their uncompromising attitude toward the observation of regulations is especially visible on the roads.

Police patrol cars are easily recognizable not only from their black and white coloring but also due to the officers' manner of driving. They move along the streets according to the traffic regulations, or in other words, 10 to 15 km/h slower than the city's traffic. They also

Figure 14.3:   New Year ceremony of martial arts in the police hall.

Source: Website of Shiosaka Jenichiro, accessed from [http://warmupsurf.com/Shiosaka].

wait at stop signs for a little bit longer than is required. Demonstrative compliance with all of the existing rules is a distinctive feature of the professional behavior of Japanese police officers. In Japan, clean vehicles are a common sight, but police cars are exceptionally so. There are usually two policemen in a patrol car. They always wear their protective helmets, their safety belts are always fastened and their faces are ritually solemn. One cannot fail to notice such a car even from far away.

Japanese traffic police detect speeders in ambush-like "speed traps." By using radar, the police can detect the speed of a vehicle while standing still or while in movement, and their radar can detect the speed from behind, in front or the side of the vehicle. In the Japanese shops, one can find a great variety of anti-radar devices, but this is quite beside the point. With copious funds and their own research institute, the national traffic police are always one step ahead of the civilians, regardless of their equipment. The Japanese police are normally rather sympathetic to violators, as could be expected from our previous discussion of law enforcement. When stopping a motorist for speeding, they express deep concern about the incident, give their sympathies and advice on how to move through the unpleasant formal procedures quickly. Upon finishing the report and giving the motorist a speeding fine, they would suggest the motorist be more careful in future and bid him or her farewell.

However, this applies only when the policemen are on duty. Otherwise, they behave like everyone else and often have their own skeletons in the closet. In July 2003, a retired police officer and respected member of the local community in Nagasaki named Shigeichi Sasaki drowned his son in a street gutter with two accomplices in order to obtain more than 100 million yen (about US$800,000) in life insurance. Using the skills of his former profession, he managed to make the murder look like a traffic accident. Police reopened the investigation two years later after receiving information from local residents. As a policeman, Sasaki had taught the residents to be on alert for criminal activity; ironically, the citizens had been so well taught that they helped police to uncover his crime.

The problem of intoxicated driving in Japan is rather interesting. The officially allowed blood alcohol content is regulated but it seems to be a secret known only to the experts. During my first years in Japan, I was absolutely certain that driving in Japan following the consumption of any amount of alcohol was not tolerated in the least. As all foreigners were, I had been politely warned about this regulation several times. One day, I happened to come across a newspaper article that, after 1 June 2002, the law regulating blood alcohol content would be changed: "taking into consideration an increased number of traffic incidents", the norm was reduced from 0.25 to 0.15 mg/ml by a breath test. This meant that one drink will put most people over the limit, which is stricter than Australia and much stricter than New Zealand or the United Kingdom. I was rather surprised by the news but my Japanese acquaintances surprised me even more by saying that they knew nothing about either the former or the newly introduced limits. They were sure that no alcohol at all was permitted while driving, and three cab drivers told me likewise. Intrigued, I cut out the newspaper article and showed it to my Japanese friends who were surprised in turn.

It is evident that, in Japan, the principle of "prevention is more important than punishment" orchestrates all of the activities of the police. Despite the fact that official documents contain full information about the permissible alcohol limits, the police do not talk too much about this. It seems that the perceived zero-tolerance of the police toward intoxicated driving is a product of the media who reinforce the idea that no drinking is allowed when one is driving as the police are watching and they are strict and principled.

There are not many intoxicated drivers in Japan compared with other countries. According to statistics, only 7 percent of the intoxicated drivers who are detained can be described as "occasional drinkers" while more than half are alcoholics, making intoxicated driving more of a medical problem in Japan. This is why the Japanese government not only introduces stricter penalties for intoxicated driving but also develops programs to identify and treat alcoholic drivers. The penalties for drunken driving have increasingly become harsher. In June 2007, new amendments were introduced to increase the maximum period of suspension from driving from three to five years, and the fine from 500,000 yen to 1,000,000 yen (from US$4,000 to 8,000).

The police note that strict measures work. Since 2000, the number of people killed in traffic accidents has steadily declined. The year 1970 was the most tragic, when road accidents claimed the lives of 16,765 people. The situation has since improved considerably; in 2007, about 6,000 people lost their lives on the road, approximately the same number as did in 1953. It should be noted that the number of vehicles on the roads has increased by more than threefold since the 1950s. Such features of the Japanese character as care, precaution and respect for rules make Japanese roads the safest in the world.

From June 2008, all passengers were required to fasten their rear seat belts while driving along high speed roads. An October 2008 survey revealed that about 60 percent of Japanese passengers fasten rear seatbelts on the highways, while in the distinctively law-abiding Miyagi Prefecture, 90 percent of passengers were observing the new law less than six months after it was introduced. Although the law allows backseat passengers to remain unfastened when riding on city streets, 30 percent of backseat passengers choose to secure their belts.

The Japanese traffic police often take to the streets to educate motorists about the dangers and consequences of inappropriate speed, and they do this in an amusing way. Several patrol cars drive along the city streets, observing all of the road signs and speed limits. Soon, a traffic jam forms but no one dares to overtake the police. All drivers are forced to move at the prescribed speed until there is a chance to change their route and break free from the black and white overseer vehicle. The police have no other purpose than to develop in motorists the habit of driving at the required speed.

New Problems on the Horizon

Until the middle of the 1990s, the Japanese police could truly serve as a model of professionalism and high morality. Policemen from New York and other mega-cities used to learn from the Japanese police. The only scandal occurred in 1978 when a police officer from Tokyo was charged with the rape and murder of a female student. Following that incident, a new phrase appeared in the media: *seifuku fushin* (distrust of the uniform). Nevertheless, public stability and a low crime rate have ensured a reasonably positive image of the police. In 1996, the crime detection rate in Japan accounted for 41 percent (in the United States, it was 22 percent and in France, 27 percent) while the murder detection rate reached an incredible 98.5 percent (in the United States, it was 67 percent and in France, 75 percent). The inevitability of punishment resulted in a reduction in serious crimes. During the 40 years after World War II, Japan's police have notched up impressive progress. From 1951 to 2000, the number of murders in Japan dropped by 68 percent while that for robberies dropped by 43 percent.

This began to change with the end of economic growth. In the 1990s, all social and economic benefits fell while the pressures and pace of life soared. Family values were weakening and community cohesion was crumbling. The crime rate steadily climbed, and from 1995 to 2001, the number of serious crimes (murders, rapes, armed robberies and assaults resulting in grave injuries) more than doubled from 22.9 to 47.8 cases per 100,000 population (*Nihon Tokei Nenkan*, 2003). The overall crime detection rate fell from 41 to 24 percent (Roberts and LaFree, 2004). Although the severity of the social problems had not reached the levels of the industrialized Western countries, alarm bells were ringing in Japanese society. The rise in crime and social instability as broadcast nationwide by the media stirred public anxiety and disenchantment with the police.

A shocking case riveted public attention in January 2000 when in the small town of Kashiwazaki (Niigata Prefecture), an abducted 19-year old girl was found in the house of an unemployed man. The man had kidnapped her from a school yard when she was only nine and kept her in the house ever since. This struck a hard blow to the image of the police who had failed to find the girl for 10 years. The police had been well aware that the man had previously attempted to kidnap another child. The man lived with his mother but she claimed ignorance since "she never went up to the first floor which was occupied by him." None of the neighbors appear to have suspected anything either. "Where are our community traditions and knowledge of the situation among the neighbors?" the Japanese asked each other in bewilderment. Local police chiefs were fired but without much publicity in order not to further agitate society with the sordid details.

The situation was aggravated by a series of scandals involving police officers across the country from Hokkaido to Kyushu. Such officer violations as abuse of power, beating of subordinates, concealment of information, blackmail, sale of classified information and use of drugs had never been pinned on the Japanese police before. During seven "hot news" months from September 1999 to March 2000, 166 crimes were reportedly committed by the police and 113 police officers and police department employees were charged. Finally, 434 people were either fired or punished. According to former police officer A. Kuroki, this was only the tip of the iceberg (Johnson, 2003).

Previously, the Japanese police had commanded a rather high reputation, with 74 percent of public trust. Only the Japanese court system enjoyed higher respect with a 79 percent approval rating. After the scandals broke, the police's rating crashed to an unprecedented 52 percent. Compared with the state railways' 75 percent confidence rating and the state medical institutions' 73 percent level of trust, such a collapse of respect for the national police force was a catastrophe. The head of the national police had to resign. Policemen from Kashiwazaki visited the family of the kidnapped girl, who were living about 50 kilometers from the house where she had been held for 10 years, and apologized for their negligence.

In 2000, Japan's Justice Minister received the results of a five-year investigation into the problems of the country's police force by a special commission. According to the commission's leading expert Yuki Nishimura who spoke to Newsweek, "Japan's national crime database is beyond salvage, law-enforcement concepts are decades out of date and investigators are often their own worst enemies. They routinely withhold information from crime reports, fail to share evidence across jurisdictional boundaries and lack even basic knowledge in crime analysis. They must be taught to gather information and analyze it in ways that can be used by others. But the police force is conservative. Many officers believe in the old system." Hiroshi Kubo, the author of several books on problems of the Japanese police, concluded: "Problems hidden deep inside Japan's law-enforcement system are floating to the surface. If things don't change, Japan is headed for a crisis" (Wehrfritz and Takayama, 2000).

Japanese criminologists agree. The police are traditionally viewed as a sacred organization and it is uncommon to criticize them publicly. It is true, though, that until recently, they did not give much grounds for speculation. This is why experts evaluating the work of law enforcement bodies often come to opposite conclusions. D. Bailey, an expert on police work, wrote in 1991 that in the eyes of the Japanese, where the criterion of truth is the consensus of the majority, the national police look surprisingly favorable. According to

American standards, the number of committed violations is small and rather insignificant in nature. But Hiromi Ochiai, a journalist with *Asahi Shimbun*, reported in 1998: "What does the word 'lawlessness' mean? According to the dictionary this is 'a place where the law is not observed.' I think that the Japanese police represent extreme lawlessness. B. Akagi, a former police officer, stated in 2000: "Corruption is a chronic disease of the Japanese police" (Johnson, 2003).

David Johnson conducted a survey in 2003 to compare typical lapses in judgment committed by American and Japanese police officers as well as their attitude to these shortcomings. Having completed the survey with the Japanese police, Johnson found that they are more uncompromising with minor violations than are their American colleagues, for example, receiving small presents from citizens who have received help in a difficult situation from a police officer. Aware of the Japanese tradition of a decent outward appearance (*tatemae*), Johnson notes that "since the mechanisms for exposing misconduct are undeveloped in Japan, police behavior may well be worse than it appears." Indeed, the violations in the above example from late 1999 to early 2000 might have been endemic, but they only surfaced once the traditional respect for the Japanese police had been eroded by breaches of the public's trust.

On the problems of the Japanese police system Johnson presents documented facts as well as the conclusions of former police officers, criminologists and researchers studying police activities. He points out three main problems: "the embezzlement of money from police slush funds, endemic corruption in Japan's pachinko industry and police tolerance of organized crime." Unlike in the West, Japanese police are more inclined to control undesirable activities rather than prohibit them outright. On the other hand, there is no structure that controls the police. Johnson sounds quite pessimistic when talking about administrative reform: "The problem of police corruption in Japan is not a matter of a few 'rotten apples' but of a failed organization... Significant reform requires conditions that now are absent and seem unlikely to emerge anytime soon. For the foreseeable future, Japanese police seem likely to remain above the law" (Johnson, 2003).

The reasons for such a wide range of opinions on the work of the Japanese police are broad. On the one hand, the maintenance of public order and the prevention of crime were traditionally considered to be sacred duties. People who routinely engaged in such missions deservedly held themselves in high esteem and enjoyed a great deal of respect. Japanese mothers used to tell their misbehaving children that they would take them to the police for reeducation if they did not behave. If parents could not help their adult children to solve a problem, the children would be advised to consult the local police. The main job of a Western policeman, however, is to fight crime with the help of the law. The Japanese police officer, besides his important primary duties, also acts as an instructor, adviser and educator. David Bailey, an expert on the Japanese legal system, said: "American police officers have the authority of man-made law; Japanese police have the authority of unspoken moral consensus" (Bailey, 1991, as cited in Tsuchimoto, 2000). Public respect and consensus give the police broad powers and many deviations from the letter of the law are allowed. It is believed that, for the sake of public security, minor violations can be ignored. Such behavior by the police is expected by the public who view them as instructors rather than punishers, and objections are seldom raised.

On the other hand, their special public mission makes the police force one of the most closed groups in Japanese society. Confucian norms regulate relations inside the group, requiring that subordinates display total openness and submission while superiors exercise supervision and control. The activities of ordinary police officers are strictly regulated and neither personal initiative nor creativity is permitted. Misconduct of one police officer casts a shadow on the entire department and, especially, on its chief. Today, such group responsibility has gradually given way to modern methods of human resource management but the traditional relationships have not vanished completely. According to Tsuchimoto: "Thirty percent of the disciplinary actions taken against police officers are still attributed to a 'lack of supervision'" (Tsuchimoto, 2000). As for moral obligations, Confucian ethics continue to guide behavior. The heads of the police departments and subdivisions often take responsibility for the misdeeds of their subordinates and sometimes they do so in the most extreme ways.

A few years ago, the Japanese prosecutor's office uncovered disciplinary violations by a certain group of police officers. It was revealed that some probation officers would blackmail suspects and then present distorted information to the law enforcement bodies. These violations had taken place several years before the case caught the attention of the media and the officers' direct supervisor, who was unaware of the violations and who had nothing to do with them, had already retired. Nevertheless, the supervisor committed suicide as the facts were uncovered. In his suicide note, he explained that he could not live with the burden of responsibility for the misdeeds of his former subordinates.

Such relationships between superiors and their subordinates, together with the closed nature of the organization, serve as the main reason for the cover-up of violations inside the police force. It is sufficiently well documented to the point of being common knowledge that police all over the world abuse their special position within the legal system, and the list of violations is approximately the same regardless of country. This is why it is difficult to put much faith in the crystal-clear reputation of the Japanese police. The Japanese police scandals of the 1990s warrant such skepticism. The first reaction of all of the heads of the Japanese police departments was predictably the same: they had by all means tried to prevent the scandal from spreading and to salvage the image of the organization. In Japan, it is not difficult to control police news coverage since the police themselves decide whether the information should be made public. Within each prefecture, the inspector who controls the activities of the local police, reports his findings to the head of the local police department. Therefore reports of police officer violations go directly to the officers' superior, who is supposed to have foreknowledge of the violations. According to both written and non-written professional ethics, a policeman at fault should report the misconduct to his direct superior. In such cases, he may count on the protection and support of the organization which will impose a penalty but will nevertheless prevent the information from getting out. Violations committed by the police in Japan receive broad news coverage only when reporters get too nosy and uncover the violations. This results in significant consequences, as was the case in 1998–1999. In actuality, these violations were not minor infractions but real crimes. It became clear that the invisible line that has always separated the Japanese police from the civilian population is gradually becoming indistinct and, in some cases, has completely disappeared. This situation does not apply only to the police, as in Japan the official investigation of any organization are internal due to the high social status of the group or organization.

Today, more brazen and more violent crimes, unknown to previous generations, are committed in Japan. Globalization has impacted not only the world economy but also crime. The Japanese police are currently faced with problems that were previously nonexistent. To develop his skills; an athlete needs a worthy sparring partner; the recent activities of the Japanese police prove this old sports adage. For many years, the police have been working as they did in previous times when "water was wetter and people were better." Therefore, from time to time, the Japanese police appear not to be up to the task when tough, resolute and coordinated actions are required in the fight against serious opponents.

In May 2007 in Aichi Prefecture, the police had to deal with an armed criminal who had taken several hostages. During the rescue operation, one officer was killed and another was seriously wounded. Further analysis revealed that police did not respond quickly enough and had made mistakes that resulted in the casualties.

However, it is too early to discuss any legal apocalypse in Japan. The fact that the relatively rare violations of the police (compared with other countries) caused such agitation makes it clear that the police are still held in high esteem. Evidently, Japanese society and the law enforcement bodies realize the necessity of change. This, together with a low crime rate, will hopefully give the Japanese legal bodies sufficient time to restructure the system. A survey held in 2005 showed that, over the last five years, the population's faith in the police has increased to 65 percent, although the Japanese still tend to trust the police less than they trust their national newspapers and television (*Nihonjin no kachikan,* 2005).

Chapter 15

Romanticizing Suicide

Without Regard to Religion

A "nation of suicide" is how Westerners sometimes refer to Japan, pointing out the nation's permissive attitude toward voluntary deaths. Many centuries ago, the concepts of Shinto, Japan's native religion, revealed to the Yamato people that neither hellish tortures nor heavenly paradise awaited them after death. With the later influence of Buddhism, the Japanese learned a philosophical approach in which human life is fragile and inevitably followed by death, just as the day is followed by night. The samurai moral code glorified death and attributed to it an aura of courage and nobility. "The Way of a samurai is found in his death. Discussions regarding death without reaching one's goal being equivalent to dying like a dog are the idle talk of egoistical people. One who has failed to achieve his goal and continues to live is a coward" (Yamamoto, 2004). The code of honor did not differentiate between violent and voluntary deaths; ritual suicide at the order of a superior was a widespread practice. Over time, the samurai attitude toward death in general and suicide in particular spread to all levels of Japanese society. The idea that a dignified death is better than a miserable life became dominant in Japan, which is why ritual suicide has a specific place in Japanese culture.

In its classic form, ritual suicide (*harakiri* or *seppuku*, literally stomach-cutting) was carried out according to the requirements of the code of honor and the system of moral obligations (*giri*). During the medieval internal wars, vassals often committed ritual suicide called *junshi* (*oibara, tsuifuku*) upon the death of their lord to demonstrate their eternal loyalty. Originally, it was only performed when the lord was slain in battle or murdered but later, *junshi* could also be carried out irrespective of whether the lord had died of an illness, fallen on the battlefield, or committed ritual suicide. As with all the other forms of ritual suicide, *junshi* was originally reserved only for samurai.

Following the medieval internal wars, attitudes toward this ritual started to change. Ieyasu Tokugawa (1543–1616) wrote that "the ritual is old but unwise, and nothing justifies its necessity." In 1661, 36 samurais of the Nabeshima clan announced their decision to commit *junshi* upon the death of Naohiro Yamagi, one of the clan's founders. Much effort was applied to talk them out of their intention and immediately thereafter the ritual was prohibited in Nabeshima County.

Soon, the government, too, reflected on the incident and found it highly irrational to lose the nation's best warriors for the sake of the ritual. Two years following this case, the government banned *junshi* entirely, stating that it was a wartime relic. To curb the practice, the government announced that the lord of any samurai who committed *junshi* in such situations would lose the right to his inheritance. The government knew well that the samurai would not dare to threaten the honor of their future lord so the deadly ritual began to fade. However, in many other cases, suicide was still considered a matter of honor and dignity.

In the second half of the 19th century, the governor of Kanagawa Prefecture, Hori Oribe, received a letter from a secretary-interpreter to the US ambassador, Henry Heusken, to which he took offense. The governor asked the minister of foreign affairs, Nobumasa Ando, to expel the American offender but was refused. The Oribe family decided that the double offence — from the foreigner and from the minister — was unbearable and the governor committed ritual suicide in the presence of his family. Relatives of the Oribe family began searching for Heusken in order to execute vengeance. Bearing in mind the customs of their country, the Japanese guards of the American diplomat abandoned him and Heusken was murdered. It was then Ando's turn to face vengeance, but Ando showed much courage and, together with his guards, resisted the attack by the enraged relatives of the Oribe family. Both sides suffered losses, but the minister was lucky to escape fatal injuries. After the two attacks,

Figure 15.1: Ritual suicide (*harakiri, seppuku*).

the vengeance of the Oribe family clan was considered fulfilled as well as was public opinion concerning the family honor. However, after committing a double crime — the murder of the foreign diplomat and the attack on the minister — the Oribe family had to disappear from society for a time.

The importance attributed to the code of honor and mutual moral obligations made acts of vengeance extremely widespread in Japan in the Middle Ages. Such cases became so common that the shogun had to enact special rules specifically related to vengeance murders in order to separate them from ordinary and contract killings. The already-mentioned decrees of Ieyasu Tokugawa, which after his death became a set of laws, stated: "It has been a custom in Japan for a long time that a man cannot live under the same sky with the enemies of his father, mother or senior brother. Starting from now, if a person

Figure 15.2

Source: Website of msn auction accessed from [http://auction.jp.msn.com].

wants to carry out an act of vengeance, he must notify local authorities and state how many days or months he plans to follow his intention. This declaration must be written down in a special book. Without such precautions, a person performing an act of vengeance will be considered an ordinary murderer" (Venyukov, 1871).

The code of honor, with ritual suicide as its most important element, did not assume its distinguished place in Japanese culture straight away. From the 13th to the 16th century, the country was in the midst of internal wars during which loyalty and courage went hand in hand with conspicuous betrayals and treachery. It must be said that there were certain reasons for such behavior.

The samurai class appeared at the end of the 12th century. At that time, samurai warriors were relatively few; their cold steel arms were ineffective and their technical engineering capabilities were very limited. For a rather long time, numerical superiority in warriors remained a key factor for victory in any battle. As a rule, the forces of the warring sides were more or less equal and it was rather difficult to achieve significant superiority. In cases where one party managed to do so, another party might easily avoid the battle in order to reorganize its force. The safest tactic was to make secret arrangements with an enemy camp in advance to radically shift the balance of power on the battlefield. No other technique could produce such an overwhelming effect so it was used widely. Moral principles initially were not considered to amount to much in battle. Taking the enemy's side was regarded as a legitimate tactic, and after the battle, no opponents were left to cast judgment on the winner.

European wars of the time were sparked by national, ethnic and religious causes. Russians fought against the Tatars, the British against the French, the Christians against the Muslims, the Catholics against the Orthodox. Such confrontations were truly uncompromising and left no place for traitors. Under such conditions, it was rather difficult to take the enemy's side due to moral considerations and this was tricky for tactical reasons. A defector had little chance of winning the confidence of his bitter foes.

The situation was completely different in Japan. The nation was homogeneous, warring clans spoke the same language, worshipped the same gods and had an almost identical upbringing. The fights were held for the sake of political influence or for access to material resources. Surely, private goals were also pursued. Ties of friendship with one clan could be altered promptly for an alliance with another, if such a coalition promised more benefits and power for the family, the clan's business and the province. The Japanese did not have strong moral or ideological principles denouncing treachery. The widely used expression *gekokujo* (inferiors win over superiors) correctly described this tactic. However, following the era of Tokugawa rule, treachery was criticized as the main cause of anarchy and social disorder. The Japanese addiction to conspiracy, intrigue and betrayal was further nourished by their inclination to secret or back-door arrangements. The Japanese commanders did not possess the oratory skills to deliver rousing speeches to their warriors, but they were very proficient in plotting artful and effective arrangements.

Japan's history has many examples of military campaigns that were won by betrayal. In the famous naval battle of Dannoura (1185), the enemy family clans of Taira and Minamoto had approximately equal power, about 400 ships each. When Tanzo, one of the

Taira allies, switched sides and took two hundred ships with him, the Minamoto troops immediately outnumbered the Taira warriors by three to one and triumphed in the battle. After winning the battle, the Minamoto family remained the most powerful military clan in Japan for many years. When the armies of Ishida and Tokugawa fought a decisive battle at Sekigahara (in 1600), one of Ishida's warlords, Hideaki Kobayakawa (1577–1602), switched sides and hit Ishida's troops with his 15,000 warriors at the peak of the battle, thus paving the way for Tokugawa's victory. These arrangements were made beforehand but Tokugawa did not trust his secret ally until the last moment.

The acts of changing sides became so common in military tactical schemes that by the end of the 16th century, when Toyotomi Hideyoshi launched a military campaign to invade Korea, one of his commanders betrayed him and joined the enemy army. Having become a leader of the Korean troops, he later fought against his countrymen (Shiba and Kin, 1972).

According to Japanese etiquette rules, a respected guest should be offered a seat that faces the entrance door which is the best seat in the house. The reason for the guest's visit — whether to negotiate, to have dinner or simply to chat — does not matter. This tradition dates to the Middle Ages when warriors played their larger-than-life military games. Medieval Japan formed its own wartime etiquette involving spies, hired assassins (*ninja*), constant conspiracies and coups. In order to convince an honorable guest that no secret plots awaited him in the house, he was offered a seat facing the entrance. In case of a sudden attack, he would have time to spring to his feet and whip out a sword. There is no need to follow this rule today but the tradition is still observed.

In the 17th century when the Tokugawa clan seized power, the lords decided to put an end to betrayals and treachery. The new peaceful period faced its own concerns and challenges. Loyalty and commitment were the enduring moral values and generations of warriors had been trained to honor them. In the following centuries, society's tolerant attitude toward ritual suicides had resulted in a rash of suicide cases. There were cases in Japanese history where suicides were not caused by inevitability but by an inability to resolve a situation.

In 1868, when the last shogun Yoshinobu Tokugawa (1837–1913) renounced power in favor of the Meiji Emperor, most of his followers disagreed with his plan and proposed to fight to the end. During a meeting in which the warriors were discussing their options, some warriors failed to deal with the stress when the crucial decision had to be made and committed suicide without waiting for the outcome of the meeting (Shiba, 2000).

However, the lenient attitude toward suicide had its limits and applied only to cases when voluntary death resolved the conflict between feelings and obligations in favor of the latter. When a suicide was committed to avoid responsibilities, it was strictly denounced. For example, a double suicide of lovers (*shinju*) who could not be together due to certain circumstances was condemned. Married people who fell in love with others usually chose this way of dealing with their unsolvable problem. In an era where the interests of the clans dominated everything, Japanese men had to love either a wife or a courtesan and never to let emotions interfere with or surpass their public duties.

Suicide was considered a dignified death when it was well-thought through, thoroughly planned and emotionless. These attributes were indispensable in a successful suicide. On the contrary, a suicide committed spontaneously or in the heat of passion was believed to be unwise and was thus condemned.

After analyzing the plots of typical novels of the Tokugawa Period, A. R. Mazellier wrote the following: "Japanese writers tell a story about a sailor who...survived a shipwreck and upon returning home found his wife married to another man. Without any complaints, as if finding the situation quite natural, he sat down near the fireplace and started to tell of his adventures. He then suddenly jumped to his feet, took out a sword, killed his wife, killed her new husband and thereafter committed suicide. One of the writers finishes his story with an exclamation: 'Who could have expected such tactful behavior from a commoner!'" Such a decay of moral norms is simply disgusting, the European researcher stated (Mazellier, 1913).

The popularity of this subject and the positive remarks made by Japanese novelists are explained by two factors: the hero showed self-control in not revealing his emotions in a critical situation, and although all the characters died, the man's honor was saved. According to the laws of the Tokugawa Period, a husband who found his wife in the arms of her lover had the right to deal with the situation immediately: either to forgive or to kill the lovers. In the latter case, he did not bear criminal responsibility for their murder.

Throughout Japanese history, one can find many examples of suicides committed according to classical canon. The rules require that much consideration be given to the last moment of life, to the careful planning of the details and to a well-weighed analysis of all of the consequences.

A famous hero of the Russo-Japanese war, General Maresuke Nogi, waited for several years for the chance to commit a sophisticated ritual suicide. The general had to delay the planned suicide in order to obey the will of Emperor Meiji, who had forbidden Nogi to perform this deadly intention during his lifetime. The emperor died in July 1912 and exactly 40 days later, Nogi performed the long-planned act. Before committing suicide he gave a press conference.

On a warm autumn evening of 1997, 85 years after Nogi's suicide, three Japanese businessmen, complete strangers, met in the lobby of a small hotel in the suburbs of Tokyo. After drinking some beer and having a light dinner, they went to their rooms. Later that evening, the three committed suicide by hanging themselves from the ceiling fan. It is very difficult to imagine a similar situation taking place in another country. The triple suicide was caused by the financial crisis that Japan had suffered in 1997. In total, 3,500 Japanese nationals committed suicide that year. Business and financial fiascos are the second most common cause of suicide in Japan (about 40 percent of the total), and the absolute number is steadily rising. In 2003, the number of suicides committed by victims of financial problems hit a tragic record of more than 8,000 people.

Until 1873, suicides partially served as a substitute for the death penalty. In Japan a voluntary death was considered more dignified than a violent one, but the privilege was given only to the samurai. One French diplomat described the process.

"The whole procedure, court hearings and execution of the verdict are performed with a great solemnity. In such cases...[they] erect on four pillars a spacious platform surrounded by a bamboo barrier, the inner side of which is upholstered with a white silk material. Armed guards protect all access to the barrier. From one door...an accused man comes out followed by two friends or witnesses of his own choice, and his advocates. From another door...the prosecutors and judges come out. The accused man, dressed in white, same as his witnesses, sits down in the middle of a white carpet bordered in red, opposite the complainants... The judges place themselves on the right and left sides. The advocates stand at a considerate distance. All participants are formally dressed. Only one person, in military uniform armed with a sword, stands behind the accused man. His duty is to cut off the head of the criminal, if the latter is too slow in committing suicide upon hearing the verdict... They say that when sentenced to death, samurai rarely display any fear when performing hara-kiri" (Humbert, 1870).

In 1873, all forms of suicide were prohibited, but signs of traditional attitudes toward ritual suicide can still be seen in modern Japan. High-ranking officials often prefer committing suicide to enduring public shame. Medieval moral instructions prescribed: "If someone accuses you, it is a dishonor for all your lifetime" (Sato, 1999). According to Buddhist ethics, death cleanses a person of all his misdeeds in life and his descendants should not recall them. A man who redeems his fault at the cost of his life is freed of charges and automatically rehabilitates his reputation. A suicide committed under such circumstances is called *inseki jisatsu* (responsibility-driven suicide).

In 1998, the famous 64-year old Japanese film director, Juzo Itami, committed suicide after some media publications claimed that he had had an affair with a young woman. In his suicide note, he wrote that only through his death could he prove his innocence. The case was broadcast in Western media as an example of the illogical behavior of the Japanese, as according to Western principles, one's innocence should be proven in court rather than by committing a suicide. According to Japanese culture, such suicides are considered as an indirect and thus more elegant admittance of guilt and readiness to atone by paying the ultimate price. Under similar discreditable circumstances, Japan's Agriculture, Forestry and Fisheries Minister Toshikatsu Matsuoka committed suicide on 28 May 2007 amidst an embezzlement scandal.

Suicides committed by Japanese top officials and businessmen before or during investigation have another rational motivation. In the Tokugawa Period, crimes against the state and society were punished more severely than were crimes against individuals. Due to austere laws and an elaborate torture system, accusatory verdicts were quite numerous. Some travelers who witnessed the legal system at that time said: "It is explained by the fact that the people in charge of punishing crimes of the first category will surely be sentenced to death if they treat criminals softly" (Ziebold, 1999).

A death sentence was always followed by property confiscation and by persecution of the criminal's family without regard to social status. Postwar reforms have not changed the age-old tradition and it remains relevant in modern Japan. Recent notorious cases of ostracism displayed toward the families of convicted men demonstrate this. In such circumstances, the suspect's suicide, besides other considerations, is also an act of noble concern for the future of his family and friends.

It is rather interesting that this tradition was founded by prosecutors of the Tokugawa Era. European men living in Japan at that time wrote in their reports that in a situation when there was grave evidence against the suspect, the prosecutors would signal to the executioner to quickly kill the poor man before he started to testify against himself. Later they would announce that the suspect had died during an investigation and his guilt remained unproven, meaning that his family members could be free of dishonor and harassment (Ziebold, 1999).

Modern Technologies and a Sensible View of Death

Over the past 150 years, Japan has changed considerably. After 1945, the country started to steadily develop its economy and social policies. The well-being of its citizens was rapidly improving as was the system of social guarantees. Despite all of these favorable factors, the suicide rate in Japan remained disproportionally high. The country suffered three peaks of suicides during the postwar period. The first one occurred in 1958, when the economy was experiencing an economic boom after the wartime devastation, with more than 23,500 nationals committing suicide. The second blow hit Japan in 1986, exactly in the midst of the "bubble economy," when the general state of things was rather good. More than 25,000 people committed suicide that year, after which the rate declined only to spike again in 1998. Since 1998, the suicide rate has remained rather high — more than 30,000 people per year, with an increase in 2003 when the number surpassed 34,000.

In 1971, Japan decided to follow the example of Great Britain and opened a hotline to receive calls from people in distress in Tokyo. Today, more than 7,000 psychologists work in 49 offices (called *inochi no denwa*, "life-saving telephone") providing assistance to people in dire straits. In 2006, they received more than 704,000 calls, of which more than 48,000 (about 7 percent) were calls from potential suicide victims.

Based on data provided by the World Health Organization (WHO), Japan has the 10th highest suicide rate in the world, with an average 25 suicides per 100,000 population per year (WHO, 2003). Among the leaders in these sad statistics are Lithuania, Russia, Belarus, Latvia, Ukraine, Sri Lanka, Slovenia, Estonia and Kazakhstan. Although the 10th position is not the worst, the Japanese are dissatisfied with the fact that all of the Western European countries, which Japan normally views as good examples, have suicide indexes that are much lower than Japan's. Among the G8 nations, Japan's suicide rate was second only to Russia's, a disappointing state of affairs for both countries.

Japan began to study the experience of Finland which has achieved the best results in reversing the high suicide rate. In 2002, the number of suicides in Finland dropped by 30 percent compared to 1990. The Japanese government set an official goal of bringing the country's suicide rate to 20 cases per 100,000 population by 2016.

Japan's statistics have some definite features and peculiarities that characterize the nation's suicide culture.

Suicide rates are the highest among the elderly despite the fact that Confucian principles advise that the elderly should be given the most care. On average, people over 54 opt for voluntary deaths twice as often as do younger people. The leaders in this age group are those over 75 years old, with an annual rate of 42 suicide cases per 100,000 population (the country's average index is 25 per 100,000 population). The leading cause behind voluntary deaths in this age group is serious disease, accounting for 45 percent of all cases.

This occurrence probably has many reasons, including some that are universal. Aging people usually do not have any illusions concerning human life. It is likely that the Japanese, who typically keep both feet on the ground and are not inclined to have their heads in the clouds, realize more clearly the severity of the final stages of life. In many Christian countries, the church plays a key role in comforting and reassuring those who are suffering from fatal conditions, providing support to those with incurable diseases, disabilities, suffering the deaths of loved ones, moral conflicts and dilemmas. Actually, this might be the church's main mission and Christian tradition encourages a dying person to see a priest.

Japanese religion, however, is more of a ritual rather than a deep devotion. When asked about the meaning of sutras recited before home altars, a Japanese man will usually answer: "I am not sure but I suppose they mean something good." They treat religion the way they treat therapists, appealing for help only when problems arrive and they pay no attention to them when everything is fine. Religious rituals help them overcome their current troubles and ease life stresses but in serious matters like life and death, they are of little help. According to polls, only about 20 percent of the Japanese have an earnest attitude toward religion (*Nihonjin no kachikan*, 2005). This is one-fifth of the adult population, although it should be considered that the survey reflects the subjective opinions of the people interviewed. The Japanese tradition of suicide upon the order of a superior shows the major role that people play in issues of life and death. While Christians seek advice from a God living in their hearts, the Japanese seek order from other people. Thus, it is not surprising that Japan actively advocates euthanasia, the practice of voluntarily ending the life of a person suffering from a terminal illness. Polls show that Japan takes third place, after the Netherlands and Denmark, in the number of euthanasia supporters (Takahashi, 2003). The Japanese parliament has already begun considering recommendations to legalize the practice.

Meanwhile, in the absence of legal regulations, Japanese doctors who are dealing with patients in critical condition have worked out their own practical ethics. These perfectly reflect national morals about a person's life and the inevitability of death, but are not in line with the Hippocratic Oath. A survey of 1,200 large Japanese hospitals revealed that almost one-third of them (31 percent) had chosen to stop providing life-support therapy for patients with incurable illnesses, or sometimes simply refused to treat them. In 40 percent of such cases, the fatal decision was taken without consultation and was based on the opinions of a couple of doctors. It can be assumed that the actual percentage is much larger since two-thirds of the surveyed hospitals did not consent to disclose such data (*Yomiuri*: 27 July 2008).

According to sociologists, the Japanese attitude toward death in general and to suicide in particular is influenced by traditional ethics that forbid behavior and actions that can cause difficulties for other people (Traphagan, 2004). For centuries, special Buddhist temples (*pokkuri-dera*) were provided for the elderly who came to pray for an easy and quick death. The natural and burden-free passing of an elderly person was considered the most comfortable option while suicide was believed to be "a dirty thing" and a special ritual had to be undertaken to cleanse the place after the incident. Like in many other cases, here one can observe the application of a basic principle of Japanese ethics that classifies all actions as either "for you" or "for others." The already-mentioned double suicide of lovers belongs to the first type and is therefore condemned. The suicide of an elderly person, although less desirable than a natural death, is more acceptable since the motivation of not burdening other people is clearly present in this type of voluntary death. This is why all ritual forms of suicide (*junshi, seppuku,* kamikaze) as actions committed "in the interests of other people" have their own names and are separated from an ordinary suicide in its Western understanding (*jisatsu*).

The highest suicide rate in the world, when analyzed by profession, is observed in the Japanese military. The Japan Self-Defense Forces, the country's alternative for a regular army, enlists about 236,000 people; therefore the absolute number of suicide cases might seem low — 78 cases in 2002. However, if calculated according to the WHO's method, this number exceeds the Japanese national average at 33 cases per 100,000 population. Without a scrupulous analysis of the causes, it can be assumed that samurai morals and traditions still greatly influence the behavior of Japanese military men.

In dead-end situations during the Pacific campaign of World War II, Japanese soldiers and officers often committed suicides en masse to the astonishment of the American troops. When confronted by the hopelessness of the situation, the Defense Commander of Saipan Island, Lieutenant General Yoshitsugu Saito, ordered the remaining able-bodied troops, about 3,000 men, to charge forward in the final, absolutely futile, attack. Behind the troops came the wounded soldiers who could move. Those who were not able to move were killed in order not to surrender to the American army. Many of the attacking Japanese soldiers did not even have arms. It was an act of mass suicide — they were moving forward in order to die on the battlefield. They reached their goal — all of the Japanese soldiers were killed in that attack. General Saito committed suicide in the traditional samurai way and his aide-de-camp helped him finish himself off.

There were also many other astounding episodes. Surrounded by the American troops, the Japanese soldiers dressed in clean clothes would line up and undermine themselves with grenades one after another. Before that suicidal act, they forced the civil population of the island, including women, children and the elderly, to commit suicide rather than surrender. Those who could not commit suicide themselves were killed by the troops. Some officers cut off their subordinates' heads and then killed themselves with samurai swords.

All these actions seemed to be medieval savagery to the American army but for the Japanese, they were acts of samurai honor intensified by imperial ideology and propaganda. The only difference was that, in the era of Tokugawa, people were ready to die for their shogun or warlord, while, in July of 1944, they died for the emperor. And likewise, the warrior who lost his battle could save his honor by the only possible way — to kill himself and his relatives. The international convention regulating treatment of prisoners of war was adopted in 1929, 15 years before the above-mentioned battle but could in no way influence deep-rooted ideas of the Japanese troops about battlefield behavior.

On 15 October 2007, a 52-year old police officer of Aichi Prefecture committed suicide. As it turned out, he was summoned to the administrative police inspectorate in connection with a complaint filed against him by a young woman who charged that the officer had made untoward advances toward her. The officer would have probably faced punishment or, at the most, dismissal from the police force but he chose another option.

Civilians in Japan quite often also commit suicide in response to traditional beliefs. They are most often office workers who commit suicide as a result of continuous stress at work. According to data provided by Japan's Ministry of Labor and Welfare, in 2006 there were 66 such cases, a 57 percent increase over the previous year. All of the victims worked hard for their companies and were stressed by their inability to cope with the extensive amount of work. Their inner feelings and motivation were hardly very different from those experienced by medieval warriors serving their lords.

Japan takes the first position in the world in the number of group suicides. An ordinary Japanese man spends the largest part of his life in a group, therefore it is not surprising that in a critical life-ending situation, he prefers to be part of a group. Until recently, the most widespread type of group suicide in Japan was jumping from a bridge, but today technological progress offers more options.

The wave of group suicides arranged on the Internet started in the second half of the 1990s. The Japanese, who worship both technological innovations and group behavior, immediately became leaders in Internet-arranged group suicides, and sites devoted to them are widely available and popular. Several strangers usually correspond with each other over the Internet and set the time, place and details of the planned action. Police regularly receive reports about parked cars with sleeping people inside, but find burned coal and several corpses at the scene.

The Japanese commit suicide in a thorough and careful manner after much preparation. In October 1998, seven Japanese men committed suicide by the above-described method of asphyxiation inside their vehicle. One of them called his friend on a mobile telephone in advance to tell him the approximate location of the car so that the police could easily find it. Many people planning to commit suicide leave notes for the police to avoid any unnecessary investigations. Usually such notes contain explanations for the suicide, requesting that the case not be considered a murder but a voluntary death. Later, relatives and friends may receive letters of apology that the person is deeply sorry to have upset his family by his suicide.

In 2005, a total of 34 cases involving 91 victims were registered. This was a three-fold jump compared to 2003, the first year for which such statistics are available. The government was forced to take measures and in 2005, a complex set of actions was devised to prevent the novel disaster from spreading. According to police reports, 14 people were rescued within the first few months of the program.

Japan features another type of group suicide that rarely occurs in other countries — family suicide (*ikka-shinju*). Reports about family suicides appear in the Japanese media with alarming frequency. The deadly decision is certainly taken by parents, those who have lost their way in life or are facing financial difficulties. Eighty percent of family suicides are suicides of mothers with children, and is common enough to have led to the creation of its own term: *oyako shinju*.

Today, the most popular place in Japan for committing suicide is the forest area of Aokigahara, which covers more than 3,500 hectares near the famous Mount Fuji. This area is one of the most popular suicide spots in the world and is reportedly ranked third after San Francisco's Golden Gate Bridge and Toronto's Bloor Street Viaduct. The main characters of a popular Japanese novel that was published in the late 1970s, a young man and his lover, committed a double suicide in Aokigahara and hundreds of imitators rushed to the area, turning the life of the locals into a nightmare as, in the 1990s, tens of unidentified bodies were discovered annually in the forest. Local authorities were forced to put up special boards reminding all those wishing to commit suicide about the value of human life and their duties toward their parents who granted that life to them.

The Japanese have a highly developed behavioral conformity that can take surprising forms. When a new novel or film featuring an original method of suicide appears, it immediately garners a crowd of followers. The Japanese like to copy the behavior of other people more so than people of other nations. Several years ago, the country experienced a tragic outbreak of hooligan actions when unknown villains put poisonous substances in foodstuff in the supermarkets. They injected toxic substances into cans of coffee, tea and other drinks and replaced the contaminated products onto the shelves. It was unclear who had initiated these indiscriminate actions and for what purpose as any shopper could become a potential victim. Nevertheless, the perpetrators began copying one another and the cases became more and more frequent. Police identified these actions as forms of showing off, hooliganism or a protest against society. Later, the authorities took some measures to limit the reporting of potentially risky examples in the media.

However, when a heinous crime occurs, it is impossible to avoid media attention and extensive coverage. On 8 June 2008 in the Akihabara District of Tokyo, seven people were killed and 10 injured as a result of a random stabbing rampage. In the following two months, police registered seven similarly violent scenarios, although with less grave consequences. On average, one random attack was carried out every six days which is unprecedented in Japan. In this way certain "set patterns" thrust their way, for good or for ill, into a society founded on unity and conformity.

One of the key principles of Japanese behavioral traditions is to avoid creating problems for other people, and society demands that this should be observed even in tragic suicide cases.

On 6 November 2007, a 38-year old railway employee, on his day off and planning to spend it in Tokyo, arrived in the Ikebukuro District. The day turned doubly tragic as a 25-year old woman attempted suicide by jumping out of a building — and fell onto the man and killed him. The sudden and unfair death of a young and healthy man came as a hard blow to his family, which, moreover, could not count on any financial compensation. According to Japanese laws, the guilty party in a person's death should pay financial compensation amounting to the victim's anticipated wages for the remainder of the latter's expected natural life. Having concluded their investigation, the police filed an appeal with the prosecutor's office which demanded fining the woman. However, the woman was mentally ill so the particulars of the case are vague, despite other cases on record where passers-by were killed or injured by people attempting suicide.

The increased number of suicides that cause injury or death to unrelated people forced the police to file charges against families whose members chose voluntary deaths. In recent years, the Japan Railways has introduced a rule allowing it to claim financial compensation from families whose members commit suicide by throwing themselves onto the rails, which results in traffic halts and the interruption of schedules. In 2008, nearly 2,000 people committed suicide by jumping in front of a train. The fines are especially high when involving a Bullet Train *Shinkansen* moving at a speed of 240 kilometers per hour. The measure may be harsh but it has the clear goal of making potential suicide victims think more about other people; if they do not care about strangers, maybe they will think about their loved ones who will suffer emotionally and financially.

Chapter 16

Body Language

Japanese-Style Movements

Over the centuries, the Japanese climate, diet and lifestyle, evidently different from those common to Europe, have affected characteristic features of the national body constitution and movements. Many aspects remain unexplored in this field; this is why I will attempt to examine only those facts that lie on the surface.

Anyone who has observed the Japanese in their everyday life cannot fail to notice some peculiarities of their movements. The first thing that catches the visitor's attention is the accuracy and speed of the Japanese's hand movements. The Japanese do not use hand gestures very often. Etiquette requires that proper speech communication uses no gestures. The Japanese use their hands exclusively for working, a task they perform skillfully. The Japanese art of paper folding (*origami*), widely recognized in many countries, requires much manual dexterity. Japanese children have numerous games and amusing exercises involving movements of their fingers or hands such as *kendama*, *otedama* and *sasebo goma*. When solving math problems or when reflecting upon something, many students and pupils habitually twirl a pencil or a pen through the outer side of their fingers. I have not seen children, or adults for that matter, of other nationalities mimic this movement. It is commonly known that packaging skills are considered an intricate art in Japan. These skills have their roots in the art of *furoshiki*, a decorative silk cloth, which the Japanese have used for ages for wrapping things of different shapes. Such wrapping was very convenient and visually pleasing for the transportation of items but it required much handiwork. Manual dexterity was also necessary when working with an abacus (*soroban*) or when tying an *obi* sash on a woman's kimono. Many Japanese have a passion for pachinko (slot machines), which also develops the nimbleness of their fingers. Some speculate that the hand muscles of the Japanese and all Asians are more accustomed to the intricate movements from writing Asian scripts.

When the Japanese perform back and forth motions, they apply their efforts in a way quite different from the European style. For example, a Japanese carpenter working with a single-handled saw or a plane applies force when pulling the instruments toward him while a European carpenter does it in the opposite direction. When canoeing, a European man will pull equally back and forth but apply force when drawing the paddles toward himself, lifting the paddles out of the water before the next stroke. The sailing of Japanese plank-built boats (*temmasen*) requires circular movements made by a single paddle and a sculler can apply force in both directions.

The Japanese consider the true value of movements to be in speed, precision and accuracy. The ideal movement must be automatic, repetitive and of a limited extent. According to the classic concept of *Do* (originally, a Buddhist way of mental training), the process of acquiring an absolute mastery in any field represents a lifetime's investment and always receives prime attention. This is why

Figure 16.1:   A Japanese carpenter.

Figure 16.2: Japanese plank-built boat, *temmasen.*

Japanese athletes, artists and craftsmen view the process of mastering their personal skills as an ultimate goal, which often happens to be more important than the achievement itself. It is believed that a true expert in any field can apply special techniques only if he has mastered them to absolute perfection; a failure to follow this postulate indicates mental immaturity (Kanayama, 1988).

Physical strength and an extended range of movements do not play an important role in Japanese culture compared with, for example, Western traditions. The Russian folk hero *bogatyr*, similar to the Greek Hercules and not very different from the American Paul Bunyan, is usually described in the following terms: "He moves his right arm and here is a street, he moves his left arm and there is a side street; he walks a horse with the left hand, and uproots oak trees with his right hand." Such descriptions demonstrate feats of great physical strength and a broad range of movement. Japanese sumo wrestlers have enormous physical strength but this does not guarantee a victory, although strength is obviously obligatory. The fascination for this sport is caused not by a demonstration of colossal physical power but by its combination of speed, coordination of movements and the outstanding ability of the sportsmen to control their emotions.

Heroes of Russian folk tales usually hit the ground with all their might to turn into animals or magical persons. "A frog slipped from the plate, hit the ground and turned into a beautiful lady." "*Burya-bogatyr* hit the ground, turned into a falcon and flew after her." The Japanese consider such body movements as excessively abrupt and rough. Heroes of Japanese tales also regularly turn into different animals but they do it in a modest and quiet way: they might cover their head with a leaf, recite a magic spell or do something completely inexplicable. Actually, in all East Asian tales, transformations into animals are performed in a graceful manner: heroes of Chinese tales drink magic mixtures, heroes of Vietnamese tales smell flowers and so on.

The speed and the accuracy of movements (especially of the upper, or "instrumental," body) have crucial importance for other national sports, including judo, archery, and kendo. Judo originated in the 19th century from the Japanese technique *jujutsu* (literally, "the art of flexibility"), which has its roots in the 15th century. Judo relies on the skillful application of your own maneuvers and the movements of your opponent, allowing you to defeat him without great strength. This type of martial arts requires good balancing skills, speed and accuracy; physical strength is not an essential factor.

According to the observations of Japanese anthropologists, the Japanese differ from Europeans in their postures and involuntary movements when they react to sudden and imminent danger. Yuji Aida noted that, in such situations, the Japanese take an absolutely defensive pose, turning their backs to the danger, squatting down, and shielding their heads with their arms. In similar situations, Europeans stand up straight and face the threat, sometimes even moving slightly forward to deal with the peril. If there is a child nearby, a European man will put the child behind his back and then strike a "battle-ready" pose while a Japanese man will embrace the child to shelter him with his body as if trying to become a single unity (Aida, 1970).

If this observation is true, then the actions of the European man reduce his own chances of survival but at the same time increase the chances of the child. By taking a defensive posture and embracing the child the Japanese man shares the child's fate. From here we can trace some common cross-cultural differences.

According to European traditions, saving the life of a child by using any available means is a top priority, and parents are expected to cast aside any thoughts of their own safety when rescuing a child. In Japan, a Confucian approach prevails and demands unity between the parents and their children. In the Middle Ages, this dogma, combined with the principle of group responsibility, was applied to the cruel practice of punishing all members of the family, including children, for the misdeeds of their parents. The punishment could even include the death penalty. Thus, if the parents were destined to die then it was considered right for the children to share their fate. Such attitudes were the basis of the Europeans calling the Japanese a cruel and barbaric nation. This example clearly illustrates a cross-cultural difference in attitudes toward the fate of the family and the individual. Today the Japanese group suicides of parents with children (*oyako shinju, ikka shinju*) echo this ancient tradition.

The defensive posture taken by the Japanese in dangerous situations reflects another important aspect of the Japanese view of life: they tend to adapt their inner feelings and reactions to an external situation without trying to change the situation in their favor. For ages, the Japanese have not sought to deal with the outside world or to change it actively to their advantage. They viewed the world as a given condition for their existence or as a certain reality that should be accepted without complaint. In the Meiji Era, such a world perception caused the spread of the practical philosophy of "existence in harmony with reality" (*genshosoku jitsuzairon*).

The spoken Japanese language is rich with words describing human conditions or senses that a man can experience only when in contact with the outside world (in the sense of external to his being). If a Japanese man is hit on his hand, he will most surely utter *itai* (it hurts). If he is pleasantly surprised by something, he will exclaim *ureshii* (I'm glad). If he is disappointed, he will say *kuyashii* (I'm vexed), and so on. Among these almost reflexive responses marking his emotional state, the most frequently used words are *abunai* (it's dangerous) and *kowai* (I'm scared). According to a purely subjective impression, there seems to be no other country in the world where people would so often and so eagerly admit that they feel fear or danger.

When my son went to a Japanese school for the first time, the school's deputy administrator immediately took responsibility for him. Foreign pupils were not numerous at that time and the administrator, a polite man with tired eyes and overloaded with duties, offered to teach the Japanese language to my son. As an educator, he wanted him to get acquainted with foreign culture as soon as possible. He volunteered to come to our home after classes to give lessons. When I offered to drive him from the school to our residence, he modestly but firmly rejected my proposal, saying that a school teacher should not receive such favors from a university professor. According to Japanese ethics, a superior person should not provide service to an inferior one. When asked about his plans to buy a car, he readily admitted to his fear of driving and to his concern for his two children. If he has an accident, his family will have no one to rely on. I was puzzled to hear that Japanese roads could be considered dangerous but did not say a word since the man was very firm in his opinion.

In the old days when the Japanese composed proverbs and sayings, they commonly used the word *kunshi*, which was borrowed from Chinese. *Kunshi* was used to refer to people of noble origin who were respectable, educated and wise. In short, all those people whom one can and should try to imitate. Japanese folklore has retained many sayings attributing different merits and virtues to these people. Prudence, cautiousness, self-control and similar qualities take central place in the image of the *kunshi*. The Japanese dictionary *Kojien* contains many proverbs and sayings praising these qualities: *kunshi wa ayauki ni chikayorazu* (a wise man should not approach danger); *kunshi wa santan wo saku* (a wise man should avoid three main risks [a wise man's pen, a samurai's sword and an advocate's speech]; *kunshi wa hitori wo tsutsushimu* (a wise man should be cautious even when he stays alone); and *kunshi wa hyohen su* (a wise man should change his opinion) (Shinmura, 1998).

Contemporary life in Japan often demonstrates quite well these enduring values.

On 3 May 2000 in the Japanese city of Fukuoka, a frantic 17-year old student armed with a kitchen knife rushed onto a passenger bus. After taking the bus hostage, he ordered the bus driver to head for Tokyo, some 1069 kilometers away. Within a few hours, they had covered about 300 kilometers, making several stops on their way. The young offender was very nervous and inflicted injuries, which were fortunately not serious, on several people. At the next stop, the police began negotiations, urging him to surrender. Many of the passengers jumped out of the windows, injuring themselves in the process. There were strong men among the passengers who could easily have restrained the hijacker but they all behaved according to a practical philosophy *genshosoku jitsuzairon* (existence in harmony with reality) and nobody blamed them for non-resistance. The Japanese police support the same principle and always urge citizens to keep away from suspicious-looking people and to avoid dangerous situations. In case of an emergency, it is recommended that one should leave the scene immediately and report the incident to the police.

This example is one of many illustrating the typical reaction of the Japanese toward danger. Such examples confirm the correctness of the observations made by Aida.

The ideals of well-considered and cautious action are common not only for the individual Japanese but for society as a whole, including the government. There are many examples demonstrating this fact. Each year, new medications are introduced throughout the world. Many of them are effective and safe for use, but Japan is always the last among the developed countries to accept them. The standard delay in the acceptance of new drugs is typically five or six years. The Japanese Ministry in charge of these issues usually takes this time to monitor the results of the mass use of new medications in the United States and Europe. Only in cases where no negative results have been revealed during this time period does the ministry approve a new drug for sale in Japan. Meanwhile, intelligent and well-informed Japanese patients are ready to cast prudence to the winds in order to get new medications not yet available in Japan. In recent years, they have found opportunities to purchase them over the Internet. I have many times been asked to help get various medication and quite often, my attempts were ruined by the unbreakable wall of Japanese norms and regulations. The purchase of medications that can be bought over the counter in Western countries is strictly controlled in Japan by the Ministry of Health, Labor and Welfare. All medical practitioners faithfully obey the instructions. You will not be able to find disposable syringes in Japanese drugstores nor will you find the most common drugs used for intramuscular injections. Such medications must not be given to patients even if the latter have prescriptions, and only medical personnel working in hospitals or clinics have access. The Japanese doctors are truly astonished when told that these are sold at drugstores in many countries.

The Japanese habit of avoiding danger and trouble by adapting themselves to the situation was apparently observed by Vasily Golovnin (2004), who got along with the Japanese rather well: "The Japanese...lack only one quality that we consider beneficial: I mean courage, bravery, audacity, which we sometimes call heroism."

Given that Golovnin's remarks were written at the beginning of the 19th century, we can partly agree with the statement about the absence of courage, especially among the common people. However, this apparently cannot be said about samurai warriors who for the most part followed the code of honor: "You must be sure that if you are to be killed in the battle, your corpse must face the enemy" (Yamamoto, 2004). Courage, bravery, defiance of danger and a fearlessness of death were cultivated for centuries in the samurai class, although it comprised only a small part of Japanese society. The major part of the population, consisting of peasants, craftsmen and townspeople, followed an entirely different lifestyle, one which obliged them to be dutiful and obedient.

Societies leading a sedentary lifestyle can develop their warrior and settlement skills through only two kinds of vital activities — hunting and cattle-breeding. Both require constant movement and an ability to adapt quickly to a new environment and to stand against unavoidable and sudden perils. It is necessary to battle neighboring settlers to win the best livestock and pasture land. The Japanese neither bred cattle nor hunted; they were, and always have been, agrarian people devoted to rice planting and to fishing. Both of these activities did not require individual artfulness and courage but instead, patience, diligence, compliance and cooperation with others. Therefore, these qualities were developed in the Japanese people over the centuries until the survival of the fittest became dominant in their character.

Looks and Appearances

The Japanese perception of the human body and its related physiological aspects at one time differed greatly from the European view. This is partly the result of racial differences and partly the result of cultural traditions and aesthetic tastes. Like all Oriental nations, the Japanese differ from Europeans and Americans in their height and body proportions. The Japanese typically have a long torso, flat buttocks and shortened limbs that often suffer from curved bones. At the beginning of the 20th century, A. Nikolaev gave the following description of Japanese body features:

"Wide head, long face and torso, short legs. Due to a low nasal bridge, the face does not have a prominent profile thus it looks wider than it is in reality. The forehead is usually low and the upper lip is very close to the nose. The eyes are always dark. They look cross-eyed but it depends on the eyelid's position. The legs are crooked, not graceful; especially the women's legs, but the arms and neck are extremely fine" (Nikolaev, 1905).

Japan was flooded by foreigners following its opening to the rest of the world in 1853. Western men did not miss a chance to compare the attractiveness of their girlfriends with the Japanese beauties. Lev Mechnikov wrote the following: "Sometimes it is possible to see a very attractive face in the crowd of young people, the features are very pleasant and the expression is even more beautiful; but on the whole, the Japanese body type is ugly, awkward, clumsy and has the distinctive feature of looking like a harsh caricature. It is difficult to see a Japanese woman in her 30s who would not look like an utterly unattractive old lady. Early marriages, as well as a habit of carrying babies on their back by tying them with special straps, damage the figures of the Japanese women and lead to frequent curving of the backbone. The widespread use of whitening makeup gives the skin a deadly, dingy look. Remarkably, the Japanese men tend to admire Western women more than their compatriot females. Those of them who had the chance to meet women of a Caucasian type later treat the best Japanese beauties with an incurable disregard" (Mechnikov, 1992). It is possible that Lev Mechnikov coincidentally mentioned the age of 30 years as crucial for the Japanese women, but in the Tokugawa Era, this age was believed to be the latest at which women could have babies. After 30, most women stopped sleeping with their husbands, their task of giving birth to the next generation having been accomplished.

After seeing Western models of female beauty, the Japanese started to feel a kind of inferiority complex for a rather long time. In a 1912 novel by Saneatsu Mushanokoji, *Seken shirazu* (*Babe in the Woods*), the author expressed his feelings through the words of his heroine: "I love paintings depicting Western women; the looks and figures of the Japanese women do not attract me." Once the two cultures met, the Japanese aesthetic views of female beauty formed by woodblock prints (*ukiyo-e*) yielded to traditional European concepts.

Until the 20th century, geisha and actresses were considered the most attractive women in Japan. The first beauty competition was held in Japan in 1908 in response to a request of the United States to send a Japanese participant to the World Beauty Contest. Geisha and actresses who professionally maintained their beauty did not participate in the contest and the title of Japan's Prime Beauty was won by Hiroko Suehiro, a student of *Gakushuin* Imperial Women's College. The Japanese had to wait for a beauty queen until 1959 when Akiko Kojima won the Miss Universe title. Their second victory did not come until May 2007 when Riyo Mori, a 20-year-old dancer from the Shizuoka Prefecture, was crowned the planet's prime beauty. The Japanese noted with satisfaction that the winner was born in Japan and national cosmetics companies could use this fact to promote their products, which until then were not very popular outside Japan.

Figure 16.3: Japanese women (from a 19th century photo).

Many Europeans who visited Japan in the 20th century noted the crooked legs of the Japanese people; its frequency could not be missed. The cause is still not determined, but it is possible that diet, lifestyle and traditional Japanese clothing all play a part. For a rather long period of time, an elegant gait was considered one of the attributes of female attractiveness in Japan. A woman had to mince along, with her feet turned inside. Such manner of walking indeed looks charming and very feminine when a woman wears a kimono. Perhaps this gait can be partly explained by the cut of the kimono: its skirt is narrow and allows only baby steps. Tiny steps move the body smoothly and gracefully while a kimono hides a not-very-elegant, according to European standards, foot posture.

Such a peculiar gait can also be explained by the specific character of the frequent habitual movements and postures of Japanese women. For example, sitting with the toes facing inward enables a classical and polite posture called *seiza*: on the knees, with legs tucked under thighs, and with a straight back. Until recently, women used to spend much of their time sitting in this posture, and it can often be seen today as well. Besides, this foot posture is useful for balancing when a person gets down on his knees from a standing position with his back being absolutely straight, as prescribed by Japanese etiquette. Japanese women had to perform such movements many times a day.

Gregory Vollan made a supposition that the Japanese women's practice of carrying their babies on their back was the cause of the trouble: "Many people say that this manner of carrying babies on the back is harmful both for those who carry and for those being carried, the latter have crooked legs as a result. The fact that the Japanese have crooked legs is indisputable, but whether it is caused by their sitting with tucked legs or by their habit of carrying babies in this special manner is not yet decided" (Vollan, 1906).

Whatever the case, this toe-in manner of walking is a fixed habit. Despite the fact that nowadays Japanese women spend much more time wearing European clothes rather than traditional kimonos, many of them still have an awkward gait. This is indirect evidence of the influence of traditional postures that are more frequently used in

Figure 16.4:   *Seiza,* a basic kneeling position.

everyday life than are kimonos, and is especially visible in provincial regions where foreign influences are not as strong and where traditions are kept more rigorously. In large cities, Japanese women are quick to adopt the external attributes of Western style and behavior.

In the Middle Ages, a woman's education was strictly controlled by her family and by society. Furthermore, this education was based on moral norms worked out by the warrior class. By the beginning of the 18th century, those norms formed a system that is still in play (at least to a degree) today. In 1716, a behavioral manual was published for women that later set a record for the number of reprints. The publication was called *Onna daigaku* (*The Greater Learning for Women*) and contained 19th main postulates for women's education. Rule number 2 said: "A woman should win hearts by the beauty of her soul, not by the beauty of her body." Although the instruction was addressed to ordinary women and not to professional entertainers of men working in special houses, such entertainers did not count only on their natural attractiveness. Many geisha spent years learning their craft in special schools to be able to satisfy not only the physical desires of men but also their spiritual needs. A woman's education in the fine arts, her ability to maintain appropriate conversation, to recite poetry and to play musical instruments were valued as much as was her physical beauty.

The Aesthetics of Nakedness

Historically, the Japanese attitude towards many aspects of a man's appearance also greatly differed from European traditions. Disparities are particularly obvious in the perception of nakedness. In European culture, undressing is allowed in two cases: when it is necessary to perform natural hygienic procedures or to attract the attention of the opposite sex. The first case addresses the demands of human existence. The second applies more to women, who are allowed to show some parts of the body if done so according to acceptable standards of the day. In European tradition, partial stripping remained an important element of erotic culture for a long time and was a publicly recognized sign of flirting. Today, people can undress in other situations, such as on the beach and after sports, but these activities were not common in the past. As recently as 100 years ago they were a novelty, so I will not take them into consideration here. The basic concepts of physical aesthetics had long been developed before the modern age.

In neither of the two cases did Japanese perceptions about nakedness coincide with European ideas. In the earliest days, the Japanese used to undress only for natural processes and for hygienic procedures. To excite the erotic feelings of another person by exposing one's body parts was out of the question. Foreigners visiting Japan in the second half of the 19th century immediately spotted this peculiarity of the relations between the sexes.

According to A. Nikolaev: "The Japanese have their own understanding of modesty. They consider nakedness of the body inappropriate in cases when it is used to affect the sensuality of another person. Japanese women blush with shame when they see a European lady in a revealing bare-necked dress" (Nikolaev, 1905).

According to Aime Humbert, the sensual indifference of the Japanese to the sight of a naked body is explained by "their lack of feeling for beautiful plasticity and that's why it does not influence their imagination, meanwhile our imagination is always in a state of excitement due to our fashion, manners and lifestyle" (Humbert, 1870). This fact led the Europeans to affirm that there was no erotic tradition in Japanese culture, just simple physiology.

Like all other aspects of Japanese life, intimate affairs were regulated and there existed special places where they could be, and should be, performed. Girls studying in geisha schools learned to entertain guests in different ways but "their main duty was to use their beauty and sultry show in order to stimulate desire in young men visiting the [tea] houses, for this purpose they often dance completely naked and make different movements, many of them far from decent, at the same time they all must remain virgins... [The Japanese] dances consist of grimacing and mimicking, their facial gestures are awful and most of their body movements are obscene" (Bartoshevsky, 1999).

However, geishas working in the pleasure quarter of Yoshiwara did not show either their body or their face to the guests. The body was clad from head to toe in a kimono, and only the neck remained open. The neck, especially its back, for a long time was considered a symbol of femininity as well as a woman's most erotic area. Not only did a kimono hide the body, but whitening makeup and blushes masked the face, the eyebrows were heavily made up and as a result, a woman's natural skin was unseen. Japanese men had only limited chances for a visual evaluation. Such women who chose the entertainment of men as their profession were well known for their wit and cleverness. It seems that these qualities were a key secret of their charm and success with men, and they indeed won the men's hearts through the beauty of their soul instead of the beauty of their bodies. Men of all cultures would agree that the beauty of the soul is best shown through elegant conversation.

Today, women working in the traditional Japanese recreational places (in hot-water spas and in traditional inns called *ryokan*) still maintain a special and absolutely open style of communication with their clients. The topics discussed are so frank that they can easily embarrass a European traveler not accustomed to the practice. Such conversations are not necessarily scandalous, but are usually based on

Figure 16.5: *Geisha.*

purely physiological matters that are not suitable for public discussion, not to mention with foreign strangers.

While visiting a Japanese hot spa, I once found myself in the midst of a good-humored discussion of the intimate parts of European men. The conversation was initiated by the women serving the dinner table. They thought it was inappropriate to serve the table and then leave the guests without entertaining them in conversation. The foreigners exchanged puzzled glances, obviously not knowing how to react to such provocative questions and remarks. Such talk is an echo of the innocent simplicity of relations common in Japanese public places in the old days.

Aime Humbert suggested seeing this as a manifestation of people's education "which permits both sexes to speak indifferently of everything without the slightest periphrasis, or any respect for persons, even children." Such excessive directness of speech is common for the Japanese of all classes; this is why it cannot be interpreted as loose conduct (Humbert, 1870). The Polish ethnographer Vaclav Seroshevsky made a similar judgment of these Japanese manners: "An unemotional looseness of behavior deeply penetrates Japanese habits and is considered by many people not as a defect, but more like a funny joke. Juicy conversations are a favorite topic for all classes of the society. Sultry pictures, books and statues are available to everybody, they are cheap and widespread, although it should be mentioned here that they do not contain a hundredth grain of the cynicism and refined lechery of the Chinese goods of the same purpose" (Nikolaev, 1905).

In more general terms, this is part of the Japanese natural perception of everything related to the human body and its functions. Japanese culture is without many of the taboos and restrictions that are common in European culture. This frankness comes as a shock to foreigners. The secretary of the American Embassy, A. Portman, in his letter to Heinrich Schliemann wrote that, in the Japanese capital alone, there were about 100,000 prostitutes. The vast majority of them were not professionals, but ordinary women, almost all of them married, who earned a living for their families in such a way. In the Tokugawa Period, husbands viewed their wives as partners in their family business — they had to give birth to the family's heirs and maintain the household. While geisha women were trained for sensual relations, wives were necessary to share household duties and responsibilities. This is why the attractiveness of wives was often used as a means of profit. For example, a man may have helped his neighbor by lending him some money without any interest or helped him purchase goods, or whatever. The neighbor would heartily thank the man who might artlessly utter: "Could you possibly lend me your wife for a while? She won't be any the worse for it." "Why not?" the neighbor thinks. "My neighbor is a good man, he often helps me out." According to Japanese historians, wives were often lent out in the past (Furukawa, 2008).

In wealthy samurai households, the process of giving birth to an heir was deliberately regulated by servants who had been specially taught. To prevent any unplanned accidents, the couple was watched and aided during the most intimate moments. The servants were present at all times to monitor the process and to do whatever was necessary to help the pair conceive an heir. In modern pornographic films, you will not see anything that was not the duty of those attentive and helpful women servants.

The first European men to visit Japan would have been even more surprised if they learned of the education of the samurai elite, but strangers were prohibited in the castles' interior rooms and their secrets were guarded thoroughly. Here we can refer to a "Secret instruction" (*Hiji sakuho*) composed by a woman in the middle of the 17th century that was addressed to the court ladies of an Edo castle. It described in full detail which actions to perform, and when and how each should be performed, with a young male heir to mold him into a sexually active and powerful master who could later produce numerous and healthy offspring. Like male instructors who physically exercised the boy to make him a strong warrior, specially educated court women performed age-old manipulations of his intimate parts to prepare him for the important mission of reproduction. The sequence and character of the manipulations, which were based on Chinese concepts about the interaction between male and female parts, were fully described. The specific actions prescribed depended on the boy's age, with different procedures for boys of nine, 10 and 13 years of age. Some actions were quite innocent and were of a more hygienic character, while other manipulations could be described in modern police reports as "sexual actions performed toward a minor in a perverted form."

Such perception of intimate affairs was a continuation of pedagogical traditions that are described in Chapter 9. According to these traditions, the mentality of any adult person almost always represents the educational efforts of his family and society; this is why these efforts should be on the fullest scale, and to be consistently and thoroughly planned. The sexual education of samurai nobility was planned to the smallest detail and accurately executed. Just as the contents of castle toilets were considered by Japanese sewage cleaners as a high quality fertilizer, the sperm of a future shogun was almost equal in esteem and thus had to be of the best quality. The quality had to be maintained from a very early age of the future heir. The related body parts had to be practiced and trained while the sperm itself was to be saved without any wastage. In the process of intimate training, court women were obliged to strictly follow these instructions to ensure that procreation occurred successfully after the wedding ceremony. The future noble samurai, in their childhood, had to withstand without complaint all of the manipulations performed by the court ladies and women servants.

The unrestrained attitude of the Japanese to all sexual pleasures remained dominant for many years and began to change only in the second half of the 19th century. Such an attitude, borrowed from China and based in Buddhist philosophy, was also held toward homosexual relationships.

Medieval Buddhist temples had their own secluded and closed world where life proceeded calmly and smoothly without changing for decades. According to Buddhist concepts about the original sinfulness of female nature, women were forbidden to enter this private world. Therefore, during years of living together, monks devoted all of their love and feelings to younger novices. In Buddhist temples, the culture of homosexual love prospered and flourished. Over the centuries, homosexual activity was part of the traditionally close

Figure 16.6: Preparing a future samurai for a male adult life.

relationships between mentors and disciples and was not considered a vice. The earliest record of such relations can be found in the mythological chronicles of the eighth century *Nihon Shoki* (*Annals of Japan*). In many Buddhist temples, the cult of young disciples was officially recognized. Young disciples were dressed in nice clothes, wore pretty haircuts and makeup and they often served as models for paintings and sculptures depicting the young Buddha. From the 12th to the 14th century many love stories were written describing homosexual relationships between masters and disciples (Takahashi, 1943). During internecine feuds, the practice also spread widely among warriors who spent much of their time in military campaigns. Revealing the social and moral norms of that time, Japanese poet Saikaku Ihara (1642–1693) wrote that "a young man without a senior lover is almost the same as a woman without a husband" (Yamamoto, 2000).

During peacetime in the Tokugawa Era the joys of homosexual love have their own place in the service industry. Soon enough, there appeared a professional class of male courtesans *(kagema)* aged from

12 to 16 years who serviced older men. In large cities such as Edo, Kyoto and Osaka, special teahouses were opened, the gay clubs of the Tokugawa Age. According to accounts, at the beginning of the 18th century there were 24 such teahouses in the capital alone. Representatives of all classes visited them but Buddhist monks were always the first among the regular visitors. The Buddhist monks had taken a vow of chastity, and although many representatives of the priesthood from time to time secretly visited pretty geisha in the red-light district of Yoshiwara, they still had to use a cover as doctors since the haircuts were the same for both professions; god's servants only had to change their dress. But such maneuvering was not necessary if they were visiting a teahouse for men. As for young male prostitutes, we can see here again how a traditionally professional approach to any business influenced their lives. When they ceased to satisfy men as young boys, they shifted to servicing noble ladies who had lost their husbands at war or simply those women who sought sexual joys outside of marriage.

Figure 16.7:   Male friendship.

Despite the further denouncement of homosexual love by European culture, modern Japan still has a very tolerant attitude as long as it is kept within appropriate contexts and does not extend beyond them. Non-traditional sexual preferences are not criminalized and gay clubs function quite legally and openly; this minority group never demands the special attention of society. Polls show that public opinion on the issue rests squarely in the middle of the range of world attitudes. If absolute approval and support of homosexual relations is to be given 10 points, then the index of approval in Japan is 4.5 (the 25th position in the world's list of countries). The highest value (index of 7.8) is held by the Netherlands (Takahashi, 2003).

Here it is necessary to mention another aspect of Japanese uniqueness. Europeans visiting Japan in the 19th century were sure that a naked body could stir emotions in any situation, while Japanese people believed that a human body had many other functions and could only be sensual if presented in the proper context at the appropriate time. They saw nothing exciting in other cases and did not feel any shame for it. Few Europeans could fail to notice this unusual Japanese habit and to point it out in their notes.

"In those cases when it is necessary to undress — for example, during certain activities or when bathing — the Japanese did not feel any shame... Even in such Europeanized cities as Nagasaki, Yokohama and Kobe, large round bowls for bathing are often placed in gardens, in full view of neighbors with whom they might keep talking while bathing or...in stores and the door is kept open for customers during this time" (Shreider, 1999). "Baths in Japan are mostly public everywhere; men bathe at the same time as women do" (Bartoshevsky, 1999). "Dresses serve for sheltering the body from the elements but not for covering the nakedness of the body since the Japanese find nothing shameful in walking around stark naked... In Japanese provincial bathrooms, young women serve the customers. Such women, without shyness, enter a bathroom where you are bathing and offer their services to help you dry with a towel when you are leaving the bathtub" (Pozdneev, 1925).

According to Japanese historians, it never occurred to the Tokugawa shoguns to be ashamed of their nakedness in the presence

Figure 16.8:   A family bathing in the garden.

of those serving them. For a long time, they might quietly remain naked in front of women servants while changing clothes or taking baths (Furukawa, 2008).

In the 18th century, the mail was delivered by couriers who would run a given distance and transfer a sack of mail to the next courier, like a baton. Europeans recalled that besides wearing a loincloth, such couriers only had red and blue tattoos which covered most parts of their bodies, thus hiding their nakedness in a small way. Until the second half of the 19th century, the Japanese bathed in public baths and walked home absolutely naked if the weather was favorable. "Baths in Japan perform the same function as they did in ancient Rome. The Japanese spend hours in public baths and children, the elderly, women and young men all enjoy bathing together. They all sing, talk and scream in different voices... I often happened to see how the Japanese would jump out of hot baths stark naked and red as a beet and run along the street, obviously not afraid of catching a cold" (Vollan, 1906).

Figure 16.9: Mail courier of the Tokugawa age.

If there was no shame in running home naked after a bath, then what can be said of sumo wrestlers, who wear only a loincloth of such a size that cannot be further reduced? In combination with the constitution of these giant sportsmen who have an excessively high fat content, this traditional clothing stirs mixed reactions among foreigners of both sexes who observe the competitions for the first time even today.

The relaxed attitude toward nakedness has a long history and is connected with the communal mode of Japanese life in the old days. In rural areas, the communes united five households (*goningumi*) while in cities, ten households (*juningumi*) were so joined. As mentioned above, discipline and social responsibilities were shared within these groups. Under such conditions, it was simply impossible to shield your life entirely from your neighbors or to live separately and independently. Russian travelers almost immediately noted: "A Japanese man lives an outside life: he works, bathes and dresses in public. Even special private rooms and unpleasantly smelling boxes are not hidden in the backyards as in Russia but look directly out to the street" (Vollan, 1906). Under such conditions, literally only one

Figure 16.10:   *Sumo*: The starting position (*shikiri*).

step separates people from complete but ethically safe integration into a clothing-free community. How is it possible not to make this step when hot water springs have been boiling across the country for thousands of years and where regular supplies of water and wood are too expensive for bathing?

In spite of their surprise at the overall nakedness around them, analytically minded Europeans have arrived at a favorable conclusion of the Japanese: "However strange these manners might seem to us, it is undeniable that not a single Japanese man had the slightest idea that they might be condemned until Europeans arrived in the country. Entering public baths, European people, with their gazing and giggling, tainted as indecent those matters that had not been considered offensive in anybody's eyes before" (Humbert, 1870). "A Japanese man views a naked body with entirely different eyes from a European man, to whom nudity is a forbidden fruit. A Japanese man...indifferently passes by bathing...women and he does not develop any frivolous ideas in his mind... Women do not feel any shame when they breastfeed their babies in theaters, attend public baths and in general they are not embarrassed by their nakedness" (Vollan, 1906).

The anxious attitude of European men toward nakedness and sensual pleasures is certainly explained by the Christian religion. For centuries, it named the human body as a source of sinful thoughts that should be avoided and sinful desires that should be suppressed. In the Middle Ages, when Japanese men and women bathed in common bathrooms, Christian morality forbade European men to see even their wives undressing. Today, more liberal Western customs have triumphed over religious dogmas and Europeans can display sarcasm toward Islamic canons that forbid women from "bathing in the same sea together with men." Not long ago, however, had the Japanese not been so respectful toward Europeans, they would have laughed in a similar manner at the European's puritanical approach.

The Japanese had other reasons as well as etiquette in their attitude toward delicate matters. Once having learned from French guests about the use of the finest silk handkerchiefs, the Japanese ladies noted immediately that "not a single woman, even a very common one, will take in her hands and put into her pocket a piece of cloth that she has used for wiping her nose" (Humbert, 1870; Vollan, 1906). Unlike Europeans, the Japanese started to use paper tissues ages ago. Lev Mechnikov once wrote that if the Japanese "have to take over many things from Europe, then Europe, in her turn, has many things to learn from Japan concerning cultural and liberal issues" (Mechnikov, 1992).

The peculiarity of Japanese etiquette is largely defined by the prolonged isolation of the country. As Nikolai Bartoshevsky noted: "Every little thing tells you that the people here followed a route that was completely different from ours, and that history led them and us to entirely different results" (Bartoshevsky, 1999). The differences have lessened with time but many of them remain and influence our comprehension of Japanese culture. For example, one Japanese etiquette rule requires that a person should not walk with his mouth stuffed with food; in fact, one must not eat, drink or smoke while walking. You are allowed to do all of these things when you sit or at least are standing still. However, this restrictive rule is not followed in other countries. In Canada, people walk along the sideways carrying large mugs of coffee and drinking it in the street. Almost everywhere in the world it is believed that one should eat very quietly, without making noise in order not to spoil the appetite of other

Figure 16.11:   Naked riksha-pullers.

people. In Japan, one can chomp, smack, noisily slurp noodles and even belch after having a good dinner since this is not considered ill-mannered. As has been mentioned, the Japanese had a more relaxed attitude toward natural physiological processes. Such an attitude led Europeans to accuse the Japanese of a lack of refinement.

Since the Europeans had developed many advanced and useful things, the Japanese did not remonstrate with them. Together with useful knowledge, they also acquired European etiquette, including the habit of being ashamed of nakedness. Today, the joint bathing of men and women is absolutely out of the question, and only in a few traditional mineral water spas is common bathing seen. People do not wash themselves at such baths but go there to improve their health. There are not many such places left in Japan; the existing ones are well known and very popular. This is so partly due to the healing proper-ties of the water, partly due to age-old traditions and partly due to the novelty as where else in modern Japan can one publicly and legally get naked?

Having once adopted a restrictive attitude toward nakedness, the Japanese, as they often did, implemented the principle to its utmost. At the end of the 19th century, British ladies and gentlemen were regularly shocked by meeting half-naked and often completely naked natives in the most inappropriate places. The government took firm and irrevocable steps to introduce European civil manners to the Japanese people. The police started to patrol the streets in an effort to identify inappropriately dressed women, workers, rickshaw cab drivers and other commoners. Joint baths were banned and the adoption of separate bathrooms was strictly controlled.

One hundred years later, the Japanese have changed completely. In addition to the reasons described in Chapter 8, the Japanese do not enjoy either bathing in the sea or sunbathing because they do not like to expose themselves to the sun; in fact, they protect themselves from it by using umbrellas, hats and elbow-length gloves. The perennial Russian dream, "if only summer would come soon so I could rush to the sea" is unlikely to be shared by the Japanese. The sea is everywhere and within 100 kilometers from any place in Japan, within reach in two hours from even the most remote places.

However, Japanese young people follow fashion and fill Japan's beaches in August, striving for bronze skin. Bathing suits are usually one-piece and you will see no men in Speedos. Here everything is done according to American beach fashion with parrot-bright boxer-short style bathing suits that reach to the knees.

There are no strict rules regarding shorts but rules regulating clothing on the upper body are quite severe. A man must not display his bare chest unless he is within 100 meters of a beach. The rules are not broken even if he plays football or works under the scorching sun. In extreme heat, the Japanese take with them several tee shirts and change them very quickly. Suntan-hungry Russian male visitors in such weather act as they habitually do in their own country by stripping to the waist and walking around the city enjoying Japanese scenery and soaking in the ultraviolet rays. The Japanese nervously cast side-long glances at them.

The cause of such an extreme modern clothing code is quite simple: it is the Japanese adherence to accepted rules of behavior taken to the hilt. One of the rules says that the form of clothing should be appropriate for the place and time of activity. Even the slightest deviation results in sharp criticism.

The governmental campaign called Cool Biz (Chapter 8), which aims to reduce carbon emissions, has caused some unplanned difficulties.

Having taken off their jackets and ties in the hot summer, Japanese employees were able to increase the temperature of their offices to 28 degrees celsius. Soon one of the female employees working for a Tokyo-based company filed a protest: male workers sweat so heavily that their white shirts stick to their bodies, inappropriately showing the shapes of their torsos. She felt terribly uncomfortable in trying to avoid looking at these men. Since every deviation from accepted norms should be filed and recorded, she claimed that this case violated her right to a sexually comfortable environment, the Japanese equivalent of American sexual harassment. The Japanese managers agreed that this was not a pleasant working environment, but added that they had similar complaints regarding the women in offices. In extremely hot weather, female employees may wear open blouses, wear laces on these blouses resembling underwear or even go without stockings. In short, summer heat breaks all of the rules. Business consultant Chiyoko Anju finally voiced the public verdict: "Wearing clothes that expose skin or casual attire creates an image of a selfish person who's brash or showy" (*Yomiuri:* 4 August, 2008).

In short, when looking at modern Japan, it is very difficult to believe that their great-grandmothers and even their grandmothers 100 years ago "without any shame took baths...in...the presence of unknown men and bathed in the sea" (Nikolaev, 1905), "breastfed babies in public and, while working, did not cover their breasts, wearing only skirts" (Vollan, 1906) and did other things that are absolutely unthinkable today.

The only people reminiscent of the old times are Japanese schoolgirls. It seems that they are secretly competing to wear the shortest skirt possible. This fierce competition attracted the attention of one Japanese magazine whose reporters decided to measure the remaining length of schoolgirls' uniforms and crown the champions of Southwestern Japan. The competition was confidently won by schoolgirls of the Kyoto administrative district with an average skirt length of 16.7 centimeters above the knee.

In all other spheres, however, attitudes concerning clothing style are becoming stricter. Such a rapid 180-degree turn in manners and habits once again demonstrates how effectively the Japanese government

Figure 16.12: Japanese schoolgirls.

has worked with the education of the population and how quickly people's tastes and preferences can be changed. Once the Japanese government has set a goal, it applies all of its resources to achieve it. In its turn, the population, which is used to control and guidance, shows an unbelievably high receptivity. As a result, the idea or political course announced by the government soon enough, as Vladimir Lenin put it, "spreads among the masses and becomes a real force." It is also one of many Japanese "miracles."

One more change in Japanese public opinion in the 20th century is worth mentioning here. It proves the same facts: effective government work with the population and the population's willing reaction. In this case, however, the government has nothing to be happy about.

This concerns the readiness of modern Japanese men to protect their country and risk their lives for its sake. It is known that until 1945, most Japanese thought that sacrificing their lives for the motherland and for the emperor was the sacred duty and the great honor of every citizen. Detachments of kamikaze pilots, Japan's suicidal attack force, were not formed simply by all of the patriots wishing to give their lives for their country but only by the creme de la creme. When the war concluded, militarism was proclaimed as evil and a new peaceful and democratic future was set as the goal. The mechanism for ideological education was fueled again but this time in the "right direction." According to polls, the Japanese people, so patriotic not so long ago, are not ready today to stand up for their country in cases of armed conflict. As of 2001, in the case of war, only one in six men said that he would voluntarily defend the country (16 percent), while one out of every two (47 percent) said that he would not. Japan came in last among 59 countries participating in the poll. For comparison, the average world index of patriotic feelings was four times higher than the Japanese (68 percent versus 16 percent) (Takahashi, 2003).

Afterword

It is usually more interesting to write an afterword than it is to read it, so I will try to make it short.

Writing about cultural issues and the lifestyles of other nations is tricky as there is always a risk of criticism and subjectivity. It is a universal truth that every bird likes its own nest and every person naturally believes that his own nation is the best. Foreign lifestyles and habits often seem bizarre and occasionally annoying. All human beings have the same tribal psychology. This is reflected in war movies as one's own country men are displayed at their best and most righteous.

Proof of this can be found in contemporary publications and research literature as well. Almost everything that is written in Japan about Russia and the Soviet Union, with the exception of classical literature and the arts, is determinedly critical. Friendliness and goodwill toward the discovery of the worldview of another nation are indeed rare. At the same time, Japanese authors eagerly write in much detail about their national culture and traditions as being remarkably exceptional. This tendency is reciprocated in the attitude of the West toward Japan. I have found the overwhelmingly critical perception of the Japanese lifestyle and way of thinking puzzling. Almost every facet of Japanese life that does not correspond with Western norms becomes the subject of criticism in the English-speaking media. A few aspects receive initially modest praise from Western commentators only to be followed by more criticism.

The same situation is true of Russia. It is not easy to find a kind word about this country in the English-speaking press, except among a few thoughtful researchers. The Russian press suffers the same bias to some extent but in the Russia-West-Japan triangle, it occupies the least hostile position. As far as it concerns Japan, Russia's attitude is more than friendly.

Such an attitude can possibly be explained by two factors. The first concerns World War II, which is still quite memorable for the Russians. The end of the war with Japan in 1945 came comparatively easily for Russia and was less costly in terms of men and materials than did the war with Germany. The second reason can be found during the Cold War when the media of the two countries reported much prejudiced information, planting deep hostility between them but with different results. In the USSR, less than half of the population believed the media reports while in Japan, the percentage of trust, as always, was much higher. The territorial dispute over the four islands seized by the USSR in the closing days of the war and later claimed by Japan has remained a thorny issue for several decades. According to the latest polls, three-quarter of Russians regard Japan with sympathy while the same majority of the Japanese dislike Russia.

It is not easy to suppress one's personal opinions when writing about a foreign country. In analyzing the Japanese reality, I have tried to avoid excessively categorical and unproven judgments and assessments based on my personal likes and dislikes. There are plenty of such books about Japan and only a few of them can be considered to be informative. As a rule, these books tell more about their authors and their experiences than about Japan.

A certain degree of subjectivity would probably be found in this volume as well. This book contains only those issues that have drawn my interest, touched my heart in some way and remained in my mind. My vision of Japanese life and culture is presented in the form of short essays. And the part of the Japanese world that lies beyond is surely larger than the one described here. Therefore, there is much left for other writers to explore.

References

English

Ames, W. (1981). *Police and Community in Japan*. Berkeley: University of California Press.

Aston, W. (1871). *A Short Grammar of the Japanese Spoken Language*. Belfast : F.D. Finlay.

Beals, G. (2001). Recession rags: Japan's young new designers are creating functional clothes with conscience. *Newsweek* (9 July 2001).

Benedict, R. (1994). *The Chrysanthemum and the Sword: Patterns of Japanese Culture*. Boston: Tuttle Co.

Bower, B. (2004). Beg your indulgence. *Science News* 165 (26 June 2004).

Chamberlain, B. (1886). *A Simplified Grammar of the Japanese Language*. London: Trübner. Yokohama: Kelly and Walsh.

Conduitt, A. and Conduitt, A. (1996). *Educating Andy*. Tokyo: Kodansha.

Diamond, J. (2005). *Guns, Germs, and Steel: The Fates of Human Societies*. New York: W.W. Norton.

Foote, D. (1991). Confessions and the Right to Silence in Japan. In *Georgia Journal of International and Comparative Law* 21.

Haberman, C. (1988). In Japan, Visitors Will Be a Little Less Alien. *New York Times*, (21 February 1988).

Haley, J. (1989). Confession, repentance and absolution. In *Mediation and Criminal Justice: Victims, Offenders and Community*, M. Wright and B. Galaway (eds.). London: Sage Publications.

Hasegawa, N. (1965). *The Japanese Character. A Cultural Profile*. Translated by J. Bester. New York: Greenwood Press.

Hoffman, J. (1876). *A Japanese Grammar*. Leiden: E. J. Britt.

International Labour Organization (1993). *World Labor Report* 1324.

Johnson, D. (2003). Above the Law? Police Integrity in Japan. *Social Science Japan Journal* 6.

Jones, C. (2006). Grim bar system may hurt legal reforms. *The Japan Times* (9 May 2006).

Kajihara, K. (1997). The student's impression which is expected by an enterprise. *Management Consulting Journal*, 44, 100–103.

Kakuchi, S. (2006). Japan: Crimes of the father leave children forever ostracized. *Global Information Network* (12 April 2006) New York: Global Information Network.

Kawashima, T. (1967). The status of the individual in the notion of law, right and social order in Japan. In *The Japanese Mind*, C. A. Moore (ed.) Tuttle Co.

Kishimoto, H. (1967). Some Japanese cultural traits and religions. In *The Japanese Mind*, C. A. Moore, (ed.) Tuttle Co.

Kitamura, K. (2006). For curious Japanese, nibbles of foreign cultures. *New York Times* (30 July 2006).

March, R. (1996). *Reading the Japanese Mind*. Tokyo: Kodansha.

McVeigh, B. (2002). *Japanese Higher Education as Myth*. New York: M. E. Sharpe Co.

Miller, R. A. (1982). *Japan's Modern Myth. The Language and Beyond*. New York-Tokyo: Weatherhill.

MIPRO (1980). *Generating the Japanese Market*. Tokyo: Manufactured Imports Promotion Organization.

Miyano, M. (2000). *Japanese Perception of Social Justice: How Do They Figure Out What Ought To Be?* Faculty of Literature, Chuo University.

Nakamura, H. (1967). Basic features of legal, political and economic thought in Japan. In *The Japanese Mind*, C. A. Moore (ed.), 143–163 Tuttle Co.

Nakamura, H. (1967). Consciousness of the individual and the universal among the Japanese. In *The Japanese Mind*, C. A. Moore. (ed.), 179–200 Tuttle Co.

Nakamura, H. (1960). *The Way of Thinking of the Eastern People*. New York: Greenwood Press.

Nguyen, D., Yanagawa, Y. and Miyazaki, S. (2005). University education and employment in Japan. *Quality Assurance in Education*, 13, 202–218.

Ohnishi, N. (2007). Pressed by police, even the innocent confess in Japan. *New York Times* (11 May 2007).

Organization for Economic Cooperation and Development (2005). *Health Statistics*.

Reischauer, E. (1977). *The Japanese*. Cambridge, MA: Harvard University Press.

Rice, J. (2004). *Behind the Japanese Mask: How to Understand the Japanese Culture — and Work Successfully with It*. Oxford: How To Books.

Roberts, A. and LaFree, G. (2004). Explaining Japan's postwar violent crime trends. *Criminology* 42, 179–210.

Teichler, U. (1997). Higher education in Japan: A view from the outside. *Higher Education*, 34, 275–298.

Terada, Shin'íchi. Japan urged to be creative to stay competitive. *Japan Times* (16 August 2008).

The Australian (25 October 2007).

The Economist 382 (10 February 2007). p. 65.

The Japan Times (30 June 2009).

The Seattle Times (18 November 2007).

Thornton, E. (1993). Japan's struggle to be creative. *Fortune* 127, Issue 8.

Traphagan, J. (2004). Interpretations of elder suicide, stress and dependency among rural Japanese. *Ethnology* 43, Issue 4.

Tsuchimoto, T. (2000). Light and shadow in Japan's police system. *Japan Quarterly* 47, Issue 2, 41–49.

Vogel, E. (1979). *Japan as Number One: Lessons for Americans*. Cambridge: Harvard University Press.

Walmsley, R. (2007). *World Prison Population List* (7th ed.). King's College, London: International Centre for Prison Studies.

Wehrfritz, G. and Takayama, H. (2000). Japan's old-style police force is failing to curb a rise in violent crime. *Newsweek* (21 February 2000).

Winston, K. (2003). On the ethics of exporting ethics: The right to silence in Japan and the U.S. *Criminal Justice Ethics* 22.

World Health Organization (2005). *Data and Statistics*.

World Health Organization (2003) *Suicide Rates by Country, Year and Gender (as of May 2003)*.

Yukawa, H. (1967). Modern trends in Western civilization and cultural peculiarities in Japan. In *The Japanese Mind* C. A. Moore (ed.). Tuttle Co.

Japanese

Aida, Y. (1970). Nihonjin no ishiki kozo. Fudo, rekishi, shakai. Kodansha.

Asahi Shimbun (15 May 2003).

———— (25 July 2008).

Devits, L. and Devits, D. (1996). *Nihonjin no raifu sutairu.* Translated by T. Sengoku. Sumairu shuppan.

Doi, T. (2001a). *Amae no kozo.* Kobundo.

Doi, T. (2001b). *Zoku. Amae no kozo.* Kobundo.

DSKK (2006). *Mottomo yukona nito taisaku wa jakunen koyo no misumachi kaisho.* Daiichi seikei keizai kenkyujo.

Ebisawa, A. and Ouchi, S. (1980). *Nihon kirisutokyoshi.* Nihon kitoku kyodan syuppankyoku.

Furukawa, A. (2008). *Edo no rekishi wa taisho jidai ni nejimagerareta.* Kodansha plus Alfa shinsho.

Gendai nihonjin no ishiki kozo (2004). NHK hoso bunka kenkyujo. NHK books,.

Haga, Y. (1979). *Nihonjin no hyogen shinri.* Chuo koronsha.

Hamaguchi, E. and Kumon, S. (1989). *Nihonteki shudanshugi.* Kakuhaiyu.

Hirota, M. (1994). Minshu no kokoro. *Nihon no kinsei.* Chuo koronsha.

Immigration Bureau of Japan (2007). *Information Bulletin Board.*

Inoue, T. (1977). *Sekentei no kozo.* NHK books.

Ishikawa, M. and Naoe, H. (1978). *Bushi no ko, shomin no ko,* p.1. *Nihon kodomo no rekishi,* v. 4. Daiichi hoki.

Iwate Nippo. (13 April 2006).

Japan Student Services Organization. (2008). *Ryugakusei koryu kenkyukai kaigi.* Dokuritsu gyosei hojin Nihon gakusei shien kiko.

Kanayama, N. (1988). *Hikaku seikatsu bunka jiten.* Daishukan shoten.

Kanji, N. (1982). *Nihon no kyoiku, doitsu no kyoiku.* Shincho sensho.

Katayama, S. (1974). *Kyoiku chokugo. Shiryo.* Koryosha shoten.

Kawakami, M. (1989). *Nihon ni daigaku rashii daigaku wa aru no ka?* Kyoritsu shuppan.

Kawasaki, T. (1999). *Rosia no yumoa. Seiji to seikatsu o waratta sambyakunen.* Kodansha.

Koseisho (2008). *Labor Statistics.* Ministry of Health, Labor and Welfare. Statistics and Information Department.

Lévi-Strauss, C. (1976). *Yasei no shiko.* Translated by A. Ohhashi. Misuzu shobo.

Levine, R. (2002). *Anata wa dono gurai matemasu ka?* Soshisha.

Maruyama, Y. (1992). Joho to kotsu. *Nihon no kinsei 6.* Chuo koronsha.

Minami, H. (1994). *Nihonjinron. Meiji kara kyo made.* Iwanami shoten.

Mito, Y. (2001). *Teikoku hassha. Nihon no tetsudo wa naze sekai de mottomo seikaku na no ka.* Shincho bunko.

Miyamoto, M. (1994). Zainichi nihonjin. *The Japan Times.*

Momo, H. (1983). *Jodai gakusei no kenkyu.* Yoshikawa kobunkan.

Mori, S. (1999). *Nihonjin ni totte kagaku to wa nani ka.* Hokuto print.

Mori, S. (2005). *Nihon wa naze isakai no oi kuni ni natta no ka.* Chuo koron shinsha.

Muraoka, M. (2006). *Bijinesuman kotoba no mana.* Sogensha.

Nihon Tokei Nenkan (2003). *Japan Statistical Yearbook.* Statistics Bureau, Director-General for Policy Planning & Statistical Research and Training Institute.

Nakane, C. (2000). *Tateshakai no ningen kankei.* Kodansha.

Nihon Keizai Shimbun. (30, June 2001).

Nihonjin no kachikan (1970). Nihon chiiki kaihatsu sentahen. Shiseido.

Nihonjin no katikan henka (2005). Dentsu soken.

Nishide, H. (2006). *Oshigoto no mana to kotsu.* Rurashi no ehon. Gakken.

Noiman, K. (2001). *Iketenai nihon Nihonjin no honto no tokoro.* Intermedia syuppan.

Sekai nijusankakoku kacikan deta bukku. (1999). Dentsu soken, Yoka kaihatsu senta. Doyukan.

Shiba, R. and Kin, D. (1972). *Nihonjin to nihon bunka.* Chuo shinsho.

Shibata, M. (1986). *Ho no tatemae to honne.* Yuhikaku.

Shinmura, I. (1984). *Kojien.* Iwanami shoten.

Somusho (2006). Statistics Bureau, Director-General for Policy Planning (Statistical Standards) and Statistical Research and Training Institute.

Sugimoto, Y. and Mouer, R. (1982). *Nihonjin wa nihonteki ka: tokushuron wo koe, tagenteki bunseki e.* Toyo keizai.

Takagi, T. (1996). *Ayamaranai amerikajin, sugu ayamaru nihonjin.* Soshisha.

Takahashi, T. (1943). *Kinsei gakko kyoiku no genryu.* Nihon syuppan haikyu.

Takahashi, T. (2003). *Nihonjin no kachikan. Sekai rankingu.* Chuo koron shinsha.

Takeuchi, Y. (2000). *Nihonjin rashisa to wa nani ka.* PHP bunko.

Tokieda, M. (1978). *Nihon bumpo. Kogohen.* Iwanami zensho.

Tsunoda, T. (1986). *Nihonjin no no.* Daishukan shoten.

Umesao, T. and Kato, H. (1993). *Nihonjin no kokoro. Bunka miraigaku e no kokoromi.* Asahi shinbunsha.

World Health Organization (2005). *Data and Statistics.*

Yasusada, H. (1934). *Nihon shukyoshi.* San'yo shoin.

Yomiuri Shimbun. (21 March 2004–15 July 2009).

Russian

Alpatov, V. (2003). *Yaponiya: yazyk i obshchestvo.* Moscow: Muravei.

Alpatov, V. and Vardul', I. (1983). *Yazykoznanie v Yaponii.* Moscow: Raduga.

Anarina, N. (1984). *Yaponskii teatr No.* Moscow.: Nauka.

Bartoshevsky, N. (1999). Yaponiya (ocherki zapisok puteshestvennika vokrug sveta). In: *Kniga yaponskih obyknovenii.* Edited by A. Meshcheryakov. Moscow: Natalis press. 348–358.

Benedict, R. (2004). *Chrizantema i mech. Modeli yaponskoi kultury.* Moscow: Rosspen, 2004.

Bernstein, N. (1905). *Muzika i teatr u yapontsev.* Sankt-Peterburg.

Bogdanovich, T. (2002). Ocherki iz proshlogo i nastoyashchego Yaponii. *Istoriya Yaponii.* Moscow: Monolit-Evrolints – Traditsiya. 59–145.

Chanoyu (2008). Internet site http://www.chanoyu.ru/center.

Daidoji, Y. (2000). Budo shoshinshu. In: Kniga samuraya. St. Petersburg: Evraziya, 14–72.

Dybovsky, A. (2007). Ritual i igra. O nekotorykh osobennostyakh rechevoi kommunikatsii v yaponskom i russkom yazykovukh kollectivakh. http:// russia-japan.nm.ru.

Frederic, L. (2007). Povsednevnaya zhizn' Yaponii v epokhu Meiji. Translated by A. Ovezova. Moskow: Molodaya gvardiya.

Golovnin, V. (2004). Zapiski o priklyucheniyakh v plenu u yapontsev. Moscow: Zahkharov.

Hashimoto, S. (1983). Voprosy izucheniya rodnogo yazyka. In: Yazykoznanie v Yaponii. Edited by V. Alpatov and I. Vardul'. Moskow: Raduga. 42–59.

Hesse-Wartegg, E. (1904). Yaponiya i yapontsy. Zhizn, nravy i obychai sovremennoi Yaponii. S.-Peterburg: Izdatel'stvo A. Devriena.

Humbert, A. (1870). Zhivopisnaya Yaponiya. S.-Peterburg: Obshchestvennya pol'za.

Kawabata, Y. (1985). Otrazhonnaya Luna. Moscow: Raduga.

Mazellier, A. (1913). Ocherk sem'i v Yaponii. Translated by A. Zhuravsky. In: Vestnik Azii, No. 13. Harbin.

Mazurik, V. (2003). Chainaya chashka i eyo funktsiya v yaponskom chainom deistve. In: Veshch v yaponskoi kul'ture. Moskow: Vostochnaya literatura.

Mechnikov, L. (1992). Yaponiya na perelome. Vladivostok: Far-Eastern University Press.

Meshcheryakov, A. and Grachov, M. (2002). Istoriya drevnei Yaponii. S. Peterburg: Giperion.

Meshcheryakov, A. (1999). Kniga yaponskikh obyknoveniy. Moskow: Natalis Press.

Meshcheryakov, A. (2004). Kniga yaponskikh simvolov, Moskow: Natalis Press.

Nihon Shoki (1997). v. 2. Translated by L. Ermakova and A. Meshcheryakov. S. Peterburg: Giperion.

Nikolaev, A. (1905). Ocherki po istorii yaponskogo naroda. v. 2. S. Peterburg: Obshchestvennaya pol'za.

Pozdneev, D. (1925). Yaponiya. Strana, naselenie, istoriya, politika. A. Iordanskii. Moskow: Gosvoenizdat.

Sato, H. (1999). *Samurai. Istoriya i legendy.* S. Peterburg: Evraziya.

Shiba, R. (2000). *Poslednii shogun. Zhizn' Tokugawa Yoshinobu.* Moskow: MIK.

Shishkina, G. (2003). Veshch v sovremennoi yaponskoi kul'ture. In: *Veshch v kul'ture.* Moskow: Vostochnaya literatura.

Shreider, D. (1999). Yaponia i yapontsy (fragmenty iz knigi). In: *Kniga yaponskikh obyknovenii.* Edited by A. Meshcheryakov. Moskow: Natalis Press. 359–385.

Tokieda, M. (1983). *Sovremenny yazuk i sovremennoe yazukovoe sushchestvovanie.* Edited by V. Alpatov and I. Vardul'. Moskow: Raduga.111–122.

Venyukov, M. (1871). Izvlecheniya iz zakonov Gogensamy. In: *Obozrenie yaponskogo archipelaga v sovremennom ego sostoyanii.* Vol.3. S.-Peterburg.

Vollan, G. (1906). V strane voschodyashchego solntsa. Moscow-S.-Peterburg: Tovarishchestvo M. Volfa.

Yamamoto, T. (2000). Hagakure. In: Kniga samuraya. Translated by R. Kotenko, A. Mishchenko, S. Petersburg: Evraziya.

Yamamoto, T. (2004). Hagakure. In: Kodeks bushido. Translated by A. Bochenkova. V. Gorbat'ko. Moskow: Eksmo.

Zapiski u izgolov'ya. Zapiski iz kel'i. (1988). In: Klassicheskaya yaponskaya proza XI-XIV vekov. Moscow: Khudozhestvennaya literatura.

Ziebold, Kempfer, Tunberg *et al.* (1999). Vpechatleniya puteshestvennikov kontsa XVII — nachala XIX veka. In: Kniga yaponskikh obyknovenii. Edited by A. Meshcheryakov. Moscow: Natalis press. 319–358.

Personal Index

Subject Index

Japanese Glossary Index

www.ingramcontent.com/pod-product-compliance
Lightning Source LLC
Chambersburg PA
CBHW071729270326
41928CB00013B/2609